WO[MEN]
~~AND~~ RELIGION !

Too Smart

A Feminist Sourcebook
of Christian Thought

ELIZABETH CLARK
and HERBERT RICHARDSON

HARPER & ROW, PUBLISHERS
New York, Hagerstown, San Francisco, London

For
Wilhelm Pauck,
Cyril Richardson,
and
George Huntston Williams
Teachers of Christian History

FIRST EDITION

Designed by C. Linda Dingler

Library of Congress Cataloging in Publication Data

Clark, Elizabeth, 1938-
    Women and religion.
    (A Harper forum book)
    Includes bibliographical references.
    1. Women (Theology)—Addresses, essays, lectures.
2. Women and religion—Addresses, essays, lectures.
I. Richardson, Herbert Warren, joint author. II. Title.
BT704.C53 1977   261.8'34'12   76-9975
ISBN 0-06-061398-X

Acknowledgments

Grateful acknowledgement is made for the selections in this volume used as noted, with the permission of the following publishers:

ARNO PRESS INC. for selections from Elizabeth Cady Stanton, *The Woman's Bible*, Parts 1, 2, and Appendix. Reprinted by Arno Press, Inc., 1972.

CONCORDIA PUBLISHING HOUSE for selections from Martin Luther, *Luther's Works*, Vol. 1, ed. Jaroslav Pelikan. Copyright © 1958 by Concordia Publishing House. Used by permission of Concordia Publishing House.

FORTRESS PRESS for selections from Martin Luther, "The Estate of Marriage" in *Luther's Works*, Vol. 45, *The Christian in Society II*, ed. Walther I. Brandt. Copyright © 1962 by Fortress Press.

HARPER & ROW PUBLISHERS, INC. for selections from Julian of Norwich, *The Revelations of Divine Love*, trans. James Walsh. Harper & Row, Publishers, Inc., 1961.

HARPER & ROW PUBLISHERS, INC. for selections from "The Gospel of Mary" in *Gnosticism: A Sourcebook of Heretical Writings from the Early Christian Period*, ed. Robert M. Grant. Copyright © 1961 by Robert M. Grant.

HARVARD UNIVERSITY PRESS for selections from Jerome, Letter 22, "To Eustochium: The Virgin's Profession" in *Select Letters of St. Jerome*, trans. F. A. Wright. Harvard University Press, Loeb Classical Library, 1933.

JOHN KNOX PRESS for selections from *Christmas Eve* by Friedrich Schleiermacher, trans. Terrence N. Tice. Copyright © 1967 by M. E. Bratcher. Used by permission of John Knox Press.

JONATHAN CAPE LTD for selections from Margery Kempe, *The Book of Margery Kempe*, 1426, ed. W. Butler-Bowen. London: Jonathan Cape, 1936.

PENGUIN BOOKS LTD for selections from *Aeschylus: The Eumenides, The Orestian Trilogy*, trans. Philip Vellacott (1964) pp. 166-182. Copyright © Philip Vellacott, 1956.

THE PUSHKIN PRESS for selections from J. Sprenger and H. Kramer, *Malleus Maelficarum*, trans. Montague Summers. London: The Pushkin Press, 1948.

THE RELIGIOUS EDUCATION ASSOCIATION OF THE UNITED STATES AND CANADA for Mary Daly's "The Women's Movement: An Exodus Community." Reprinted from the September/October 1972 issue of *Religious Education* by permission of the publisher, the Religious Education Association, 409, Prospect St., New Haven, CT 06510. Membership or subscription available for $20.00 per year.

T. & T. CLARK LIMITED for selections from Karl Barth, "The Doctrine of Creation" in *Church Dogmatics*, Vol. 3, sec. 4, ed. G. W. Gromiley and T. F. Torrance. Edinburgh: T. & T. Clark Ltd., 1961.

THE WESTMINSTER PRESS for selections from *Alexandrian Christianity*, Vol. II, The Library of Christian Classics, ed. Henry Chadwick and J. E. L. Oulton. Published in the U.S.A. 1954. Used by permission of The Westminster Press.

Contents

Preface

This volume was developed as a response to two needs. First, the burgeoning interest in women's studies suggested that primary source texts should be gathered and edited for use in courses. In addition, the dawning consciousness of the bias against women in Western religion coupled with a will to correct that bias demanded that studies be made of the ways that discrimination against women has manifested itself throughout the history of our culture.

Besides providing selections from the works of writers who shaped attitudes toward women in their own times or in later eras, the editors have also sought to demonstrate, through introductory essays, that the "woman issue" provides an interpretive key to the rest of an intellectual position. It is not separable from theology, ethics, hermeneutics, social theory, or attitudes towards authority, nature, thought, and action. We think that patriarchy has been, in one form or another, the most pervasive and destructive manifestation of inhumanity in history. When the author of Genesis 3 described Yahweh's punishing Eve for her sin by subjecting her to Adam, he enlisted God on the side of patriarchy. Since our society's structures are undergirded by our religious symbols, the launching of a different social order requires a critical analysis of the Christian religion. The emancipation of women, we are sure, will demand a new understanding of God.

Despite the prevalence of patriarchalism in Christianity, we have been encouraged to uncover some thinkers and movements whose importance has been largely overlooked by "mainstream" historians. For example, we consider Margery Kempe and Mother

Ann Lee to be brilliant and heroic innovators. Our book then attempts to present both the champions of male dominance and the foresighted explorers of a more just world.

We have listed basic bibliographical suggestions within the notes at the back of the book which refer to the individual essays. By no means definitive, they are intended to help students pursue further research.

Some years ago, one of the authors of this volume published *Nun, Witch, Playmate*, in which he proposed to prepare a book of readings to accompany that work. Since then, the women's movement has grown to be a major force in American life, and so he here fulfills that promise better than he had ever hoped or intended.

We wish to thank Union Theological Seminary and the School of Religion at the State University of Iowa for their hospitality during the period when this book was being prepared. Our colleagues at Mary Washington College and St. Michael's have given us continuous encouragement, which we gratefully acknowledge. Many individuals have provided counsel and special assistance at various steps along the way: Nathaniel Brown, David Cain, Kate Dickson, Frank Flinn, Susan Hanna, Mary Beth Iskat, William Kemp, Elizabeth Kirk, Warren Lewis, George Oliver, Elaine Pagels, Georgiane Perret, William Phipps, Wayne Smith, and Rose Yunker. We are also especially aware that this project would not have been begun or completed without the encouragement and editorial direction of Marie Cantlon at Harper & Row.

Elizabeth Clark   Herbert Richardson
Department of Religion   Institute of Christian Thought
Mary Washington College   St. Michael's College
Fredericksburg, Virginia   Toronto, Ontario

April 27, 1976
Mary Wollstonecraft Day

1. Introduction

This volume contains representative readings epitomizing attitudes towards women in the Western religious tradition. This tradition is unremittingly patriarchal, although one can trace a development in which various aspects of patriarchy are begrudgingly qualified. The earlier identification of the female with the sexual and the male with the spiritual was opposed by Christianity, which acknowledged the equal spiritual dignity of both men and women. The medieval depreciation of marriage was rejected by the Reformation, which saw in the marital relation between men and women something of the highest religious value. Christianity's lack of a feminine image of God and its emphasis on a masculine Messiah were corrected by modern religious movements which not only conceived God as feminine, but also acknowledged female religious leadership—including even female Messiahs!

Progress towards a more enlightened view of women is thus real, but it is also painfuly slow and it proceeds against a constant patriarchal opposition which has become more outspoken with the passage of time. Hence, we find the most influential theologian of the twentieth century, Karl Barth, reiterating the most patriarchal themes, insisting that woman should recognize that "in order she is woman, and therefore B, and therefore behind and subordinate to man." Why, asks Barth, "should not woman be the second in the sequence, but only in sequence? What other choice has she, seeing she can be nothing at all apart from this sequence and her place within it? And why," he asks rhetorically, "should she desire anything else?"[1]

Where should we now begin our historical account? Editors addressing themselves to the history of attitudes toward women find their problem complicated by the fact that their judgments must be based on written documents which cover only a brief span of humanity's life. The mystery persists: what happened in the periods before those depicted in the literary remains? Is there any evidence to suggest that at the dawn of human culture, matriarchies, in which women ruled over men, really existed?

Matriarchal theories gained considerable popularity in the late nineteenth century through writers like J. J. Bachofen[2] and (to a lesser extent) Lewis Henry Morgan.[3] Bachofen, a jurist and lover of classical civilization, held that matriarchy was a universal stage in mankind's development; he assumed that Greek and Roman mythology described the actual history of those cultures. Legends telling of the Amazons, for example, were simply the dim reflections of an aberration which had occurred in the development of woman's role; women warriors really had banded together in exclusively female groups. Morgan took a different approach; he investigated contemporary primitive societies, particularly nonpatriarchal ones (the Iroquois was a tribe to which he devoted special attention) to see if they might provide us with clues to life in distant ages. Most scholars now reject Bachofen's belief that myth mirrors history, but Morgan's assumption (that the social patterns of present primitive cultures are analogous to those of past millennia) is one shared by many contemporary anthropologists. Although the theory of matriarchy (in the strict sense of the word) has been largely abandoned,[4] scholars do note the occurrence of matrilineal societies, in which the line of descent is reckoned through the female, and matrilocal ones, in which the place of residence is determined by the woman's kinship group, not by the man's. Common sense might lead us to postulate that females had a status more equal to men's in times and cultures in which their labor as food growers and gatherers was essential to the life of the group;[5] however, it remains difficult to substantiate such assumptions, given the great variation in social organizations throughout human history.[6] Since convincing evidence for matriarchy is nonexistent, we shall begin our anthology with selections which reflect the values of the ancient literate world—patriarchal values.

In the types of societies which are represented by the first documents in this book—Athenian society of the fifth century, B.C. and the Hebrew community of biblical times—some characteristics typical of patriarchy in this first historical period of our study can be noted.[7] In the personal sphere of life, classical patriarchy assumes that the "real people" are men; women, to one degree or another, are thought to be nonpersons who have no public identity. Males make the laws, set the values, and control the lives of those subordinate to them—not only women, but children, and men excluded from the ruling group. Women are viewed as distinctly different creatures from men, and are usually considered to be deficient in intellect as well as in physical strength. Their capabilities limit them largely to the domestic sphere, although we should remember that the "domestic sphere" of ancient times might be considered broader than that of the modern Western nuclear household. Because females were assumed to have weak minds and did not receive the same education as men, males in patriarchal societies thought that there was little likeness between themselves and women, with the consequence that friendship between members of the two sexes was considered unusual if not impossible.[8] More attention was paid to what women did with their bodies than to how they utilized their minds, in part because female sexuality was viewed as something dangerous which needed to be controlled. The image of woman as temptress, luring innocent men into sexual escapades, was prevalent in patriarchy. Since patriarchy emphasized upholding the legitimacy of the kinship line, "proper" women must have their chastity guarded, even if this forced them into lives of semiseclusion, as perhaps "middle-class" women of fifth century Athens experienced.[9]

Many of these characteristics, exhibited in the *Oresteia* and the Old Testament, are discussed in greater detail in the introductions to those selections given below. A few examples, however, may here be given. In Aeschylus' trilogy, the rule of Argos by a woman, Clytemnestra, was deemed improper by the male population of the city. Her sexual infidelity to her husband, the king, was seen as one stage in the events leading to her murder of him—an act, the chorus reminds us, which savors of the evil to which women have always been prone, as is recounted in well-known legends.[10]

The Furies, representative of the ancient female guardians of fertility, behave in an irrational, hysterical manner—the way which patriarchy has affirmed is "typical" of women. The male-oriented Olympians, on the other hand, represent the new rational order of justice which Athens (and Aeschylus) was striving to promote. One message of the *Oresteia*, then, is that civilization and justice are the creations of the male sex.

In the Old Testament, patriarchal characteristics are displayed just as fully. Men are both the political rulers and the religious leaders. The Hebrew Scriptures abound with laws to ensure the sexual purity of women and guarantee that legitimate children be born to the male. The woman as sexual temptress is a recurring character: the story of Delilah is but one example.[11]

Patriarchy also had its religious manifestations. God (or the gods) was portrayed as male. An obvious objection to this point is that the Greeks had female deities. But most of the important Olympian goddesses, by the time we meet up with them in myth and legend, have lost their "femaleness," particularly their fertility associations (if they ever had them[12]) and have become engrossed in masculine occupations,[13] engaging in feats of military prowess (Athena) and in hunting activities (Artemis). Even Aphrodite, a love goddess, was associated with the sphere of the lusty erotic life rather than with reproduction per se. In the *Eumenides*, from which our first selection is taken, Athena appears as the very prototype of the "male-identified" woman, who sides with the men and exempts herself from traditional female roles. Although at a later point in history, women might live in the free, "male" fashion of the Greek goddesses, the women of the fifth-century Athens could scarcely use Athena, Artemis, or Aphrodite as "role-models" for their own lives. And the chief god of the Olympian pantheon, Zeus, as is well known, is not only a male, but a playboy par excellence. In the Old Testament, Yahweh performs the masculine tasks of leading his people to war and giving them the law; the "sexlessness" of God appears to us to be a concept developed by later theologians, not one prominent within the Old Testament itself.[14] We also learn in the Hebrew Scriptures that women were excluded from positions of religious leadership and from essential cultic functions; perhaps menstruation and childbirth were thought to render them periodically unclean.

Both in ancient Greece and in Israel, women's social world was determined by their inclusion in male-dominated families; their chief function within the family group was to bear legitimate children. They had little or no public identity and were seen largely in the domestic role. The laws and customs regulating their social lives suggest that they might be considered the "property" of the male, as is evidenced in some of the Scriptural passages below, such as the infamous story of the Levite's concubine.[15]

In the *Eumenides*, even women's importance as mother is challenged: it is the father, Apollo claims, who is the true parent of the child; the mother merely tends the plant which another has deposited with her![16] The emphasis placed on childbearing in the Old Testament indicates a woman's prime source of worth; there is no greater curse which can fall upon her than the inability to produce offspring—note the grief of Sarah, Rachel, and Hannah at their childless condition.[17] Such attitudes do not necessarily mean that women were degraded; to the contrary, their sexual, maternal, and domestic services were highly valued, but, nonetheless, they were unusually excluded from the centers of power and influence.

Although the word *patriarchy* is often used rather loosely to denote male dominance in Western society from early times to the present, we believe that there have been some advances from this state of affairs—as well as regressions to it.[18] We by no means claim, as do some Christian enthusiasts, that the coming of Christianity brought a radical revision of the social order which upgraded the status of women.[19] All the same, the early Christian era witnessed several developments which we consider to be progress. To what extent they simply reflected the gradual emancipation of women in the Roman Empire is difficult to judge.[20]

Christianity—which taught that we are all one in Jesus Christ—made possible associations between men and women which would have been deemed inappropriate by the Judaism of that time. Jesus himself may have set the pattern of freer and more open relationships between the sexes.[21] Some New Testament passages indicate that woman joined with men in advancing the cause of the infant religion and perhaps even traveled about with the disciples and apostles.[22] The spiritual equality of the sexes and their mutual efforts on behalf of Christianity meant that friendships between males and females were now imaginable. Whereas "proper" women in either Greek or Hebrew society did not associate unchaperoned with men other than their husbands or male kin,[23] the early Christian era witnessed unrelated men and women cooperating in joint prospects. The fourth-century church father Jerome, some of whose writings are presented below, gathered about him a circle of female companions with whom he discussed Scripture and to whom he taught Hebrew. Although others looked askance at such relationships, they signaled the dawning of an increased appreciation of women's intellectual and spiritual capacities—the capacities which make friendship possible.

Some Christian women carried the idea of friendship with men even further. The agapetae or subintroductae of the early church were usually virgins or widows who set up housekeeping with men also dedicated to chastity and attempted to live in "spiritual marriage," an association of companionship and mutual support which purportedly excluded sexual activity. The church took a dimmer view of the strength of human nature than these couples did and repeatedly attempted to outlaw the practice.[24] Nevertheless, the very phenomenon testifies to a different notion of male-female relationships than had been present earlier.

We also find that women in the early Christian era acquired at least limited access to positions of religious leadership which had been denied to Jewish women. Although it is unclear what official status the New Testament women who prophesied or bore the name of "deacon" held, there was an order of widows in early Christianity, and, in the fourth century, of deaconesses, who, at least in the East, received a clerical ordination.[25] It was, however, among the heretical and sect groups, such as the Gnostics, that women were considered to be capable of instructing men (as is suggested by the selection below from The Gospel of Mary) and were permitted to exercise full clerical office. Moreover, among the Gnostics, we discover that God was frequently depicted as being female as well as male, mother as well as father.[26] This tendency toward the feminization of the Godhead did not take hold very firmly among the "orthodox" churchmen, although occasional passage which stress God's female characteristics can be found: "And God himself is love; and out of his love to us became feminine. In his ineffable essence he is Father; in his compassion to us he became Mother. The Father by loving became feminine; and the great proof of this is he whom he begot of himself; and the fruit brought forth by love is love."[27]

In patristic Christianity, moreover, there was a significant social development which affected the lives of many women. Celibacy and virginity, advocated by Paul, were popularized in the fourth century and gave to Christian women an option other than marriage and motherhood. Proponents of sexual liberation tend to mock the extravagant denunciations of sexual activity we find in the Christian literature of this period. These passages are present, to be sure—the reader has only to note Jerome's satiric jibes at marital relations and Augustine's embarrassment at male erection[28] —to see what the critics are talking about. We believe, however, that the attack upon sex was not always or necessarily antifeminist; it had some unexpected benefits for the status of women. Domesticity was the only "career" available to women in the ancient world, and in the absence of reliable methods of birth control (coupled with the patristic denunciation of contraception and abortion[29]), marriage might well involve submission to the male and repeated pregnancies. The virginal life, on the other hand, freed women from the cycle of childbearing and dependence upon men. It is in this context that we can at least partially understand Jerome and one of his later confreres, John Chrysostom,[30] who utter rather vile words about women in general but extravagantly praise their female friends who had undertaken the celibate life, thereby raising themselves above the level of ordinary women still immersed in sexual and domestic functions. The virgins had chosen the better part, Jerome declared; he compared them to the "hundred fold harvest" of Mark 4, whereas married people were likened only to the "thirty fold harvest."[31] Of course, it points to the *hubris* of such men that they tended to describe these women as "male" or "manly."[32] All the same, new opportunities were opened to women in the "career" of virginity. Not only did they escape male domination and the very real dangers of childbearing in that era,[33] they also had available to them a far richer mental and spiritual life than most females of their day. If women's emancipation is concerned with the expanding of options, this step is a significant one.

Secondly, as we move beyond the patristic era into the Middle Ages, we discover that woman's profession of celibacy was formally organized in the institution of the convent. Before the advent of monasticism, women rejecting sexual life were left to their own resources to find suitable places of residence and means of support. From the fourth century on, however, women began to gather in convents (Jerome's female companions organized one of the first, in Bethlehem). Women who chose the nun's role were initiated into the confirming bonds of sisterhood—a word which has been adopted and invested with secular meaning by contemporary feminists. Moreover, as the convents developed in the medieval period, they often became influential forces in Christian society. Some abbesses exerted power far beyond that permitted to most married women of their day, controlling both towns and territories in the environs of their convents and male monastic establishments which sprang up in conjunction with the female institutions.[34]

A second move away from classical patriarchy begins in the High Middle Ages and continues into the Puritan era. In this period, the idea of romantic love between the sexes was exalted.[35] The erotic ideals of the Greeks—which had tended to be homosexually oriented—were now seen as appropriate to heterosexual relationships,[36] and in the love poetry of the age, women were extolled as the bearers of virtue and sources of inspiration for male courage and chivalry. The phenomenon of courtly love paralleled another significant development: the Marian cult. The rise of devotion to Mary indicated that one woman, if no other, could be religiously glorified, freed from the sinful condition of fallible humanity, and raised to a semidivine status. Mary became a mediator ("Mediatrix") between God and mankind, an exemplar of the gracious love and forgiveness of the deity. As has been pointed out by recent feminists, it may be foolish to place undue emphasis on the popularity of the Marian cult in this period; the elevation of Mary probably did very little for the advancement of womanhood in general at this time.[37] Nevertheless, perhaps one small step was taken in the direction of affirming female worth.

Thirdly, the religious/erotic mysticism of medieval piety with its stress on God's passionate love for his "bride," the Christian community (or its particular representatives), blatantly portrayed the relation between the transcendent Creator and his mortal creation in terms derived from originally erotic poetry, such as the Song of Songs. That the Christian community and individual males could put themselves in the role of the "bride," the female recipient of God's caressing love, testifies to a feminization of piety.[38]

Likewise, the description of Christ as female, a "mother," as in the selection given below from the female mystic, Julian of Norwich, witnesses to the same tendency. In light of these evidences of a slowly developing esteem accorded women, Thomas Aquinas's discussion of the female as a "misbegotten male" (a definition which he derived from Aristotle)[39] is a reversion to misogynistic values, just as the witchcraze of the late medieval and Renaissance periods, as depicted below in the *Malleus Maleficarum*, appears as a "backlash," a return to oppressive attitudes at a time when loftier notions of women's status had already been imagined, if not put into effect in real life.

To the social world of women, the Protestant Reformation brought a changed conception of marriage. No longer were childbearing and the allaying of male lust the chief or only purpose of the institution; rather, it received a new dignity as an "estate" commanded by God.[40] Although Luther's praise of marriage set the stage for further reflection by his associates and spiritual heirs, he did not define marriage primarily as companionship, as did the later Protestants, especially the Puritans. For them, marriage was a partnership into which a couple freely entered for the enrichment of their own lives and characters, as well as for the creation of children and for sexual expression. This newer understanding of marriage, as represented in our selection from Milton, gradually became normative among Protestants. Catholicism, however, was rather slow in adopting it. Thus the Vatican's belief, expressed as late as 1930 in the *Casti Connubii*, that the threefold ends of marriage are the begetting of offspring, fidelity, and the "sacramental bond," appears to us to be more appropriate to earlier centuries than to the twentieth. However, recent documents from Roman Catholicism, such as "The Church in the Modern World" (*Gaudium et Spes*) produced by the Second Vatican Council, have expressed more enthusiastically the view of marriage as a partnership for the development and mutual enjoyment of the husband and wife.[41]

In addition, Luther's theory that all Christians, even if they were farmers and housewives, had a "vocation" in which they might demonstrate Christian virtues meant that married women could proudly assert that their lives had sacred significance equal to and even beyond that of Catholic nuns. Although the nuns continued to wield more influence in the larger world than did most married women of the lower or middle classes, a religious esteem which formerly had been granted only to the few who had exempted themselves from customary female roles was now extended to the thousands of women who were wives and mothers. Luther's view of "vocation" as far as it relates to the status of women can indeed be judged from two different perspectives: on the one hand, it stressed—as Catholic theology had not—the holiness of women engaged in sexual and domestic functions, but in championing that position, it encouraged nuns to desert the convents, where they had more opportunity to exhibit religious leadership and to live in a sisterhood independent of men. Whether Luther's stress on the "vocation" of marriage was a step forward or backward depends on one's vantage point.

A third shift away from traditional patriarchalism gained impetus from spiritualistic Christianity and the movements of social perfectionism which arose between the seventeenth and the nineteenth centuries. The heightened sense of individuality expressed by the participants in some of the religious sects which developed in this period was especially beneficial for women. Believing that the Spirit was the decisive influence on a person's life, these Christians postulated that it might arouse and summon women to activities which earlier Christianity had not considered fitting for females.[42] Thus the Quakers and, after them, the Shakers asserted that women as bearers of the Spirit were equal to men and might be called by God to positions of religious leadership. Moreover, many of these spiritualistic groups believed that they were already experiencing the Kingdom of God here on earth, which encouraged them to think that traditional ideas of women's roles and the marital relationship had been superseded, replaced by a God-given equality of the sexes.

Secondly, some of these movements, in holding the concept of the basic likeness of the sexes, brought the idea of androgyny to the fore. Men and women eagerly explored what it felt like to recognize and develop within themselves the qualities which customarily had been ascribed to the opposite sex. The great nineteenth-century theologian Schleiermacher, for example, yearned to express the femaleness of his character, and even regretted not having been born a woman—a view totally baffling and upsetting, even a century later, to a theologian like Karl Barth, who affirmed anew the orthodox tradition. A more explicit acceptance of androgyny emerged in the writings of the Catholic thinker Franz von Baader (a selection of them is printed below), who believed that Adam's originally androgynous state was the "image of God" (Gen. 1:26) which men and women should now strive to recapture, recreating themselves as whole human beings once more. The concept of androgynous likeness between the sexes was affirmed by the English Romantics, especially by Coleridge. Revived in the twentieth century by Virginia Woolf, the idea has been given fresh meaning by contemporary feminists.

The nineteenth century also saw the rise of movements which led to greatly increased social freedom for women. The feminism of this era is often associated exclusively with the issue of suffrage, but getting the vote was only one of its achievements. The suffragists persisted in the face of tremendous opposition from males (as well as from their conventional sisters) to win educational opportunities for women, which kindled their professional aspirations. The first women lawyers, physicians, scientists, and ministers who had received intellectual training identical to men's appeared in this century. Married women won the right to hold property in their own name and to initiate divorce proceedings. Time-honored interpretations of women's legal status were challenged and important gains made, although many battles still today remain to be fought out in the courts. Some feminists such as Sarah Grimké and Elizabeth Cady Stanton recognized that the social attitudes of Western Christendom, particularly attitudes toward women, had been largely derived from a traditional reading of the Bible and asked Christians of their era to examine Scripture with new eyes. (Examples of what that reevaluation might involve are given below.) Working together on these political, social, and intellectual projects gave women a sense of sisterhood, of cooperation in common tasks beyond those of the domestic arena; in earlier centuries, such feelings might have been difficult to arouse in women not part of convent life.

In the middle and late nineteenth century, another social change which had enormous consequences for male-female relationships took place: the creation and improvement of more reliable methods of contraception, such as the condom and the diaphragm.[44] For the first time, effective regulation of their reproductive lives began to be an option for thousands of women. Others in this era, like John Humphrey Noyes at the Oneida Community, perfected the time-honored practice of *coitus reservatus* in an attempt to enhance the joyfulness and the love involved in sexual union and to decrease the possibility of excessive pregnancies, which Noyes saw as a blight upon women's physical, intellectual, and emotional health. Further elaboration of Noyes's unique concepts of marriage and "male continence" (his name for *coitus reservatus*) can be found in the selections from his writings given below.

Religiously, a number of novel theories were explored by the spiritualist groups which flourished in this era. We find the idea of a "Father-Mother God" being postulated by the Shakers and the Christian Scientists, while the notion of female Messiahship was espoused by the Shakers, who saw in Mother Ann Lee the feminine counterpart to the male savior, Jesus.[45] These two sects are also significant examples of the trend in the nineteenth century for women to be the founders of religious groups. It is extremely difficult to envision a Mary Baker Eddy or a Mother Ann Lee appearing in orthodox Christianity of the patristic period!

All these developments have contributed to women's present status. The "advances" we have suggested here were ones which at first affected only a small number of women, the elite, who for various reasons had lived in ways considered out of the ordinary in their own time. The change in the twentieth-century scene, from our point of view, is that opportunities once enjoyed by only a few—or enjoyed to the exclusion of other possible satisfactions in life—are now the right and the heritage of many females in Western society. Thousands of women now expect, as a matter of course, that they will develop nonsexual friendships with men, cooperate with other women on projects in a sisterly spirit, have careers whether or not they choose to marry or bear children, control their own reproductive faculties and determine their own sexual preferences, join the church's ordained ministry, if they so desire, and at all times to think of themselves as intellectual and spiritual equals with men: these notions surely do mark progress over former times. Secular society, in fact, now appears to be more advanced than the mainline churches in its acceptance of feminist ideals. The failure of orthodox Christianity to keep apace with what women actually are thinking and doing is sharply pointed up in our last selection by Mary Daly. Although the situation in America often appears discouraging when we survey the still-present sex-role stereotyping inflicted upon children and the economic discrimination against women, from a long-range point of view, women now have more opportunities than ever before in history and are uniting to overcome the remaining vestiges of patriarchy. The final battles, to be sure, may well be among the most difficult, as those who have worked for the goals of the contemporary women's movement know full well. But as Elizabeth Cady Stanton extolled modern womanhood in her interpretation of the parable of the wise and foolish maidens in Matthew 25:[46]

The wise virgins are they who keep their lamps trimmed, who burn oil in their vessels for their own use, who have improved every advantage for their education, secured a healthy, happy, complete development, and entered all the profitable avenues of labor, for self-support, so that when the opportunities and the responsibilities of life come, they may be fitted fully to enjoy the one and ably to discharge the other. . . .

. . . Such is the type of womanhood which the bridegroom of an enlightened public sentiment welcomes today; and such is the triumph of the wise virgins over the folly, the ignorance and the degradation of the past as in grand procession they enter the temple of knowledge, and *the door is no longer shut.*

2. Aeschylus: Queens, Goddesses, Furies

Aeschylus's *Oresteia* is a political, social, and religious interpretation of an old Greek legend about a royal family doomed by the relentless pressures of an avenging fate. In the first two plays of the trilogy, Aeschylus depicts the bloody homecoming of King Agamemnon from Troy, killed by his wife Clytemnestra in revenge for Agamemnon's earlier sacrificial slaughter of their daughter Iphigenia and also, one suspects, for his infidelities. Their son Orestes understands himself to be compelled by the divine forces to avenge his dead father through the slaying of his mother.[1] He seeks out Apollo to purify him from his bloodguilt but is nonetheless hounded by the Furies, spirits seeking retaliation for his matricide. In the third play of the trilogy, the *Eumenides*, from which our selections are taken, gods and humans participate in a trial to decide the fate of Orestes. Through the decisive vote of Athena, Orestes is acquitted. The Furies renounce their vengeful role, become the "friendly ones" (the Eumenides), and accept Athena's offer of a place in Athenian religious life.

One of the major questions of the play is, how is justice, especially in homicide cases, to be attained? Aeschylus rejects the more primitive tribal notion of blood-revenge offered by the Furies as well as the notion of ritual purification represented by Apollo's solution, in favor of jury trial. Aeschylus himself had lived through the overthrow of the tyrants and the institution of democratic reforms at Athens, as well as the Greek defeat of the Persians in the early fifth century B.C. He appears to be demonstrating his approval of the "golden age" of Athens by portraying his respect for the procedures of a democratic trial.[2]

There is more, however, than a social and political message to the play. In his depiction of the Furies and the gods, Aeschylus shows us the triumph of the Olympian deities over an older order of chthonic spirits in Greek religion. Scholars are in disagreement as to the origin of the Furies (the Erinyes): were they originally ghosts of the slain person or were they merely hypostatization of curses?[3] From early times they were associated with the earth and hence later on became identified with the spirits of fertility. In Aeschylus' play, they are the champions of maternal rights who impress upon their audience the horrors of Orestes' matricide. It is revealing that the playwright paints these "female principles" as hideous old hags, irrational, repetitious, and somewhat hysterical in their demands and threats.

Over against the Furies are pitted the Olympian deities. Apollo, in defending his protégé Orestes, claims that it is Zeus' will for the young man to be acquitted; after all, matricide is not much of a crime when compared with Clytemnestra's dispatching of her husband, the king. He argues on Orestes' behalf that it is the father who is the real parent of the child, anyway; the mother hardly counts at all in the reproductive process. Moreover, he proudly boasts, men have brought forth children without the aid of women —witness Athena, who purportedly sprang from the head of Zeus.

Athena in the Eumenides is the very prototype of what contemporary feminists would call a "male-identified" woman. She is the motherless virgin goddess who sides with the male claim over against the female[5] and who by the persuasive force of her "masculine" logic is able to convince the Furies to renounce their vengeance and accept a place of honor both within the Olympian system and among the Athenians.

The Eumenides, then, can be interpreted as revealing the displacement of earlier, chthonic deities by the "male" Olympians. Although most twentieth-century scholars reject the notion that there once were matriarchal societies in the distant past, we do know that goddesses, presumably associated with fertility, were worshiped throughout the Mediterranean world in ancient times. In the Hellenistic era, there was a successful revival of female deities; they became the goddesses of purification and salvation in the so-called mystery cults. Aeschylus, of course, did not live to see the reestablishment of female deities from the second century B.C. on; for him, the triumph of Zeus, Apollo, and Athena was the triumph of justice and of "civilization."

Can the women portrayed in Greek tragedies—such as Clytemnestra in our play—be taken as reflections of typical women in fifth-century Greece? Probably not. For one thing, females such as Clytemnestra are queens representing a past era of Greek civilization and hence are hardly appropriate models from which to make deductions about the lives of females, noble or otherwise, in Aeschylus' day. And despite attempts to discount the oppressed state of Greek women,[6] scholarly opinion continues to emphasize the subordinate and nonpublic character of women's lives in fifth-century Athens.[7] The Hellenistic era and the period of the Roman Empire saw a gradual emancipation of women, although we should not imagine that even the "liberated" Roman women of the early Christian centuries shared equal political or educational rights with men.[8] They enjoyed more freedom than did "middle-class" women of Aeschylus' time, but their liberty was not of the sort envisioned by modern feminists.

The Eumenides

ATHENE returns, bringing with her twelve Athenian citizens.

APOLLO comes from the temple, leading ORESTES.

ATHENE: Summon the city, herald, and proclaim the cause; let the Tyrrhenian trumpet, filled with mortal breath, crack the broad heaven, and shake Athens with its voice. And while the council-chamber fills, let citizens and jurors all in silence recognize this court which I ordain today in perpetuity, that now and always justice may be well discerned.

CHORUS [Furies]: Divine Apollo, handle what belongs to you. Tell us, what right have you to meddle in this case?

APOLLO: I came to answer that in evidence. This man has my

From Aeschylus, the *Eumenides, The Oresteian Trilogy,* trans. Philip Vellacott (Baltimore: Penguin Books, Inc., 1964).

protection by the law of suppliants. I cleansed him from this murder; I am here to be his advocate, since I am answerable for the stroke that killed his mother. Pallas, introduce this case, and so conduct it as your wisdom prompts.

ATHENE: The case is open. [To the LEADER OF THE CHORUS] Since you are the accuser, speak. The court must first hear a full statement of the charge.

CHORUS: Though we are many, few words will suffice. [To ORESTES] And you answer our questions, point for point. First, did you kill your mother?

ORESTES: I cannot deny it. Yes, I did.

CHORUS: Good; the first round is ours.

ORESTES: It is too soon to boast: I am not beaten.

CHORUS: You must tell us, none the less, how you dispatched her.

ORESTES: With a sword I pierced her heart.

CHORUS: On whose persuasion, whose advice?

ORESTES: Apollo's. He is witness that his oracle commanded me.

CHORUS: The god of prophecy commanded matricide?

ORESTES: Yes; and he has not failed me from that day to this.

CHORUS: If today's vote condemns you, you will change your words.

ORESTES: I trust him. My dead father too will send me help.

CHORUS: Yes, trust the dead now: your hand struck your mother dead.

ORESTES: She was twice guilty, twice condemned.

CHORUS: How so? Instruct the court.

ORESTES: She killed her husband, and my father too.

CHORUS: Her death absolved her; you still live.

ORESTES: But why was she not punished by you while she lived?

CHORUS: The man she killed was not of her own blood.

ORESTES: But I am of my mother's?

CHORUS: Vile wretch! Did she not nourish you in her own womb? Do you disown your mother's blood, which is your own?

ORESTES: Apollo, now give evidence. Make plain to me if I was right to kill her. That I struck the blow is true, I own it. But was murder justified? Expound this point, and show me how to plead my cause.

APOLLO: To you, august court of Athene, I will speak justly and truly, as befits a prophet-god. I never yet, from my oracular seat, pronounced for man, woman, or city any word which Zeus, the Olympian Father, had not formally prescribed. I bid you, then, mark first the force of justice here; but next, even more, regard my father's will. No oath can have more force than Zeus, whose name has sanctioned it.

CHORUS: Then Zeus, you say, was author of this oracle you gave Orestes—that his mother's claims should count for nothing, till he had avenged his father's death?

APOLLO: Zeus so ordained, and Zeus was right. For their two deaths are in no way to be compared. He was a king wielding an honoured sceptre by divine command. A woman killed him: such death might be honourable—in battle, dealt by an arrow from an Amazon's bow. But you shall hear, Pallas and you who judge this case, how Clytemnestra killed her husband. When he came home from the war, for the most part successful, and performed his ritual cleansing, she stood by his side; the ritual ended, as he left the silver bath, she threw on him a robe's interminable folds, wrapped, fettered him in an embroidered gown, and struck.

Such, jurors, was the grim end of this king, whose look was majesty, whose word commanded men and fleets. Such was his wife who killed him—such that none of you, who sit to try Orestes, hears her crime unmoved.

CHORUS: Zeus rates a father's death the higher, by your account. Yet Zeus, when his own father Cronos became old, bound him with chains. Is there not contradiction here? Observe this, jurors, on your oath.

APOLLO: Execrable hags, outcasts of heaven! Chains may be loosed, with little harm, and many ways to mend it. But when blood of man sinks in the thirsty dust, the life once lost can live no more. For death alone my father has ordained no healing spell; all other things his effortless and sovereign power casts down or raises up at will.

CHORUS: You plead for his acquittal: have you asked yourself how one who poured out on the ground his mother's blood will live henceforth in Argos, in his father's house? Shall he at public altars share in sacrifice? Shall holy water lave his hands at tribal feasts?

APOLLO: This too I answer; mark the truth of what I say. The mother is not the true parent of the child which is called hers. She is a nurse who tends the growth of young seed planted by its true parent, the male. So, if Fate spares the child, she keeps it, as one might keep for some friend a growing plant. And of this truth, that father without mother may beget, we have present, as proof, the daughter of Olympian Zeus: one never nursed in the dark cradle of the womb; yet such a being no god will beget again.

Pallas, I sent this man to supplicate your hearth; he is but one of many gifts my providence will send, to make your city and your people great. He and his city, Pallas, shall for ever be your faithful allies; their posterity shall hold this pledge their dear possession for all future years.

ATHENE: Shall I now bid the jurors cast each man his vote according to his conscience? Are both pleas complete?

APOLLO: I have shot every shaft I had; and wait to hear the jurors' verdict.

ATHENE: [to the CHORUS]:   Will this course content you too?

CHORUS [to the jurors]:   You have heard them and us. Now, jurors, as you cast your votes, let reverence for your oath guide every heart.

[*The jurors vote.*]

ATHENE: My duty is to give the final vote. When yours are counted, mine goes to uphold Orestes' plea. No mother gave me birth. Therefore the father's claim and male supremacy in all things, save to give myself in marriage, wins my whole heart's loyalty. Therefore a woman's death, who killed her husband, is, I judge, outweighed in grievousness by his. And so Orestes, if the votes are equal, wins the case. Let those appointed bring the urns and count the votes.

[*Two of the jurors obey her.*]

ORESTES: O bright Apollo, what verdict will be revealed?

CHORUS: O Mother Night, O Darkness, look on us!

ORESTES: To me this moment brings despair and death, or life and hope.

CHORUS: To us increase of honour, or disgrace and loss.

APOLLO: The votes are out. Count scrupulously, citizens; justice is holy; in your division worship her. Loss of a single vote is loss of happiness; and one vote gained will raise to life a fallen house.

[*The votes are brought to* ATHENE. *The black and the white pebbles are even in number.* ATHENE *adds her to the white.*]

ATHENE: Orestes is acquitted of blood-guiltiness. The votes are even.

ORESTES: Pallas, Saviour of my house! I was an exile; you have brought me home again. Hellas can say of me, "He is an Argive, as he used to be, and holds his father's house and wealth by grace of Pallas and Apollo, and of Zeus the Saviour, the Fulfiller." Zeus has shown respect for my dead father, seeing my mother's advocates, and has delivered me.

So now, before I turn my steps to Argos, hear the oath I make to you, your country, and your people, for all future time: no Argive king shall ever against Attica lead his embattled spear. If any man transgress this oath of mine, I will myself rise from the grave in vengeance, to perplex him with disastrous loss, clogging his marches with ill omens and despair, till all his soldiers curse the day they left their homes. But if my oath is kept, and my posterity prove staunch and faithful allies to the Athenian State, they shall enjoy my blessing. So, Pallas, farewell; farewell, citizens of Athens! May each struggle bring death to your foes, to you success and victory!

[*Exeunt* APOLLO *and* ORESTES.]

CHORUS: The old is trampled by the new! Curse on you younger gods who override the ancient laws and rob me of my due! Now to appease the honour you reviled vengeance shall fester till my full heart pours over this land on every side anger for insult, poison for my pain—yes, poison from whose killing rain a sterile blight shall creep on plant and child and pock the earth's face with infectious sores. Why should I weep? Hear, Justice, what I do! Soon Athens in despair shall rue her rashness and her mockery. Daughters of Night and Sorrow, come with me, feed on dishonour, on revenge to be!

ATHENE: Let me entreat you soften your indignant grief. Fair trial, fair judgement, ended in an even vote, which brings to you neither dishonour nor defeat. Evidence which issued clear as day from Zeus himself, brought by the god who bade Orestes strike the blow, could not but save him from all harmful consequence. Then quench your anger; let not indignation rain pestilence on our soil, corroding every seed till the whole land is sterile desert. In return I promise you, here in this upright land, a home, and bright thrones in a holy cavern, where you shall receive for ever homage from our citizens.

CHORUS: The old is trampled by the new! Curse on you younger gods who override the ancient laws and rob me of my due! Now to appease the honour you reviled vengeance shall fester till my full heart pours over this land on every side anger for insult, poison for my pain—yes, poison from whose killing rain a sterile blight shall creep on plant and child, and pock the earth's face with infectious sores. Why should I weep? Hear, Justice, what I do! Soon Athens in despair shall rue her rashness and her mockery. Daughters of Night and Sorrow, come with me, feed on dishonour, on revenge to be!

ATHENE: None has dishonoured you. Why should immortal rage infect the fields of mortal men with pestilence? You call on Justice: I rely on Zeus. What need to reason further? I alone among the gods knows the sealed chamber's keys where Zeus' thunderbolt is stored. But force is needless; let persuasion check the fruits of foolish threats before it falls to spread plague and disaster. Calm this black and swelling wrath; honour and dignity await you: share with me a home in Athens. You will yet applaud my words, when Attica's wide fields bring you their firstfruit gifts, when sacrifice for childbirth and for marriage-vows is made upon your altars in perpetual right.

CHORUS: O shame and grief, that such a fate should fall to me, whose wisdom grew within me when the world was new! Must I accept, beneath the ground, a nameless and abhorred estate? O ancient Earth, see my disgrace! While anguish runs through flesh and bone my breathless rage breaks every bound. O night, my mother, hear me groan, outwitted, scorned and overthrown by new gods from my ancient place!

ATHENE: Your greater age claims my forbearance, as it gives wisdom far greater than my own; though to me too Zeus gave discernment. And I tell you this: if you now make some other land your home, your thoughts will turn with deep desire to Athens. For the coming age shall see her glory growing yet more glorious. You, here possessing an exalted sanctuary beside Erechtheus' temple, shall receive from all, both men and women, honours which no other land could equal. Therefore do not cast upon my fields whetstones of murder, to corrupt our young men's hearts and make them mad with passions not infused by wine; nor plant in them the temper of the mutinous cock, to set within my city's walls man against man with self-destructive boldness, kin defying kin. Let war be with the stranger, at the stranger's gate; there let men fall in love with glory; but at home let no cocks fight.

Then, goddesses, I offer you a home in Athens, where the gods most love to live, where gifts and honours shall deserve your kind good-will.

CHORUS: O shame and grief, that such a fate should fall to me, whose wisdom grew within me when the world was new! Must I accept, beneath the ground, a nameless and abhorred estate? O ancient Earth, see my disgrace! While anguish runs through flesh and bone my breathless rage breaks every bound. O Night, my mother, hear me groan, outwitted, scorned and overthrown by new gods from my ancient place!

ATHENE: I will not weary in offering you friendly words. You shall not say that you, an older deity, were by a younger Power and by these citizens driven dishonoured, homeless, from this land. But if holy Persuasion bids your heart respect my words and welcome soothing eloquence, then stay with us! If you refuse, be sure you will have no just cause to turn with spleen and malice on our peopled streets. A great and lasting heritage awaits you here; thus honour is assured and justice satisfied.

CHORUS: What place, divine Athene, do you offer me?

ATHENE: One free from all regret. Acceptance lies with you.

CHORUS: Say I accept it: what prerogatives are mine?

ATHENE.   Such that no house can thrive without your favour sought.

CHORUS: You promise to secure for me this place and power?

ATHENE: I will protect and prosper all who reverence you.
CHORUS: Your word is pledged for ever?
ATHENE: Do I need to promise what I will not perform?
CHORUS: My anger melts. Your words move me.
ATHENE: In Athens you are in the midst of friends.
CHORUS: What blessings would you have me call upon this land?
ATHENE: Such as bring victory untroubled with regret; blessing from earth and sea and sky; blessing that breathes in wind and sunlight through the land; that beast and field enrich my people with unwearied fruitfulness, and armies of brave sons be born to guard their peace. Sternly weed out the impious, lest their rankness choke the flower of goodness. I would not have just men's lives troubled with villainy. These blessings you must bring; I will conduct their valiant arms to victory, and make the name of Athens honoured through the world.
CHORUS: I will consent to share Athene's home, to bless this fortress of the immortal Powers which mighty Zeus and Ares chose for their habitation, the pride and glory of the gods of Greece, and guardian of their altars. This prayer I pray for Athens, pronounce this prophecy with kind intent: fortune shall load her land with healthful gifts from her rich earth engendered by the sun's burning brightness.
ATHENE: I will do my part, and win blessing for my city's life, welcoming within our walls these implacable and great goddesses. Their task it is to dispose all mortal ways. He who wins their enmity lives accurst, not knowing whence falls the wounding lash of life. Secret guilt his father knew hails him to their judgement-seat, where, for all his loud exclaims, death, his angry enemy, silent grinds him into dust.
CHORUS: I have yet more to promise. No ill wind shall carry blight to make your fruit-trees fade; no bud-destroying canker shall creep across your frontiers, nor sterile sickness threaten your supply. May Pan give twin lambs to your thriving ewes in their expected season; and may the earth's rich produce honour the generous Powers with grateful gifts.
ATHENE: Guardians of our city's wall, hear the blessings they will bring! Fate's Avengers wield a power great alike in heaven and

hell; and their purposes on earth they fulfill for all to see, giving, after their deserts, songs to some, to others pain in a prospect blind with tears.

CHORUS: I pray that no untimely chance destroy your young men in their pride; and let each lovely virgin, as a bride, fulfil her life with joy. For all these gifts, you sovereign gods, we pray, and you, our sisters three, dread Fates, whose just decree chooses for every man his changeless way, you who in every household have your place, whose visitations fall with just rebuke on all—hear us, most honoured of the immortal race!

ATHENE: Now, for the love that you perform to this dear land, my heart is warm. Holy Persuasion too I bless, who softly strove with harsh denial, till Zeus the Pleader came to trial and crowned Persuasion with success. Now good shall strive with good; and we and they shall share the victory.

CHORUS: Let civil war, insatiate of ill, never in Athens rage; let burning wrath, that murder must assuage, never take arms to spill, in this my heritage, the blood of man till dust has drunk its fill. Let all together find joy in each other; and each both love and hate with the same mind as his blood-brother; for this heals many hurts of humankind.

ATHENE: These gracious words and promised deeds adorn the path where wisdom leads. Great gain for Athens shall arise from these grim forms and threatening eyes. Then worship them with friendly heart, for theirs is friendly. Let your State hold justice as her chiefest prize; and land and city shall be great and glorious in every part.

[The play ends with a torchlight procession which ushers the Furies, now "the Friendly Ones," to their new home.]

3. The Old Testament

Some passages appropriate to be read in conjunction with this section are:

> Genesis 1–3; 12; 16; 29–30; 34; 38
> Exodus 20:14, 17; 21:7–11; 22; 22:16–19
> Leviticus 12; 15:19–32; 20:10–21
> Numbers 15:21–31
> Deuteronomy 22:5, 13–30; 24:1–5; 25:5–10
> Judges 11:29–40; 19
> Ruth
> 2 Samuel 11–13
> Esther
> Proverbs 5:1–6; 9:13–18; 31:10–31
> Song of Songs
> Ezekiel 16
> Hosea 1–3

The Old Testament view of women is more complex and varied than can possibly be described in a brief introduction; at best, a few generalizations can be hazarded. Although it has been stated that "the Old Testament is a man's 'book' where women appear for the most part simply as adjuncts of men, significant only in the context of men's activities,"[1] there are some biblical motifs which could give rise to a different interpretation. For example, the God of the Old Testament was not pictured as involved in a sexual relationship as the fertility deities of the Ancient Near East usually were. This has led theologians to argue that the biblical God transcends sex, is neither male nor female. Despite this claim, it is necessary to point out that the images used to depict God are overwhelmingly masculine: God is the King, the Judge, the Shepherd, the Warrior. Such descriptions of God are not surprising since Hebrew society was so strongly patriarchal; nonetheless they pose problems for contemporary women who find the theologians' assessment wanting.

Likewise, it has been suggested that a central biblical motif supportive of women's aspirations is freedom from oppression, perhaps best expressed in the accounts of the Hebrews' Exodus from Egypt to "a land flowing with milk and honey," a land of liberty.[2] This theme too is inspiring in principle—and a feminist interpretation of the Exodus has been developed by Mary Daly[3]—but the fact remains that the freedom spoken about is given to the Hebrew people as a whole, not to women in particular. It is dubious whether the Hebrews themselves would have interpreted the Exodus as signaling new relationships between the sexes.

When we fall back on the actual stories and accounts preserved in the Old Testament regarding women, we might easily become bewildered by the evidence. It is true that women are depicted as having some freedom of movement outside the home (especially in Genesis, the wives and daughters of the patriarchs wander about with a lack of restraint not considered proper in later Hebrew society[4]), and they are represented as engaging in tasks which were financially profitable (the industrious housewife of Proverbs 31 is an example). But the actual legal position of Hebrew women does not appear to have been as high as that of women in other Ancient Near Eastern countries such as Egypt and Babylon.[5] Hebrew women were not considered capable of adult responsibility in matters of inheritance, the taking of vows, or in initiating divorce. They were excluded by virtue of their sex from many cultic acts, in part because women's biological functions of menstruation and childbirth were thought to render her ritually unclean (Lev. 12; 15). Her domestic services were indeed valued, particularly her contribution of children to the household, but her place remained, nonetheless, subordinate to the male's. A few women are singled out as special heroines, although it must be mentioned that some of these much-touted females, such as Ruth and Esther, achieved their ends through their sexual allurement and hence lose their attractiveness as "role-models" for modern women. Others, like Deborah and Jael, made contributions to Hebrew society in their own right, but often the females described are those who brought doom and disaster to the men with whom they associated. Delilah and Jezebel stand as horrifying remainders of the destructive powers of the female sex. The "myth of feminine evil," as H. R. Hays has labeled it,[6] was entrenched in the Hebrew tradition as well as in the Graeco-Roman.

Although some might argue that it is an exaggeration to refer to Hebrew women as the chattels of their husbands or fathers, numerous laws and stories in the Old Testament invite that interpretation. Judges 19 tells the tale of the Levite's concubine, delivered by her master into the hands of rapists who abused her until she died. David's seduction/rape of Bathsheba (2 Sam. 11–12) is viewed primarily as an offense against her husband Uriah.[7] The young woman who lies about her virginity is judged deserving of the death penalty because she deceived not only her prospective husband, but also her father, under whose watchful (or in this case, not so watchful) eye she had lived (Deut. 22). Fathers, apparently, had the right to dispose of their children as they saw fit; the sacrifice of Jephthah's nameless daughter as the penalty for his thoughtless vow (Judg. 11) was a biblical story viewed with special horror by later feminists.[8] In the Decalogue, a wife is listed among the possessions of a neighbor which are not to be coveted (Exod. 20). And the practice of levirate marriage (Deut. 25) implies that the childless widow was considered the "property" of her dead husband's family. Such evidence suggests that the concept of "ownership" of females is not a totally misleading one, despite frequent protests to the contrary.

Patriarchal societies usually express a strong concern for purity of descent and legitimate succession of children;[9] the Hebrews were no exception in this regard. Although married men were not prohibited from sexual relationships with unmarried females, especially harlots, a married woman's sexual fidelity to her husband was considered essential. The mere suspicion on his part that she had "strayed," even if it was not prompted by objective evidence, could result in the wife's undergoing something like a trial by ordeal—and the husband was not judged guilty or punished if he wrongly suspected his wife and forced her to submit to the "command of jealousy" (Num. 5). It is instructive in this regard that the Hebrews used a woman's sexual deviation as a central metaphor for religious apostasy; falling away from the worship of Yahweh alone is described as "harlotry" in several biblical passages (Hos. 1–3; Ezek. 16).[10]

Sexual relations themselves were thought of as a "good," at least within the context of marriage. In general, Judaism has not condemned the pleasure of the sexual act in the way that Christianity so often has.[11] Although both Jews and Christians came to interpret the Song of Songs allegorically, the fact that such a lusty love poem could find its way into the "sacred literature" testifies to the Hebrews' positive evaluation of the sexual relation. Of course, such relations were hedged about with many tabus, particularly regarding menstruation (Lev. 15). Men worried about the wiles of "loose" women, a theme especially prominent in the wisdom literature (Prov. 5; 9). Homosexuality and other forms of "deviant" sexual behavior were condemned (Exod. 20; Lev. 18). Nonetheless, the command to "reproduce and multiply" in Genesis 1 seems to have been undertaken with a sense of joy rather than grudgingly performed out of duty to society.

Moreover, it is to the Hebrews' credit that they did not, at least in the literature contained in the Jewish canon of the Bible, interpret the stories of Genesis 2 and 3 (Eve's creation and her part in the first sin in Eden) as a justification for negative attitudes to women. Eve, strangely enough, does not function as any kind of female symbol in the Old Testament. It was, rather, the early church fathers who understood what a useful service she might render as a prototype of female sensuality, stupidity, and treacherousness.[12] Hebrew women might well have held a secondary place to men in their society, but at least they were not, in the biblical period, considered to be God's unfortunate afterthought.

In fact, recent attempts have been made, with some success, to show that the myth of Eve in Genesis 2 and 3 is in no way insulting to woman, but rather depicts her as an equal to Adam, the completion of creation.[13] Such myths, read with fresh eyes, have led at least one Old Testament scholar to remark that "depatriarchalizing" is not something we have to bring to the Old Testament text; "it is a hermeneutic operating within Scripture itself. We expose it; we do not impose it."[14] Although this viewpoint does not hold for all the Old Testament depictions of women, the story of Adam and Eve is readily subject to new interpretations welcome to biblical scholars and feminists alike.

There are many fascinating sources in post-Biblical Judaism for the study of women; alas, they cannot be dealt with here. It is hoped that other books will undertake a description of female status in the Talmudic and medieval Jewish codes of law, examine the references to Lilith and the Shekinah, and explore the attitudes toward women in early Reform Judaism, among the Hasidim, the founders of the kibbutz movement, and in contemporary Israel.

4. The New Testament

Some passages appropriate to be read in conjunction with this section are:

Matthew 1–2; 5:27–32; 9:18–26; 10:34–39; 12:46–50; 15:21–28; 19:1–15; 22:23–33; 27:55–28:20.
Mark 3:31–35; 5:21–43; 7:24–30; 10:1–16; 12:18–27; 15:40–16:20.
Luke 1–3; 7:11–17, 36–50; 8:1–3, 19–21, 40–56; 10:38–42; 11:27–28; 12:51–53; 13:10–17; 14:26–27; 15:8–10; 16:18; 18:15–17; 20:27–40; 23:49–24:53.
John 2:1–11; 4:1–42; 8:1–11; 11:1–44; 12:1–8; 19:25–20:31.
Acts 9:36–43; 12:12–17; 16:11–15; 18:1–3, 24–28; 21:8–9.
Romans 1; 16.
1 Corinthians 5–7; 11:1–16; 14:33–36.
Galatians 3:26–28.
Ephesians 5:21–33.
Colossians 3:18–19; 4:15.
1 Timothy 2:11–15; 5:3–16.
Titus 2:3–5.
1 Peter 3:1–7.

The New Testament Gospels, all of which were written at least forty years after Jesus' death, give us four different pictures of him. They were composed, so say the scholars, not as biographies but as confessions of faith, witnessing to their authors' conviction of the power of the risen Lord who, they thought, was still guiding the Christian community. We have, alas, no firsthand information from Jesus himself, as we do from Paul.

The Gospels, as far as we know, were all composed by men, or groups of men, and the new faith to which they testified was one which had arisen from the male-oriented religion of Judaism. The readers and hearers of the Gospels, although they were not living in environments as oppressive of women as postexilic Palestinian Judaism, still were not part of a world in which females had equal rights and responsibilities with men. Yet the Gospels give us a picture of Jesus as a man who mingled and talked with women, was not afraid of becoming ritually defiled by them, and did not think that their only function lay in kitchen and childbearing duties. All of the Gospels mention the female followers of Jesus and stress their roles in the resurrection events. The Gospel of Luke, in particular, written to a primarily Gentile audience, stresses Jesus' friendship with Mary and Martha (Luke 10:38–42), mentions Jesus' female traveling companions (Luke 8:1–3), and even compares God to a woman in the parable of the lost coin (Luke 15:8–10).

To what extent does such evidence suggest that Jesus was a feminist, as Leonard Swidler has argued?[1] The gospel portrayals of Jesus can be assessed from different viewpoints. Although Jesus is represented as dealing with women in a kindly fashion, he is also shown treating other kinds of outcasts—lepers, tax collectors, the poor—with similar good will and benevolence. Whether or not the depiction of Jesus in the Bible gives us the right to claim that he would favor modern feminism is a dubious matter. No doubt this topic will be much debated in the years to come, just as the question of Jesus' sexuality has recently been brought to the forefront in a number of provocative books and articles.[2]

Paul's letters, the earliest materials preserved in the New Testament, present us with an even more confusing picture. Most scholars now believe that the letters to Timothy, Titus, and the Ephesians were not written by Paul, but were products of a later time. This eliminates from Pauline authorship some of the more offensive passages about women in the New Testament. But even when we limit our investigation to those letters of Paul generally considered to be authentic, there is considerable disagreement about the interpretation of his words.

Paul's inspiring assertion in Galatians 3:28 ("There is neither Jew nor Greek, there is neither slave nor free, there is neither male nor female[3]; for you are all one in Christ Jesus") has often been cited by feminists as an injunction to bring justice to women in the social sphere. But did Paul intend for his words to carry this meaning? The New Testament certainly depicts Paul as investing his prodigious energy in the project of ensuring that Gentile converts to Christianity were accepted on an equal footing with their Jewish-Christian brethren. But, as far as we know, he did nothing to promote changing the status of slaves or women. In fact, the letter to Philemon represents Paul as accepting without question the institution of slavery, and there is little from him that evidences a strong belief in women's equality. In his letters, Paul does send greetings to women who are leaders in the churches and in the book of Acts he is represented as working with them. Moreover, in his letters he speaks of women praying and prophesying along with men in public worship (1 Cor. 11:5), something forbidden to women in the Judaism out of which Paul came. In Romans 16:1, Paul calls Phoebe a *diakonos*,[4] which suggests that women held some kind of "ordained office" in the church.[5] But to what extent do such practices indicate that Paul was a feminist?

It is futile to cite the words of 1 Corinthians 7 on the equal rights and responsibilities of the husband and wife in marriage as any indication of Paul's feminist stance, since Paul plainly thought that marriage meant bondage, not liberty, for both partners, the wife as well as the husband.[6] A more negative evidence of Paul's position might be derived from 1 Corinthians 11, in which he instructs women to keep their heads covered during worship, alluding to Eve's secondary place at creation and her primacy in rushing into sin as justifications for the practice. Valiant attempts have been made to rescue the passage from its usual interpretation and make it a proof-text for Paul's feminism, but they seem rather strained.[7] And 1 Corinthians 14:34–36 is such an embarrassment to the supporters of Paul that they generally eliminate the verses from the Pauline canon.[8] Paul's chastisements of women actually suggest that they played an important part in the early Christian church (at least in Corinth), no matter what Paul himself felt about the situation. The debate about Paul's feminism will no doubt continue.[9] But whether Paul was or was not a feminist, the actual history of the Christian church developed in a nonfeminist direction.

Most scholars agree that attitudes toward women became increasingly oppressive toward the end of the first century A.D., as the church gradually relinquished its hope for the early arrival of the Kingdom of God and settled back into the mores and customs of the world. The post-Pauline epistles bear witness to this change. In these letters, it is presumed that women will stay at home, bear children, obey their husbands, and keep silent. No more journeying about the countryside in the service of the Christian cause! The open attitudes of Jesus and perhaps even Paul have vanished by the turn into the second century. And in the centuries thereafter, it was not the mainline "orthodox" church, the Great Church, which carried the message of expanded roles for women to its conclusion; it was the "heretics," the Gnostics and spiritualists, who took seriously the hints for female emancipation which the Bible had provided. It was in these fringe groups that Paul's cry of "no male and female" was put into effect, sometimes in surprisingly radical ways.[10] Within mainstream Christianity, the Pauline "no male and female" text perhaps found its fullest manifestation within the monastic tradition, which attempted to uphold the spiritual equality—and sometimes the political[11]—of men and women.

The church fathers we will study in the following chapters occasionally—but not often—struggled to overcome the bias of their culture or their personal temperaments in regard to the equality of women. As one commentator has phrased it,

> The later Church, when it lost the vision that the Kingdom was coming, also lost the theology that enabled it to live as though the Kingdom were at hand. As a consequence, it inherited two seemingly divergent messages: the theology of equivalence in Christ; the practice of women's subordination. In attempting to reconcile them, it maintained a status-quo ethics on the social level through the subordination of women, and it affirmed the vision of equivalence on the spiritual level by projecting it as an other-

worldly reality. Throughout the history of the Church this has led to complex and confused theological arguments, with their consequent social distortions.[12]

One pair of stories found in the New Testament is of particular interest for the development of later attitudes regarding women and sexuality. The stories of Jesus' birth recounted in Matthew and Luke had enormous significance for the veneration of Mary and virginity. Although the stories differ in many details, they both agree that Mary was a virgin at the time she conceived Jesus. Already in the second century these accounts—preserved nowhere else in the New Testament and presumably unknown to Paul and other New Testament writers—had been elaborated upon to stress that Mary never lost the physiological evidence of her virginal status, not even after she had given birth to Jesus. An apocryphal gospel called "The Protevangelium of James" was one of the first to press this point of view; its author, in describing the miraculousness of Jesus' birth, depicts Mary as different in kind from other women. According to this work, after Jesus had been born in a cave, the midwife who had attended the birth met her friend Salome:

> And she said to her: "Salome, Salome, I have a new sight to tell you; a virgin has brought forth, a thing which her nature does not allow." And Salome said: As the Lord my God lives, unless I put forward my finger and test her condition, I will not believe that a virgin has brought forth."
> And the midwife went in and said to Mary: "Make yourself ready, for there is no small contention concerning you." And Salome put forward her finger to test her condition. And she cried out, saying: "Woe for my wickedness and my unbelief; for I have tempted the living God; and behold, my hand falls away from me, consumed by fire!"[13]

Salome is healed by touching the infant Jesus, and she affirms her belief in Mary's virginity.

The theme of Mary's virginal conception of Jesus took on further meaning as later Christian theologians such as Augustine asserted the theory that there was a link between sexual intercourse and the transfer of original sin. Jesus, not only because he was the

Son of God, but also because he was born of a virgin, was exempt from that sin.

By the eleventh century, it was also popularly believed that Mary also had a sin-free status, although it was not until 1854 that the Vatican decreed as a dogmatic pronouncement that Mary was "immaculately conceived" by her parents.[14] Thus Mary has been depicted as a sinless woman in Catholic teaching, a circumstance which is sometimes held to be of importance in raising the status of women. Feminists have tended to deny this interpretation, holding that the figure of Mary cannot serve as a genuine role-model for ordinary women, who can never aspire to her divinely given freedom from original sin any more than they can hope to achieve simultaneous motherhood and virginity.[15] Nonetheless, Mary played an important part in Christian thinking from at least the fourth century, if not earlier, due to the fact that she was taken by the church as the exemplar of lifelong virginity, which by that time had become the preferred mode of existence for Christians.[16]

5. Clement of Alexandria and the Gnostics: Women, Sexuality, and Marriage in Orthodoxy and Heterodoxy

The Gnostic movement, insofar as it was associated with Christianity, provided a foil for the "orthodox"[1] church's affirmation of the goodness of human sexuality and of marriage. The desire to combat Gnostic views and to restate the opinion presented in Genesis 1 and 2, that the created order had received God's blessing, led Clement to compose his treatise on marriage,[2] which comes down to us as one of the most positive statements regarding marriage and sexuality in early Christian literature. By the fourth century, the rapid development of asceticism within the Christian community would call into question even the rather lukewarm affirmation of marriage given by Clement, but, in the late second century, when Clement's attitudes were taking shape, the threat to Christian ethical teaching came largely from the Gnostic sects which had developed and spread—rather alarmingly, from the point of view of the church fathers—in the course of the one hundred years previous.

It is impossible to do more here than to suggest a few of the features of Gnosticism with which Clement was concerned. Gnosticism, as described by Hans Jonas, was part of a larger spiritual movement which swept the Hellenistic world; as a "dualistic transcendent religion of salvation,"[3] it was composed of a large variety of sects, each of which had its own particular mythology and ethic. Common to many of the sects was the view that the universe was evil,[4] created either through the malicious intent of a wicked deity or through an accident which occurred within the realm of the spiritual powers. In either case, the material world in all its ramifications was seen as the unfortunate result of divine mismanagement. The "spark" or "spirit" (*pneuma*) within humans—or true Gnostics, at least—was trapped in the fleshly covering of the body. To bring enlightenment to man, to show him the heavenly origins and destiny of his *pneuma*, was one aim of the Gnostic religion.

Gnostic hostility to the *cosmos* and to the powers responsible for its creation led to the adoption of at least two diverse ethical outlooks.[5] Some Gnostics took an ascetic approach to the material world and denied themselves, as far as possible, food, drink, and sexual intercourse. Others took the opposite stance of libertinism; their reasoning was that if the God who made the universe and gave us the Old Testament commandments was not the redeemer who brings us knowledge (*gnosis*), we should show our contempt for him by defying his laws and standards of goodness.

Many Gnostics believed that a person's "salvation" or "damnation" was not in any way dependent upon his behavior, but simply upon whether or not he had received the *gnosis*. True Gnostics, they thought, could not forfeit their salvation, no matter how reprehensible their conduct might appear to those espousing a more ordinary morality. The church fathers were highly suspicious about this "predestinarian" element in Gnostic thinking; they frequently asserted that good behavior resulting from the free choice of the individual was essential for salvation. The praise and blame assigned to a person's deeds must be related to his volition; righteousness was, in the words of Hellenistic philosophy, "up to us." It is easy to understand how, in this context, neither the predestinarian elements of Paul's teaching nor his emphasis upon God's grace could be much stressed until years after the first wave of Gnosticism had subsided. Clement was one of the church fathers most vociferous in his attack upon Gnostic determinism. His stress on the free will of human beings was, as W. E. G. Floyd has put it, his "trump card."[6]

Clement, in the selections which follow, demonstrates his opposition to both the ascetic and the libertine forms of Gnosticism. It is blasphemy to abstain from sexual relations out of hostility to the Creator and the world he made. Sexual desire is something which God has implanted within us and hence must be good. So eager to affirm the positive worth of marriage is Clement that he even asserts Paul married![7]

Christians should be taught that abstinence can be a good if— and only if—it is undertaken from the motivation of the love of God and with constant dependence upon his strengthening help. Mere physical continence by itself, such as athletes practiced, would not meet Clement's standards of Christian virginity. It may be that Clement himself would have preferred that more Christians embrace the old Stoic ideal of *apatheia*, freedom from passion, but since this goal did not seem to be a realistic one for the large mass of "simple believers," marriage should be affirmed as a kind of "middle way."[8] Even within marriage, Clement enjoins considerable restraint regarding sexual relations, which seem to be solely for the sake of begetting children.[9] But marriage, as well as celibacy, must be approved as a kind of "service and ministry to the Lord."

Let us now turn to the examination of some Gnostic material. The selection from Clement gives us few clues to the distinctive beliefs and practices of the Gnostics regarding femaleness. In two different ways, the Gnostics showed that their view of women was at variance with orthodox Christianity's. In contrast to the unremittingly "male" imagery associated with the Godhead by the church fathers, there are many references in Gnostic literature to female aspects of divinity. Some Gnostic systems describe the Godhead (*pleroma*) as composed of male and female principles. In the Valentinian scheme, for example, the Forefather, Abyss, mates with a primordial female, Thought (also called Grace and Silence), to bring forth a male aeon, Mind, and a female one, Truth—and the "begetting" continues from that point, with male and female principles bringing forth new offspring.[10] The last female aeon, Sophia (Wisdom), throws the pleroma into disruption by her passion to know Father Abyss; because of the disturbance she causes, the entire universe (and mankind) is created.[11] In other

Gnostic texts, such as the *Apocryphon of John*, instead of the conventional description of the Trinity as Father, Son, and Holy Spirit, we learn about the Father, the Son—and the Mother! "John" is given a vision in which God informs him, "I am the Father, I am the Mother, I am the Son."[12] Such female descriptions of the Godhead are almost nonexistent in traditional Christian circles of this era, but reemerge later in some Christian mystical literature (see the selections from Julian of Norwich below) and in Shaker piety.

The notion that "femaleness" could be contained within the Godhead found its social counterpart in the activities of women within the Gnostic camp. One example of the church fathers' horror at female leadership exerted among the Gnostics is Tertullian's famous outcry: "How bold these heretical women are! They have no modesty; they are bold enough to teach, to argue, to perform exorcisms, to undertake cares, and maybe even to baptize!"[13] Our selection below from *The Gospel of Mary* indicates an approval of roles for females which orthodox Christianity did not sanction. The reproval of Mary by Peter and Andrew suggests that the Gnostic writer of this gospel was aware that the church fathers did not share the high estimate of women's abilities held by his sect. It may well be that one of the chief attractions for women in the so-called heretical and schismatic groups (we think also of the Montanists) lay in the expanded field of activity allowed them.

The Coptic *Gospel of Mary* is a Gnostic writing of an undetermined sect composed probably in the second century. In the first part of the gospel,[14] the risen Christ instructs his disciples. After his departure, they remain perplexed as to his intention for their future program of action. Mary Magdalene (a favorite character in Gnostic literature) comforts them in their despair and shares with them the private revelations given her by Jesus. Some of the male disciples, especially Peter,[15] refuse to accept the notion that Jesus gave such revelations to a woman rather than to them; the situation is smoothed over by Levi, and the disciples go out to undertake their religious missions. Thus the worth of a woman is vindicated; a female has instructed male associates, much as some

Gnostic women must have preached to and taught men. Woman's role in church leadership vanishes from the scene in orthodox Christianity, reappearing briefly among some nuns of the medieval period, but coming to its own again in such spiritualistic sects as the Quakers, Shakers, and Christian Scientists many centuries later.

On Marriage

It is not our aim to pursue this subject in further detail and to mention further senseless heresies. To put them to shame we should be forced to deal with each one, and to state our objections to each point, which would extend these notes to an unconscionable length. Accordingly we may divide all the heresies into two groups in making answer to them. Either they teach that one ought to live on the principle that it is a matter of indifference whether one does right or wrong, or they set a too ascetic tone and proclaim the necessity of continence on the ground of opinions which are godless and arise from hatred of what God has created. First we may discuss the former group. If it is lawful to live any sort of life one likes, obviously one may live in continence; or if any kind of life has no dangers for the elect, obviously one of virtue and self-control is far less dangerous. If the "lord of the sabbath" (Matt. 12:8) has been given the right to pass uncorrected if he lives an immoral life, a fortiori there will be no correction for him who behaves decently. "All things are lawful, but all things are not expedient" (1 Cor. 6:12, 10:23) says the apostle. If all things are lawful, obviously this includes self-control. . . .

But how is it possible to become like the Lord and have knowledge of God if one is subject to physical pleasures? . . . We must not live as if there were no difference between right and wrong, but, to the best of our power, must purify ourselves from indulgence and lust and take care for our soul which must continually be devoted to the Deity alone. For when it is pure and set free

From Clement of Alexandria, "On Marriage," *Stromateis* 3 in *Alexandrian Christianity*, ed. J. E. L. Oulton and H. Chadwick, vol. 3 of The Library of Christian Classics (Philadelphia: Westminster Press, 1954).

from all evil the mind is somehow capable of receiving the power of God and the divine image is set up in it. "And everyone who has this hope in the Lord purifies himself," says the Scripture, "even as he is pure" (1 John 3:3).

To attain the knowledge of God is impossible for those who are still under the control of their passions. Therefore they cannot attain the salvation they hope for as they have not obtained any knowledge of God. He who fails to attain this end is clearly subject to the charge of being ignorant of God, and ignorance of God is shown by a man's manner of life. It is absolutely impossible at the same time to be a man of understanding and not to be ashamed to gratify the body. . . .

It is the manner of life which shows up those who know the commandments; for as a man's word is, so is his life. The tree is known by its fruit (Matt. 7:16), not by its blossom and leaves. Knowledge, then, comes from the fruit and from behavior, not from talk and from blossom. We say that knowledge is not mere talk, but a certain divine knowledge, that light which is kindled in the soul as a result of obedience to the commandments, and which reveals all that is in a state of becoming, enables man to know himself and teaches him to become possessed of God. What the eye is in the body, knowledge is in the mind. Let them not call bondage to pleasure freedom, as if bitterness were sweet. We have learnt to recognize as freedom that which the Lord alone confers on us when he liberates us from lusts and desires and the other passions. "He who says, I know the Lord, and does not keep his commandments, is a liar and the truth is not in him," says John (1 John 2:4).

To those, on the other hand, who under a pious cloak blaspheme by their continence both the creation and the holy Creator, the almighty, only God, and teach that one must reject marriage and begetting of children, and should not bring others in their place to live in this wretched world, nor give any sustenance to death, our reply is as follows. . . .

The task of the law is to deliver us from a dissolute life and all disorderly ways. Its purpose is to lead us from unrighteousness to righteousness, so that it would have us self-controlled in marriage, in begetting children, and in general behavior. The Lord is not "come to destroy the law but to fulfill it" (Matt. 5:17). "To fulfill" does not imply that it was defective, but that by his coming the prophecies of the law are accomplished, since before the law the demand for right conduct was proclaimed by the Logos to those also who lived good lives. The multitude who know nothing of continence live for the body, not for the spirit. But the body without spirit is "earth and ashes" (Gen. 18:27). Now the Lord judges adultery which is only committed in thought (Matt. 5:28). What then? Is it not possible to remain continent even in the married state and not to seek to "put asunder what God has joined together" (Matt. 19:6)? For such is the teaching of those who divide the yoke of marriage, by reason of whom the Christian name is blasphemed. If it is the view of these people who themselves owe their existence to sexual relations that such relations are impure, must not they be impure? But I hold that even the seed of the sanctified is holy. . . .

If, as they say, they have already attained the state of resurrection, and on this account reject marriage let them neither eat nor drink. For the apostle says that in the resurrection the belly and food shall be destroyed. Why then do they hunger and thirst and suffer the weaknesses of the flesh and all the other needs which will not affect the man who through Christ has attained to the hoped for resurrection? Furthermore those who worship idols abstain both from food and from sexual intercourse. "But the kingdom of God does not consist in eating and drinking" (Rom. 14:17), he says. And indeed the Magi make a point of abstaining from wine and the meat of animals and from sexual intercourse while they are worshipping angels and daemons. But just as humility consists in meekness and not in treating one's body roughly, so also continence is a virtue of the soul which is not manifest to others, but is in secret.

There are some who say outright that marriage is fornication and teach that it was introduced by the devil. They proudly say that they are imitating the Lord who neither worried nor had any possession in this world, boasting that they understand the gospel better than anyone else. The Scripture says to them: "God resists the proud but gives grace to the humble" (James 4:6; 1 Pet. 5:5). Further, they do not know the reason why the Lord did not marry. In the first place he had his own bride, the Church; and in the next place he was no ordinary man that he should also be in need of some helpmeet (Gen. 2:18) after the flesh. Nor was it necessary for him to beget children since he abides eternally and was born the only Son of God. It is the Lord himself who says: "That which God has joined together, let no man put asunder" (Matt. 19:6). And again: "As it was in the days of Noah, they were marrying, and giving in marriage, building and planting, and as it was in the days of Lot, so shall be the coming of the Son of man" (Matt. 24:37–39). And to show that he is not referring to the heathen he adds: "When the Son of man is come, shall he find faith on the earth" (Luke 18:8). And again: "Woe to those who are with child and are giving suck in those days" (Matt. 24:19), a saying, I admit, to be understood allegorically. The reason why he did not determine "the times which the Father has appointed by his own power" (Acts 1:7) was that the world might continue from generation to generation.

Concerning the words, "Not all can receive this saying. There are some eunuchs who were born so, and some who were made eunuchs by men, and some who have made themselves eunuchs for the sake of the kingdom of heaven; let him receive it who can receive it" (Matt. 19:11f.), they do not realize the context. After his word about divorce some asked him whether, if that is the position in relation to woman, it is better not to marry; and it was then that the Lord said: "Not all can receive this saying, but those to whom it is granted." What the questioners wanted to know was whether, when a man's wife has been condemned for fornication, it is allowable for him to marry another.

It is said, however, that several athletes abstained from sexual intercourse, exercising continence to keep their bodies in training, as Astylos of Croton and Crison of Himera. Even the cithara-player, Amoebeus, though newly married, kept away from his bride. And Aristotle of Cyrene was the only man to disdain the love of Lais when she fell for him.

As he had sworn to the courtesan that he would take her to his home country if she rendered him some assistance against his antagonists, when she had rendered it, he kept his oath in an amusing manner by painting the closest possible likeness of her and setting it up in Cyrene. The story is told by Istros in his book on *The Peculiarity of Athletic Contests*. Therefore there is nothing meritorious about abstinence from marriage unless it arises from love to God. At any rate the blessed Paul says of those who revile marriage: "In the last times some shall depart from the faith, turning to spirits of error and doctrines inspired by daemons, forbidding to marry and condemning abstinence from food" (1 Tim. 4:1, 3). And again he says: "Let no one disqualify you by demanding self-imposed ascetic practices and severe treatment of the body" (Col. 2:18, 23). And the same writer has this also: "Are you bound to a wife? Do not seek to be separated from her? Are you free from any wife? Do not seek to find one." And again: "Let every man have his own wife lest Satan tempt you" (1 Cor. 7:27, 2, 5).

How then? Did not the righteous in ancient times partake of what God made with thanksgiving? Some begat children and lived chastely in the married state. To Elijah the ravens brought bread and meat for food (1 Kings 17:6). And Samuel the prophet brought as food for Saul the remnant of the thigh, of which he had already eaten (1 Sam. 9:24). But whereas they say that they are superior to them in behavior and conduct, they cannot even be compared with them in their deeds. "He who does not eat," then, "let him not despise him who eats; and he who eats let him not judge him who does not eat; for God has accepted him" (Rom. 14:3). Moreover, the Lord says of himself: "John came neither eating nor drinking, and they say, He has a devil. The Son of man came eating and drinking and they say, Behold a gluttonous man and a wine-bibber, a friend of publicans and a sinner" (Matt. 11:18f.).

Or do they also scorn the apostles? Peter and Philip had children, and Philip gave his daughters in marriage.

Even Paul did not hesitate in one letter to address his consort.*

* Does Clement have in mind Philippians 4:3?

The only reason why he did not take her about with him was that it would have been an inconvenience for his ministry. Accordingly he says in a letter: "Have we not a right to take about with us a wife that is a sister like the other apostles" (1 Cor. 9:5)? But the latter, in accordance with their particular ministry, devoted themselves to preaching without any distraction, and took their wives with them not as women with whom they had marriage relations, but as sisters, that they might be their fellow-ministers in dealing with housewives. It was through them that the Lord's teaching penetrated also the women's quarters without any scandal being aroused. We also know the directions about women deacons which are given by the noble Paul in his second letter to Timothy (1 Tim. 5:9f.). Furthermore, the self-same man cried aloud that "the kingdom of God does not consist in food and drink," not indeed in abstinence from wine and meat, "but in righteousness, peace, and joy in the Holy Spirit" (Rom. 14:17). Which of them goes about like Elijah clad in a sheepskin and a leather girdle? Which of them goes about like Isaiah, naked except for a piece of sacking and without shoes? Or clothed merely in a linen loincloth like Jeremiah (1 Kings 19:13; 2 Kings 1:8; Isa. 20:2; Jer. 13:1). Which of them will imitate John's gnostic way of life? The blessed prophets also lived in this manner and were thankful to the Creator. . . .

The human ideal of continence, I mean that which is set forth by Greek philosophers, teaches that one should fight desire and not be subservient to it so as to bring it to practical effect. But our ideal is not to experience desire at all. Our aim is not that while a man feels desire he should get the better of it, but that he should be continent even respecting desire itself. This chastity cannot be attained in any other way except by God's grace. That was why he said "Ask and it shall be given you" (Matt. 7:7). This grace was received even by Moses, though clothed in his needy body, so that for forty days he felt neither thirst nor hunger (Exod. 24:18). Just as it is better to be in good health than for a sick man to talk about health, so to be light is better than to discuss light, and true chastity is better than that taught by the philosophers. Where there is light there is no darkness. But where there is inward desire, even if it goes no further than desire and is quiescent so far as bodily action is concerned, union takes place in thought with the object of desire, although that object is not present.

Our general argument concerning marriage, food, and other matters, may proceed to show that we should do nothing from desire. Our will is to be directed only towards that which is necessary. For we are children not of desire but of will (John 1:13). A man who marries for the sake of begetting children must practise continence so that it is not desire he feels for his wife, whom he ought to love, and that he may beget children with a chaste and controlled will. For we have learnt not to "have thought for the flesh to fulfill its desires." We are to walk honourably as in the way", that is in Christ and in the enlightened conduct of the Lord's way, "not in revelling and drunkenness, not in debauchery and lasciviousness, not in strife and envy" (Rom. 13:13–14). . . .

If by agreement marriage relations are suspended for a time to give opportunity for prayers (1 Cor. 7:5), this teaches continence. He adds the words "by agreement" lest anyone should dissolve his marriage, and the words "for a time" lest a married man, brought to continence by force, should then fall into sin; for if he spares his own wife he may fall into desire for another woman. On this principle he said that the man who thinks he is not behaving properly if he brings up his daughter to be unmarried, does right to give her in marriage (1 Cor. 7:36). Whether a man becomes a celibate or whether he joins himself in marriage with a woman for the sake of having children, his purpose ought to be to remain unyielding to what is inferior. If he can live a life of intense devotion, he will gain to himself great merit with God, since his continence is both pure and reasonable. But if goes beyond the rule he has chosen to gain greater glory, there is a danger that he may lose hope. Both celibacy and marriage have their own different forms of service and ministry to the Lord; I have in mind the caring for one's wife and children. For it seems that the particular characteristic of the married state is that it gives the man who desire a perfect marriage an opportunity to take responsibility for everything in the home which he shares with his wife. The apostle says that one should appoint bishops who by their oversight over their own house have learned to be in charge of the whole church (1 Tim. 3:4f.). Let each man therefore fulfill his ministry by the work in which he was called (1 Cor. 7:24), that he may be free (1 Cor. 7:22) in Christ and receive the proper reward of his ministry. . . .

If birth is something evil, let the blasphemers say that the Lord who shared in birth was born in evil, and that the virgin gave birth to him in evil. Woe to these wicked fellows! They blaspheme against the will of God and the mystery of creation in speaking evil of birth. This is the ground upon which Docetism is held by Cassian and by Marcion also, and on which even Valentine indeed teaches that Christ's body was "psychic." They say: Man became like the beast when he came to practise sexual intercourse. But it is when a man in his passion really wants to go to bed with a strange woman that in truth such a man has become a wild beast. "Wild horses were they become, each man whinnied after his neighbour's wife" (Jer. 5:8). And if the serpent took the use of intercourse from the irrational animals and persuaded Adam to agree to have sexual union with Eve, as though the couple first created did not have such union by nature, as some think, this again is blasphemy against the creation. For it makes human nature weaker that that of the brute beast if in this matter those who were first created by God copied them.

But if nature led them, like the irrational animals, to procreation, yet they were impelled to do it more quickly than was proper because they were still young and had been led away by deceit. Thus God's judgment against them was just, because they did not wait for his will. But birth is holy. By it were made the world, the existences, the natures, the angels, powers, souls, the commandments, the law, the gospel, the knowledge of God. And "all flesh is grass and all the glory of man as the flower of grass. The grass withers, the flower falls; but the word of the Lord abides (Isa. 40:6–8) which anoints the soul and unites it with the spirit. Without the body how could the divine plan for us in the Church achieve its end? Surely the Lord himself, the head of the Church (Eph. 1:22; 5:23), came in the flesh, though without form and beauty (Isa. 53:2), to teach us to look upon the formless and incorporeal nature of the divine Cause. "For a tree of life" says the prophet, "grows by a good desire" (Prov. 13:12), teaching that desires which are in the living Lord are good and pure.

Furthermore they wish to maintain that the intercourse of man and wife in marriage, which is called knowledge, is a sin; this sin is referred to as eating of the tree of good and evil, and the phrase "he knew" (Gen. 2:9)signifies transgression of the commandment. But if this is so, even knowledge of the truth is eating of the tree of life (Gen. 2:9; 3:22). It is possible for a sober-minded marriage to partake of that tree. We have already observed that marriage may be used rightly or wrongly; and this is the tree of knowledge, if we do not transgress in marriage. What then? Does not the Savior who heals the soul also heal the body of its passions? But if the flesh were hostile to the soul, he would not have raised an obstacle to the soul by strengthening with good health the hostile flesh. "This I say, brethren, that flesh and blood cannot inherit the kingdom of God nor corruption incorruption" (1 Cor. 15:50). For sin being corruption cannot have fellowship with incorruption which is righteousness. "Are you so foolish?" he says; "having begun in the Spirit are you now to be made perfect by the flesh" (Gal. 3:3).

Some, then, as we have shown, have tried to go beyond what is right and the concord that marks salvation which is holy and established. They have blasphemously accepted the ideal of continence for reasons entirely godless. Celibacy may lawfully be chosen according to the sound rule with godly reasons, provided that the person gives thanks for the grace God has granted (1 Cor. 7:7), and does not hate the creation or reckon married people to be of no account. For the world is created: celibacy is also created. Let both give thanks for their appointed state, if they know to what state they are appointed. But others have kicked over the traces and waxed wanton, having become indeed "wild horses who whinny after their neighbour's wives" (Jer. 5:8). They have abandoned themselves to lust without restraint and persuade their neighbours to live licentiously; as wretches they follow the Scripture: "Cast your lot in with us, let us all have a common purse and let our moneybag be one" (Prov. 1:14).

The Gospel of Mary

The Saviour said, "Sin as such does not exist, but you make sin when you do what is of the nature of fornication, which is called 'sin.' For this reason, the Good came into your midst, to the essence of such nature, to restore it to its roots." He went on to say, "For this reason you come into existence and die (. . .) whoever knows may know (. . .) a suffering which has nothing like itself, which has arisen out of what is contrary to nature. Then there arises a disturbance in the whole body. For this reason I said to you, Be of good courage (cf. Matt. 28:9), and if you are discouraged, still take courage over against the various forms of nature. He who has ears to hear, let him hear." When the Blessed One had said this, he greeted all of them, saying, "Peace be with you (cf. John 14:27). Receive my peace for yourselves. Take heed lest anyone lead you astray with the words, 'Lo, here!' or 'Lo, there!' (cf. Matt. 24:5, 23; Luke 17:21) for the Son or Man is within you (cf. Luke 17:21). Follow him; those who seek him will find him (cf. Matt. 7:7). Go, therefore, and preach the Gospel of the Kingdom (cf. Matt. 4:23, 9:15; Mark 16:15). I have left no commandment but what I have commanded you, and I have given you no law, as the lawgiver did, lest you be bound by it."

When he had said this, he went away. But they were grieved and mourned greatly, saying, "How shall we go to the Gentiles and preach the Gospel of the Kingdom of the Son of Man? If even he was not spared, how shall we be spared?"

Then Mary stood up and greeted all of them and said to her brethren, "Do not mourn or grieve or be irresolute for his grace will be with you all and will defend you. Let us rather praise his greatness, for he prepared us and made us into men." When Mary said this,

From THE GOSPEL OF MARY, in Robert M. Grant, ed., Gnosticism: A Sourcebook of Heretical Writings from the Early Christian Period (New York: Harper & Bros., 1961).

their hearts changed for the better, and they began to discuss the words of the (Saviour).

Peter said to Mary, "Sister, we know that the Saviour loved you more than other women (cf. John 11:5, Luke 10:38–42). Tell us the words of the Saviour which you have in mind since you know them; and we do not, nor have we heard them."

Mary answered and said, "What is hidden from you I will impart to you." And she began to say the following words to them. "I," she said, "I saw the Lord in a vision and I said to him, 'Lord, I saw you today in a vision.' He answered and said to me, 'Blessed are you, since you did not waver at the sight of me, for where the mind is, there is your countenance' (cf. Matt. 6:21). I said to him, 'Lord, the mind which sees the vision, does it see it through the soul or through the spirit? The Saviour answered and said, 'It sees neither through the soul nor through the spirit, but the mind, which is between the two, which sees the vision, and it is . . .' "

(And at this point, pages 11–14 of the papyrus are lost.)

". . . and Desire said, 'I did not see you descend; but now I see you rising. Why do you speak falsely, when you belong to me?' The soul answered and said, 'I saw you, but you did not see me or recognise me; I served you as a garment and you did not recognize me.' After it had said this, it went joyfully and gladly away. Again it came to the third power, Ignorance. This power questioned the soul: 'Whither are you going? You were bound in wickedness, you were bound indeed. Judge not' (cf. Matt. 7:1). And the soul said, 'Why do you judge me, when I was judged not? I was bound, though I did not bind. I was not recognised, but I recognised that all will go free, things both earthly and heavenly.' After the soul had left the third power behind, it rose upward, and saw the fourth power, which had seven forms. The first form is darkness, the second desire, the third ignorance, the fourth the arousings of death, the fifth is the kingdom of the flesh, the sixth is the wisdom of the folly of the flesh, the seventh is wrathful wisdom. These are the seven participants in wrath. They ask the soul, "Whence do you come, killer of men, or where are you going, conqueror of space?' The soul answered and said, 'What seizes me is killed; what turns me about is overcome; my desire has come to an end and ignorance is dead. In a world I was saved from a world, and in a "type," from a higher "type" and from the fetter of the impotence of knowledge, the existence of which is temporal. From this time I will reach rest in the time of the moment of the Aeon in silence.'"

When Mary had said this, she was silent, since the Saviour had spoken thus far with her. But Andrew answered and said to the brethren, "Say what you think concerning what she said. For I do not believe that the Savior said this. For certainly these teachings are of other ideas."

Peter also opposed her in regard to these matters and asked them about the Saviour. "Did he then speak secretly with a woman (cf. John 4:27), in preference to us, and not openly? Are we to turn back and all listen to her? Did he prefer her to us?"

Then Mary grieved and said to Peter, "My brother Peter, what do you think? Do you think I thought this up myself in my heart or that I am lying concerning the Saviour?"

Levi answered and said to Peter, "Peter, you are always irate. Now I see that you are contending against the woman like the adversaries. But if the Saviour made her worthy, who are you to reject her? Surely the Saviour knew her very well (cf. Luke 10:38–42). For this reason he loved her more than us (cf. John 11:5). And we should rather be ashamed and put on the Perfect Man, to form us as he commanded us, and proclaim the gospel, without publishing a further commandment or a further law than the one which the Saviour spoke." When Levi has said this, they began to go out in order to proclaim him and preach him.

6. Jerome: The Exaltation of Christian Virginity

Jerome was one of the foremost advocates of the celibate life in fourth-century Latin Christendom,[1] a century which saw the rapid development of Christian asceticism. In former times, Christians had been able to demonstrate their extraordinary devotion to God and their religion by giving themselves as martyrs; once the persecutions ended and the empire became nominally Christian under Constantine, this way of displaying loyalty to Christianity of necessity ceased. Moreover, when Christianity became a legally protected religion, many joined the faith who were not made of heroic fiber. How, under these circumstances, could one show one's superior commitment? The route of asceticism became a very popular solution to the problem as the fourth century progressed; thousands of men and women took to the deserts to lead lives of extreme simplicity with the hope of overcoming the frailty of human nature. Jerome himself got caught up in the passion for the hermit's life and spent two or three years in the desert near Antioch;[2] he did not find the experience as satisfying as he had anticipated. He is honest enough to tell one of his numerous correspondents that he himself could never reach the height of Christian perfection, despite his life of deprivation, since he had already forfeited the crown of virginity in his youth.[3] And even when as a hermit he denied his body physical comforts, he was still plagued with visions of dancing girls.[4]

In his writings, Jerome frequently reveals himself as a misogynist. He incorporated the pagan antifeminist tradition derived from such authors as Juvenal and Horace into his own literary productions.[5] Both of our selections reveal this bias. *To Eustochium*, in fact, has been called "the greatest slander of women since Juvenal's sixth satire."[6] And Jerome's treatise *Against Jovinian* has been deemed responsible in part for the misogynist strain in the literary tradition of the Middle Ages.[7]

Although Jerome could scarcely have been more vicious toward women in his writings, he was extremely supportive of them—at least to the ones who accepted his tutelage—in real life. During his stay at Rome, he acquired a circle of wealthy Roman women among his devotees.[8] To these women he taught Scripture—even going so far as to organize Hebrew classes[9]—and gave them much encouragement in the undertaking of celibacy. Their loyalty to him is revealed by the fact that some of them followed him to Bethlehem and set up a convent near the male monastic institution he established there. How to reconcile Jerome's personal devotion to and friendships with women and the misogynist tone of his satiric writings therefore remains something of a problem.[10]

The Eustochium he addresses in our first selection was the teenage daughter of one of his favorite Roman women friends, Paula. While still an adolescent, Eustochium decided to embrace the "virgin's profession"; Jerome wrote her a long letter, actually a treatise, praising her resolution to do so. He tells her that she is the first highborn Roman Christian woman to devote herself to virginity. He reminds her frequently how lucky she is to be escaping the trials of marriage—which he paints in the blackest of colors—and to be winning the love of the heavenly bridegroom, Jesus. (He does not hesitate to use overtly sexual metaphors derived from the Song of Songs to describe the relationship between the pair.) Virginity will be for her a foretaste of the angelic afterlife; it is also a means of recapturing the innocence of Eden before the Fall. Although the virginal life is a rigorous one, he is confident that Eustochium will succeed in it if she but follow his advice, which included shunning the "sham" virgins who not only associated with men, but were sometimes found to be with child by their supposedly "spiritual brothers."[11]

Our second selection is taken from *Against Jovinian*, a treatise repudiating the theories of a monk who had given up the ascetic life and had, in about 390, composed a work in which he argued against the exaltation of virginity. Jovinian reasoned that, in the eyes of God, a virgin was no better than a wife, nor would she receive a higher reward after death. (He based his opinion on the belief that baptism makes all Christians equal before God.) And there was much scriptural evidence Jovinian could marshal to demonstrate that marriage was commanded in the sacred writings. When the book became a best seller, Jerome undertook to answer its arguments. To his surprise, the Roman public considered parts of his work (the Against Jovinian) offensive, even shocking, and Jerome had to defend himself for even writing the treatise![12] Despite the plea that he held a more favorable view of marriage than some others in the Christian fold,[13] the damage had already been done. Jerome had tried to dissociate himself from the opinions of the heretical Gnostics who downgraded marriage, but apparently he had not succeeded in convincing his audience. Certainly his inclusion of a long section of a biting, even venomous, treatise On Marriage, which he attributes to the earlier Aristotelian writer Theophrastus, had not helped his cause.[14]

Such an ardent apostle of virginity as Jerome could be expected to champion the perpetual virginity of Mary, the mother of Jesus. Jerome devoted a whole treatise (the Against Helvidius, not included in our selections) to this subject. Helvidius, a Roman layman, had argued that although Mary was a virgin at the time of Jesus' conception, she did not remain one afterwards. Helvidius drew his evidence from the wording of the birth stories which implied that Joseph and Mary had married and engaged in sexual relations after Jesus' birth, as well as from the biblical passages mentioning Jesus' brothers and sisters. Jerome applied his talents as an exegete—he was probably the foremost biblical scholar of his day—to the task of explaining away or interpreting the passages Helvidius had singled out so that Mary emerged as devoted to the ideal of lifelong virginity. The brother and sisters of Jesus mentioned in the text of the New Testament are turned into relatives.[15] Jerome was so eager to advance the cause of virginity that he even depicted Joseph as a devotee of lifelong celibacy.[16]

Jerome's treatise on Mary's virginity was part of a rising interest at the end of the fourth century in the virgin birth and in Mary.[17] In 649, a Lateran Council declared the perpetual virginity of Mary to be doctrine of the Catholic church. Catholicism's devotion to Mary and to virginity has continued through the ages.[18]

Letter 22 [to Eustochium]

I am writing this to you, Lady Eustochium (I am bound to call my Lord's bride "Lady"), that from the very beginning of my discourse you may learn that I do not today intend to sing the praises of the virginity which you have adopted and proved to be so good. Nor shall I now reckon up the disadvantages of marriage, such as pregnancy, a crying baby, the tortures of jealousy, the cares of household management, and the cutting short by death of all its fancied blessings. Married women have their due allotted place, if they live in honourable marriage and keep their bed undefiled. My purpose in this letter is to show you that you are fleeing from Sodom and that you should take warning by Lot's wife. There is no flattery in these pages. A flatterer is a smooth-spoken enemy. Nor will there be any pomp of rhetoric in expounding the beatitude of virginity, setting you among the angels and putting the world beneath your feet. . . .

Oh, how often, when I was living in the desert, in that lonely waste, scorched by the burning sun, which affords to hermits a savage dwelling-place, how often did I fancy myself surrounded by the pleasures of Rome! I used to sit alone; for I was filled with bitterness. My unkempt limbs were covered in shapeless sackcloth; my skin through long neglect had become as rough and black as an Ethiopian's. Tears and groans were every day my portion; and if sleep ever overcame my resistance and fell upon my eyes, I bruised my restless bones against the naked earth. Of food and drink I will not speak. Hermits have nothing but cold water even when they are sick, and for them it is sinful luxury to partake of cooked

From Jerome, Letter 22, "To Eustochium: The Virgin's Profession," *Select Letters of St. Jerome,* trans. F. A. Wright, (Cambridge, Mass.: Harvard University Press, Loeb Classical Library, 1933).

dishes. But though in my fear of hell I had condemned myself to this prison-house, where my only companions were scorpions and wild beasts, I often found myself surrounded by bands of dancing girls. My face was pale with fasting; but though my limbs were cold as ice my mind was burning with desire, and the fires of lust kept bubbling up before me when my flesh was as good as dead.

And so, when all other help failed me, I used to fling myself at Jesus' feet; I watered them with my tears, I wiped them with my hair; and if my flesh still rebelled I subdued it by weeks of fasting. I do not blush to confess my misery; nay, rather, I lament that I am not now what once I was. I remember that often I joined night to day with my wailings and ceased not from beating my breast till tranquillity returned to me at the Lord's behest. I used to dread my poor cell as though it knew my secret thoughts. Filled with stiff anger against myself, I would make my way alone into the desert; and when I came upon some hollow valley or rough mountain or precipitous cliff, there I would set up my oratory, and make that spot a place of torture for my unhappy flesh. There sometimes also—the Lord Himself is my witness—after many a tear and straining of my eyes to heaven, I felt myself in the presence of the angelic hosts and in joy and gladness would sing: "Because of the savour of thy good ointments we will run after thee" (Song of Sol. 1:3).

If such are the temptations of men whose bodies are emaciated with fasting so that they have only evil thoughts to withstand, how must it fare with a girl who clings to the enjoyment of luxuries? . . .

You may choose perhaps to answer that a girl of good family like yourself, accustomed to luxury and down pillows, cannot do without wine and tasty food and would find a stricter rule of life impossible. To that I can only say: "Live then by your own rule, since you cannot live by God's." Not that God, the Lord and Creator of the universe, takes any delight in the rumbling of our intestines or the emptiness of our stomach or the inflammation of our lungs; but because this is the only way of preserving chastity. . . .

It wearies me to tell how many virgins fall daily, what notabilities

Mother Church loses from her bosom: over how many stars the proud enemy sets his throne, how many hollow rocks the serpent pierces and makes his habitation. You may see many women who have been left widows before they were ever wed, trying to conceal their consciousness of guilt by means of a lying garb. Unless they are betrayed by a swelling womb or by the crying of their little ones they walk abroad with tripping feet and lifted head. Some even ensure barrenness by the help of portions, murdering human beings before they are fully conceived. Others, when they find that they are with child as the result of their sin, practise abortion with drugs, and so frequently bring about their own death, taking with them to the lower world the guilt of three crimes: suicide, adultery against Christ, and child murder. Yet these are the women who will say: "To the pure all things are pure. My conscience is enough for me. A pure heart is what God craves. Why should I refrain from the food which God made for enjoyment?" When they wish to appear bright and merry, they drench themselves with wine, and then joining profanity to drunkenness they cry: "Heaven forbid that I should abstain from the blood of Christ." When they see a woman with a pale sad face, they call her "a miserable Manichaean": and quite logically too, for on their principles fasting is heresy. As they walk the streets they try to attract attention and with stealthy nods and winks draw after them troops of young men. Of them the prophet's words are true: "Thou hast a whore's forehead: thou refusest to be ashamed" (Jer. 3:3). Let them have only a little purple in their dress, and loose bandeau on their head to leave the hair free; cheap slippers, and a Maforte fluttering from their shoulders; sleeves fitting close to their arms, and a loose-kneed walk: there you have all their marks of virginity. Such women may have their admirers, and it may cost more to ruin them because they are called virgins. But to such virgins as these I prefer to be displeasing.

There is another scandal of which I blush to speak; yet, though sad, it is true. From what source has this plague of "dearly beloved sisters" found its way into the Church? Whence come these unwedded wives, these new types of concubines, nay, I will go further, these one-man harlots? They live in the same house with their male-friend; they occupy the same room and often even the same bed; and yet they call us suspicious if we think that anything is wrong. A brother leaves his virgin sister; a virgin, scorning her unmarried brother, seeks a stranger to take his place. Both alike pretend to have but one object: they are seeking spiritual consolation among strangers: but their real aim is to indulge at home in carnal intercourse. About such folk as these Solomon in Proverbs speaks the scornful words: "Can a man take fire in his bosom and his clothes not be burned? Can one go upon hot coals and not burn his feet" (Prov. 6:27)?

Let us therefore drive off and expel from our company such women as only wish to seem and not to be virgins: Now I would direct all my words to you who, inasmuch as you have been at the beginning the first virgin of high rank at Rome, will now have to labour the more diligently so as not to lose your present and your future happiness. As for the troubles of wedded life and the uncertainties of marriage, you know of them by an example in your own family. Your sister Blesilla, superior to you in age but inferior in firmness of will, has become a widow seven months after taking a husband. How luckless is our mortal state, how ignorant of the future! She has lost both the crown of virginity and the pleasures of wedlock. Although the widowed state ranks as the second degree of chastity, can you not imagine the crosses which every moment she must bear, seeing in her sister daily that which she herself has lost? It is harder for her than for you to forgo the delights that she once knew, and yet she receives a less reward for her present continence. Still, she too may rejoice and be not afraid. The fruit that is an hundredfold and that which is sixtyfold both spring from one seed, the seed of chastity. . . .

Some one may say: "Do you dare to disparage wedlock, a state which God has blessed?" It is not disparaging wedlock to prefer virginity. No one can make a comparison between two things, if one is good and the other evil. Let married women take their pride in coming next after virgins. "Be fruitful," God said, "and multiply and replenish the earth" (Gen. 1:28). Let him then be fruitful and multiply who intends to replenish the earth: but your company is in heaven. The command to increase and multiply is fulfilled after the expulsion from Paradise, after the recognition of nakedness, after the putting on of the fig leaves which augured the approach of marital desire. Let them marry and be given in marriage who eat their bread in the sweat of their brow, whose land brings forth thorns and thistles, and whose crops are choked with brambles. My seed produces fruit a hundredfold.

. . . Eve in Paradise was a virgin: it was only after she put on a garment of skins that her married life began. Paradise is your home. Keep therefore as you were born, and say: "Return unto thy rest, O my soul" (Ps. 116:7). . . .

I praise wedlock, I praise marriage; but it is because they produce me virgins. I gather the rose from the thorn, the gold from the earth, the pearl from the oyster. Shall the ploughman plough all day? Shall he not also enjoy the fruit of his labour? Wedlock is the more honoured when the fruit of wedlock is the more loved. Why, mother, grudge your daughter her virginity? She has been reared on your milk, she has come from your body, she has grown strong in your arms. Your watchful love has kept her safe. Are you vexed with her because she chooses to wed not a soldier but a King? She has rendered you a high service: from to-day you are the mother by marriage of God. . . .

In the old days, as I have said, the virtue of continence was confined to men, and Eve continually bore children in travail. But now that a virgin has conceived in the womb a child, upon whose shoulders is government, a mighty God, Father of the age to come, the fetters of the old curse are broken. Death came through Eve: life has come through Mary. For this reason the gift of virginity has been poured most abundantly upon women, seeing that it was from a woman it began. As soon as the Son of God set foot on earth, He formed for Himself a new household, that as He was adored by angels in heaven He might have angels also on earth. . . .

Let the seclusion of your own chamber ever guard you; ever let the Bridegroom sport with you within. If you pray, you are speaking to your Spouse: if you read, He is speaking to you. When sleep falls on you, He will come behind the wall and will put His hand through the hole in the door and will touch your flesh. And you will awake and rise up and cry: "I am sick with love" (Song of Sol., 5:8). And you will hear Him answer: "A garden inclosed is my sister, my spouse; a spring shut up, a fountain sealed" (Song of Sol., 5:8). Go not from home nor visit the daughters of a strange land, though you have patriarchs for brothers and rejoice in Israel as your father. Dinah went out and was seduced (Gen. 34:1). I would not have you seek the Bridegroom in the public squares; I would not have you go about the corners of the city. You may say: "I will rise now and go about the city: in the streets and in the broad ways I will seek Him whom my soul loveth" (Song of Sol. 3:2). But though you ask the watchmen: "Saw ye Him whom my soul loveth?" no one will deign to answer you. The Bridegroom cannot be found in the city squares. "Strait and narrow is the way that leadeth unto life" (Matt. 7:14). And the Song goes on: "I sought him but I could not find him: I called him but he gave me no answer."

Against Jovinian

. . . For ourselves, we do not follow the views of Marcion and Manichaeus, and disparage marriage; nor, deceived by the error of Tatian, the leader of the Encratites, do we think all intercourse impure; he condemns and rejects not only marriage but also food which God created for the use of man. . . . We are not ignorant of the words, "Marriage is honourable among all, and the bed undefiled." We have read God's first command, "Be fruitful, and multiply, and replenish the earth"; but while we honour marriage we prefer virginity which is the offspring of marriage. Will silver cease to be silver, if gold is more precious than silver? Or is despite done to tree and corn, if we prefer the fruit to root and foliage, or the grain to stalk and ear? Virginity is to marriage what fruit is to the tree, or grain to the straw. Although the hundred-fold, the sixty-fold, and the thirty-fold spring from one earth and from one sowing, yet there is a great difference in respect of number. The

From Jerome, "Against Jovinian," St. Jerome: Letters and Select Works; Nicene and Post-Nicene Fathers, 2nd ser., vol. 6, ed. Philip Schaff (New York: Christian Literature Co., 1893).

thirty-fold has reference to marriage. . . . The sixty-fold applies to widows, because they are placed in a position of difficulty and distress. . . . [And the hundred-fold applies to virgins.]

He [i.e., Jovinian] says that "virgins, widows, and married women, who have been once passed through the laver of Christ, if they are on a par in other respects, are of equal merit." . . .

. . . I entreat virgins of both sexes and all such as are continent, the married also and the twice married, to assist my efforts with their prayers. Jovinian is the common enemy. For he who maintains all to be of equal merit, does no less injury to virginity in comparing it with marriage than he does to marriage, when he allows it to be lawful, but to the same extent as second and third marriages. But to digamists and trigamists also he does wrong, for he places on a level with them whoremongers and the most licentious persons as soon as they have repented; but perhaps those who have been married twice or thrice ought not to complain, for the same whoremonger if penitent is made equal in the kingdom of heaven even to virgins. . . .

First of all, he says, God declares that "therefore shall a man leave his father and his mother, and shall cleave unto his wife: and they shall be one flesh." And lest we should say that this is a quotation from the Old Testament, he asserts that it has been confirmed by the Lord in the Gospel—"What God hath joined together, let not man put asunder": and he immediately adds, "Be fruitful, and multiply, and replenish the earth." He next repeats the names of Seth, Enos, Cainan, Mahalalel, Jared, Enoch, Methuselah, Lamech, Noah, and tells us that they all had wives and in accordance with the will of God begot sons, as though there could be any table of descent or any history of mankind without wives and children. . . . [Jovinian here lists numerous Old Testament and New Testament characters who were married yet favored by God. Jerome acknowledges these cases, but cites examples of Biblical virgins, widows, and widowers. Jovinian then takes up the issue of married clergy, to which Jerome responds.]

All that goes for nothing, says Jovinianus, because even bishops, priests, and deacons, husbands of one wife, and having children, were appointed by the Apostle. Just as the Apostle (1 Cor. 7:25) says he has no commandment respecting virgins, and yet gives his advice, as one who had obtained mercy from the Lord, and is anxious throughout the whole discussion to give virginity the preference over marriage, and advises what he does not venture to command, lest he seem to lay a snare, and to put a heavier burden upon man's nature than it can bear; so also in establishing the constitution of the Church, inasmuch as the elements of the early Church were drawn from the Gentiles, he made the rules for fresh believers somewhat lighter that they might not in alarm shrink from keeping them. . . . For he does not say: Let a bishop be chosen who marries one wife and begets children; but who marries one wife, and (1 Tim. 3:2–4, Tit. 1:6) has his children in subjection and well disciplined. You surely admit that he is no bishop who during his episcopate begets children. The reverse is the case— if he be discovered, he will not be bound by the ordinary obligations of a husband, but will be condemned as an adulterer. Either permit priests to perform the work of marriage with the result that virginity and marriage are on a par: or if it is unlawful for priests to touch their wives, they are so far holy in that they imitate virgin chastity. But something more follows. A layman, or any believer, cannot pray unless he abstain from sexual intercourse. Now a priest must always offer sacrifices for the people: he must therefore always pray. And if he must always pray, he must always be released from the duties of marriage. For even under the old law they who used to offer sacrifices for the people not only remained in their houses, but purified themselves for the occasion by separating from their wives, nor would they drink wine or strong drink which are wont to stimulate lust. That married men are elected to the priesthood, I do not deny: the number of virgins is not so great as that of the priests required. Does it follow that because all the strongest men are chosen for the army, weaker men should not be taken as well? All cannot be strong. If an army were constituted of strength only, and numbers went for nothing, the feebler men might be rejected. As it is, men of second or third rate strength are chosen, that the army may have its full numerical complement. How is it, then, you will say, that frequently at the ordination of priests a virgin is passed over, and a married man taken? Perhaps because he lacks other qualifications in keeping with virginity, or it may be that he is thought a virgin, and is not: or there may be a stigma on his virginity, or at all events virginity itself makes him proud, and while he plumes himself on mere bodily chastity, he neglects other virtues; he does not cherish the poor: he is too fond of money. It sometimes happens that a man has a gloomy visage, a frowning brow, a walk as though he were in a solemn procession, and so offends the people, who, because they have no fault to find with his life, hate his mere dress and gait. Many are chosen not out of affection for themselves, but out of hatred for another. In most cases the election is won by mere simplicity, while the shrewdness and discretion of another candidate elicit opposition as thought they were evils. Sometimes the judgment of the commoner people is at fault, and in testing the qualities of the priesthood, the individual inclines to his own character, with the result that he looks not so much for a good candidate as for one like himself. Not unfrequently it happens that married men, who form the larger portion of the people, in approving married candidates seem to approve themselves, and it does not occur to them that the mere fact that they prefer a married person to a virgin is evidence of their inferiority to virgins. What I am going to say will perhaps offend many. Yet I will say it, and good men will not be angry with me, because they will not feel the sting of conscience. Sometimes it is the fault of the bishops, who choose into the ranks of the clergy not the best, but the cleverest, men, and think the more simple as well as innocent ones incapable: or, as though they were distributing the offices of an earthly service, they give posts to their kindred and relations; or they listen to the dictates of wealth. And, worse than all, they give promotion to the clergy who besmear them with flattery. . . .

But you will say: "If everybody were a virgin, what would become of the human race?" Like shall here beget like. If everyone were a widow, or continent in marriage, how will mortal men be propagated? . . . . You are afraid that if the desire for virginity were general there would be no prostitutes, no adulteresses, no wailing infants in town or country. Every day the blood of adulterers is shed, adulterers are condemned, and lust is raging and rampant in the very presence of the laws and the symbols of authority and the courts of justice. Be not afraid that all will become virgins: virginity is a hard matter, and therefore rare, because it is hard: "Many are called, few chosen." Many begin, few persevere. And so the reward is great for those who have persevered. If all were able to be virgins, our Lord would never have said (Matt. 19:12): "He that is able to receive it, let him receive it": and the Apostle would not have hesitated to give his advice, (1 Cor. 7:25) "Now concerning virgins I have no commandment of the Lord." Why then, you will say, were the organs of generation created, and why were we so fashioned by the all-wise creator, that we burn for one another, and long for natural intercourse? . . . Are we never then to forego lust, for fear that we may have members of this kind for nothing? Why then should a husband keep himself from his wife? Why should a widow persevere in chastity, if we were only born to live like beasts? Or what harm does it to me if another man lies with my wife? For as the teeth were made for chewing, and the food masticated passes into the stomach, and a man is not blamed for giving my wife bread: similarly if it was intended that the organs of generation should always be performing their office, when my vigour is spent let another take my place, and if I may so speak, let my wife quench her burning lust where she can. But what does the Apostle mean by exhorting to continence, if continence be contrary to nature? What does our Lord mean when He instructs us in the various kinds of eunuchs (Matt. 18:12). Surely (1 Cor. 7:7) the Apostle who bids us emulate his own chastity, must be asked, if we are to be consistent, Why are you like other men, Paul? Why are you distinguished from the female sex by a beard, hair, and other peculiarities of person? How is it that you have not swelling bosoms, and are not broad at the hips, narrow at the chest? Your voice is rugged, your speech rough, your eyebrows more shaggy. To no purpose you have all these manly qualities, if you forego the embraces of women. I am compelled to say something and become a fool: but you have forced me to dare to speak. Our Lord and Savior (Phil. 2:6–8), Who though He was in the form of God, condescended to take the form of a servant, and became obedient to the Father even unto death, yea the death of the cross—what necessity was there for Him to be born with members which He was not going to use? He certainly was circumcised to manifest His sex. Why did he cause John the Apostle and John the Baptist to make themselves eunuchs through love of Him, after causing them to be born men? Let us then who believe in Christ follow His example. And if we knew Him after the flesh, let us no longer know Him according to the flesh. The substance of our resurrection bodies will certainly be the same as now, though of higher glory. For the Saviour after His descent into hell had so far the selfsame body in which He was crucified, that (John 20:20) He showed the disciples the marks of the nails in His hands and the wound in His side. Moreover, if we deny the identity of His body because (John 20:19) He entered though the doors were shut, and this is not a property of human bodies, we must deny also that Peter and the Lord had real bodies because they (Matt. 14:28) walked upon the water, which is contrary to nature "In the resurrection of the dead they will neither marry nor be given in marriage, but will be like the angels" (Matt. 22:30). What others will hereafter be in heaven, that virgins begin to be on earth. If likeness to the angels is promised us (and there is no difference of sex among the angels), we shall either be of no sex as are the angels, or at all events, which is clearly proved, though we rise from the dead in our own sex, we shall not perform the functions of sex. . . .

. . . A book *On Marriage*, worth its weight in gold, passes under the name of Theophrastus. In it the author asks whether a wise man marries. And after laying down the conditions—that the wife must be fair, of good character, and honest parentage, the husband in good health and of ample means, and after saying that under these circumstances, a wise man sometimes enters the state of matrimony, he immediately proceeds thus: "But all these conditions are seldom satisfied in marriage. A wise man therefore must not take a wife. For in the first place his study of philosophy will be hindered, and it is impossible for anyone to attend to his books and his wife. Matrons want many things, costly dresses, gold jewels, great outlay, maid-servants, all kinds of furniture, litters and gilded coaches. Then come curtain-lectures the live-long night: she complains that one lady goes out better dressed than she: that another is looked up to by all: 'I am a poor despised nobody at the ladies' assemblies." 'Why did you ogle that creature next door?' 'Why were you talking to the maid?' 'What did you bring from the market?' 'I am not allowed to have a single friend, or companion.' She suspects that her husband's love goes the same way as her hate. There may be in some neighbouring city the wisest of teachers; but if we have a wife we can neither leave her behind, nor take the burden with us. To support a poor wife, is hard: to put up with a rich one, is torture. Notice, too, that in the case of a wife you cannot pick and choose: you must take her as you find her. If she has a bad temper, or is a fool, if she has a blemish, or is proud, or has bad breath, whatever her fault may be—all this we learn after marriage. Horses, asses, cattle, even slaves of the smallest worth, clothes, kettles, wooden seats, cups, and earthenware pitchers, are first tried and then bought: a wife is the only thing that is not shown before she is married, for fear she may not give satisfaction. Our gaze must always be directed to her face, and we must always praise her beauty: if you look at another woman, she thinks that she is out of favour. . . . If a woman be fair, she soon finds lovers; if she be ugly, it is easy to be wanton. It is difficult to guard what many long for. It is annoying to have what no one thinks worth possessing. But the misery of having an ugly wife is less than that of watching a comely one. Nothing is safe, for which a whole people sighs and longs. One man entices with his figure, another with his brains, another with his wit, another with his open hand. Somehow, or sometime, the fortress is captured which is attacked on all sides. Men marry, indeed, so as to get a manager for the house, to solace weariness, to banish solitude; but a faithful slave is a far better manager, more submissive to the master, more observant of his ways, than a wife who thinks she proves herself mistress if she acts in opposition to her husband, that is, if she does what pleases her, not what she is commanded. But friends, and servants who are under the obligation of benefits received, are better able to wait upon us in sickness than a wife who makes us responsible for her tears(she will sell you enough to make a deluge for the hope of a legacy); who boasts of her anxiety, yet drives her sick husband to the distraction of despair. But if she herself is poorly, we must fall sick with her and never leave her bedside. Or if she be a good and agreeable wife (how rare a bird she is!), we have to share her groans in childbirth, and suffer torture when she is in danger. . . . Then again, to marry for the sake of children, so that our name may not perish, or that we may have support in old age, and leave our property without dispute, is the height of stupidity. For what is it to us when we are leaving the world if another bears our name, when even a son does not all at once take his father's title, and there are countless others who are called by the same name. Or what support in old age is he whom you bring up, and who may die before you, or turn out a reprobate? Or at all events when he reaches mature age, you may seem to him long in dying. Friends and relatives whom you can judiciously love are better and safer heirs than those whom you must make your heirs whether you like it or not. Indeed, the surest way of having a good heir is to ruin your fortune in a good cause while you live, not to leave the fruit of your labour to be used you know not how."

7. Augustine: Sinfulness and Sexuality

Augustine's writings on marriage and sexuality, more than those of any other church father, contributed to the development of later Roman Catholic theory regarding those topics. His words are quoted with as much approval by twentieth-century popes as they were by medieval theologians. Augustine, unlike many churchmen of the early Christian era, had enjoyed considerable sexual experience in his youth, fathering a son while he himself was still an adolescent.[1] He became convinced that the renunciation of sexual life was essential for his own espousal of Christianity; in the *Confessions* he reveals how enormously difficult this decision was for him.[2] About Augustine's nameless and long-suffering mistress who was cast off when his mother decided it was time for him to embark upon a respectable married career,[3] we are not given much information. About his mother, Monica, on the other hand, who worried much about her son's prospects in life, we hear a great deal. Augustine tells us she believed that a proper wife should serve her husband.[4] Far from rejecting her point of view, Augustine admired his mother's willing acceptance of a humble female role and remarked that her submissiveness and patience had served her well, for she had escaped being beaten by her husband, whereas women with more assertive manners had reaped a reward of curses and blows from their irate spouses.[5]

For nine years in his youth, Augustine belonged to the Manichean sect.[6] Part of Manichean ethics involved the disallowance of procreation. Manicheans believed that bringing new humans into the world only further dispersed the "sparks of light" which had become entangled with matter as a result of the defeat of Light by Darkness in a primeval battle. Although the higher rank of the Manicheans, the "Elect," apparently avoided sexual intercourse altogether, the "Auditors" of the lower levels married and engaged in sexual relations, but tried to ensure that these would be non-procreative. Over against the Manicheans, Augustine "proposed an ethic which bound intercourse to procreation and found marital procreation good."[7] It is probably not incorrect to think that Augustine's view of procreation as the chief justification of sexual relations stemmed in part from his horror of Manichean sexual practices. On the other hand, Augustine did not stress the joys of family life. In the *Confessions*, he asserts that having a wife and family is inhibiting to the contemplation, study, and friendships which men might be able to enjoy together if they were left to their own devices.[9] But if a man wished to marry and engage in sexual intercourse, he must father children; those children, Augustine thought, would burden him with responsibilities and prevent the full development of his mental and spiritual capacities. Given Augustine's acceptance of these attitudes, it is clear why he thought celibacy the preferable mode of life.

A second movement in reaction to which Augustine evolved some of his most important ideas on sexuality was Pelagianism.[10] Pelagius and his followers emphasized, as part of their defense of God's justice in his dealings with humans, man's capacity to will and do the good. Those Christians who complained that they were too morally weak to keep God's commandments were enjoined to summon up their will power and try harder. Pelagius thought that each rational adult was responsible for his own sins and flaws; neither Adam, Eve, nor the devil could be blamed for our wrongdoing. Infants, he thought, did not enter the world in a state of sin, but were morally like "blank slates." Child baptism thus made no sense in Pelagius's scheme of things and he condemned the practice.[11]

In contrast to Pelagius, Augustine stressed the importance of the doctrine of original sin. Although Adam had been created with free will and had possessed, in Eden, the ability to keep from sinning, once he made the wrong choice, he lost his ability to choose the good and implicated himself and all his descendants in sin, two central effects of which were to become mortal and to become dominated by lust. Through the sacraments, especially baptism, the worst effects of original sin are mitigated, but the body remains resistant to rational control while we are on this earth; only in heaven will true perfection be attained. There the blessed saints will be granted God's prerogative, the inability to sin.[12]

Augustine's opponents, he was aware, might argue that the theory of original sin implied a condemnation of sexuality and marriage. Although Augustine was careful not to say that there was a "biological" transfer of the parents' sinfulness to the child, the implication nonetheless remained that the sexual act was tainted, if the child so conceived was born under the influence of original sin. Paul had spoken earlier about the sin of Adam and the disobedience of the members of our bodies, but it lay with Augustine to make a firm connection between the transmission of original sin and sexual intercourse.[13]

Whatever Augustine's views on the tainted quality of the sex act, he clearly set himself as the *defender* of marriage over against writers such as Jerome. In fact, Augustine tells us that he felt impelled to write about marriage and sexuality since no one (i.e., not even Jerome) had given a satisfactory answer to Jovinian.[14] Apparently Augustine thought that Jerome had presented too negative a view of marriage, one out of keeping with the Christian faith. Moreover, also unlike Jerome, Augustine did not rail at and mock women. He shared the common views of his day regarding women's inferiority to men,[15] but he did not stress the evils of women as a justification for the adoption of the celibate life as Jerome had. Virginity he indeed held to be higher than marriage, but marriage had its own "goods." Even the sex act itself would have been part of the innocent life in Eden—although intercourse would have involved no lust on the part of the couple.[16] Yet Augustine's view of the "ideal" sexual relation in Eden does not seem to have entailed a notion of women compatible with modern sentiments. Rosemary Ruether has called Augustine's picture of Eve "depersonalized" and "unfeeling"; the woman for Augustine becomes virtually a "baby-making machine."[17] Even in Paradise, the concepts of love or companionship do not find a place in the description of the sexual relationship. Nonetheless, for his own day, Augustine was attempting to legitimate the sexual act as part of God's intention for men and women.

Augustine's attitudes on sexuality and marriage became part of the standard teaching of the Catholic church. The notion that sexual relations are best if they are engaged in for the sake of procreation alone and that children are the first "good" of marriage became commonplaces of Catholic teaching. The passages given below on contraception and abortion became one of the central texts in all Christian writing on these topics.[18] Augustine's understanding of what was "natural" in sexual relations contributed to the church's rejection of various sexual practices. Contemporary proponents of sexual liberation will no doubt find his teachings among those still necessary to combat, but from an historical point of view, we can assert that he attempted to give for his time a "balanced" outlook which veered neither toward extreme asceticism nor toward reckless licentiousness.

Because of limitations of space, selections from The City of God are not included in this volume. For readings illustrative of Augustine's views on mankind's original righteousness, the entrance of sin into the world, and the relation of both to sexuality, see The City of God, Book 13, chaps. 3 and 13, and Book 14, chaps. 16, 18, 21–24, and 26.

On Marriage and Concupiscence

Book 1, Chap. 5 no. 4. The natural good of marriage. All society naturally repudiates a fraudulent companion. What is true conjugal purity? No true virginity and chastity, except in devotion to true Faith.

The union, then, of male and female for the purpose of procreation is the natural good of marriage. But he makes a bad use of

From Augustine, "On Marriage and Concupiscence," Augustine: Anti-Pelagian Writings; Nicene and Post-Nicene Fathers, 1st ser., vol. 5, ed. Philip Schaff (New York: Christian Literature Society, 1893).

this good who uses it bestially, so that his intention is on the gratification of lust, instead of the desire of offspring. Nevertheless, in sundry animals unendowed with reason, as, for instance, in most birds, there is both preserved a certain kind of confederation of pairs, and a social combination of skill in nest-building; and their mutual division of the periods for cherishing their eggs and their alternation in the labor of feeding their young, give them the appearance of so acting, when they mate, as to be intent rather on securing the continuance of their kind than on gratifying lust. Of these two, the one is the likeness of man in a brute; the other, the likeness of the brute in man. With respect, however, to what I ascribed to the nature of marriage, that the male and the female are united together as associates for procreation, and consequently do not defraud each other (forasmuch as every associated state has a natural abhorrence of a fraudulent companion), although even men without faith possess this palpable blessing of nature, yet, since they use it not in faith, they only turn it to evil and sin. In like manner, therefore, the marriage of believers converts to the use of righteousness that carnal concupiscence by which "the flesh lusteth against the Spirit" (Gal. 5:17). For they entertain the firm purpose of generating offspring to be regenerated—that the children who are born of them as "children of the world" may be born again and become "sons of God." Wherefore all parents who do not beget children with this intention, this will, this purpose, of transferring them from being members of Christ, but boast as unbelieving parents over unbelieving children—however circumspect they be in their cohabitation, studiously limiting it to the begetting of children—really have no conjugal chastity in themselves. For inasmuch as chastity is a virtue, having unchastity as its contrary vice, and as all the virtues (even those whose operation is by means of the body) have their seat in the soul, how can the body be in any true sense said to be chaste, when the soul itself is committing fornication against the true God? Now such fornication the holy psalmist censures when he says: "For, lo, they that are far from Thee shall perish: Thou hast destroyed all them that go a whoring from Thee" (Ps. 73:27). There is, then, no true chastity, whether conjugal or vidual, or virginal, except that which devotes itself to true faith. For though consecrated virginity is rightly preferred to marriage, yet what Christian in his sober mind would not prefer catholic Christian women who have been even more than once married, to not only vestals, but also to heretical virgins? So great is the avail of faith, of which the apostle says, "Whatsoever is not of faith is sin" (Rom. 14:23); and of which it is written in the Epistle to the Hebrews, "Without faith it is impossible to please God" (Heb. 11:6).

Book 1, chap. 16, no. 14 A certain degree of intemperance is to be tolerated in the case of married persons: the use of matrimony for the mere pleasure of lust is not without sin, but because of the nuptial relation the sin is venial.

But in the married, as these things are desirable and praiseworthy, so the others are to be tolerated, that no lapse occur into damnable sins; that is, into fornications and adulteries. To escape this evil, even such embraces of husband and wife as have not procreation for their object, but serve an overbearing concupiscence, are permitted, so far as to be within range of forgiveness, though not prescribed by way of commandment (1 Cor. 7:6): and the married pair are enjoined not to defraud one the other, lest Satan should tempt them by reason of their incontinence (1 Cor. 7:5). For thus says the Scripture: "Let the husband render unto the wife her due: and likewise also the wife unto the husband. The wife hath not power of her own body, but the husband: and likewise also the husband hath not power of his own body, but the wife. Defraud ye not one the other; except it be with consent for a time, that ye may have leisure for prayer; and then come together again, that Satan tempt you not for your incontinency. But I speak this by permission, and not of commandment" (1 Cor. 7:3–6). Now in a case where permission must be given, it cannot by any means be contended that there is not some amount of sin. Since, however, the cohabitation for the purpose of procreating children, which must be admitted to be the proper end of marriage, is not sinful, what is it which the apostle allows to be permissible, but that married persons, when they have not the gift of continence, may require one from the other the due of the flesh—and that not from a wish for procreation, but for the pleasure of concupiscence? This gratification incurs not the imputation of guilt on account of marriage, but receives permission on account of marriage. This, therefore, must be reckoned among the praises of matrimony; that, on its own account, it makes pardonable that which does not essentially appertain to itself. For the nuptial embrace, which subserves the demands of concupiscence, is so effected as not to impede the child-bearing, which is the end and aim of marriage.

Book 1, chap. 17, no. 15. What is sinless in the use of matrimony? What is attended with venial sin, and what with mortal?

It is, however, one thing for married persons to have intercourse only for the wish to beget children, which is not sinful: it is another thing for them to desire carnal pleasure in cohabitation, but with the spouse only, which involves venial sin. For although propagation of offspring is not the motive of the intercourse, there is still no attempt to prevent such propagation, either by wrong desire or evil appliance. They who resort to these, although called by the name of spouses, are really not such; they retain no vestige of true matrimony, but pretend the honourable designation as a cloak for criminal conduct. Having also proceeded so far, they are betrayed into exposing their children, which are born against their will. They hate to nourish and retain those whom they were afraid they would beget. This infliction of cruelty on their offspring so reluctantly begotten, unmasks the sins which they had practised in darkness, and drags it clearly into the light of day. The open cruelty reproves the concealed sin. Sometimes, indeed, this lustful cruelty, or, if you please, cruel lust, resorts to such extravagant methods as to use poisonous drugs to secure barrenness; or else, if unsuccessful in this, to destroy the conceived seed by some means previous to birth, preferring that its offspring should rather perish than receive vitality; or if it was advancing to life within the womb, should be slain before it was born. Well, if both parties alike are so flagitious, they are not husband and wife; and if such were their character from the beginning, they have not come together by wedlock but by debauchery. But if the two are not alike in such sin, I boldly declare either that the woman is, so to say, the husband's harlot; or the man, the wife's adulterer.

Book 1, chap. 19, no. 17. Blessings of matrimony.

In matrimony, however, let these nuptial blessings be the objects of our love—offspring, fidelity, the sacramental bond. Offspring, not that it be born only, but born again; for it is born to punishment unless it be born again to life. Fidelity, not such as even unbelievers observe one towards the other, in their ardent love of the flesh. For what husband, however impious himself, likes an adulterous wife? Or what wife, however impious she be, likes an adulterous husband? This is indeed a natural good in marriage, though a carnal one. But a member of Christ ought to be afraid of adultery, not on account of himself, but of his spouse: and ought to hope to receive from Christ the reward of that fidelity which he shows to his spouse. The sacramental bond, again, which is lost neither by divorce nor by adultery, should be guarded by husband and wife with concord and chastity. For it alone is that which even an unfruitful marriage retains by the law of piety, now that all that hope of fruitfulness is lost for the purpose of which the couple married. Let these nuptial blessings be praised in marriage by him who wishes to extol the nuptial institution. Carnal concupiscence, however, must not be ascribed to marriage: it is only to be tolerated in marriage. It is not a good which comes out of the essence of marriage, but an evil which is the accident of original sin.

Book 2, chap. 35, no. 20. He answers the arguments of Julianus. What is the natural use of the woman? What is the unnatural use?

My answer to this challenge is, that not only the children of wedlock, but also those of adultery, are a good work in so far as they are the work of God, by whom they are created: but as concerns original sin, they are all born under condemnation of the first Adam; not only those who are born in adultery, but likewise such as are born in wedlock, unless they be regenerated in the second Adam, which is Christ. As to what the apostle says of the wicked, that "leaving the natural use of the woman, the men turned in their lust one toward another: men with men working that which is unseemly" (Rom. 1:27); he did not speak of the conjugal use, but the "natural use," wishing us to understand how it comes to pass that by means of the members created for the purpose the two sexes can combine for generation. Thus it follows, that even when a man unites with a harlot to use these members, the use is a natural one. It is not, however, commendable, but rather culpable. But as regards any part of the body which is not meant for generative purposes, should a man use even his own wife in it, it is against nature and flagitious. Indeed, the same apostle had previously (Rom. 9:26) said concerning women: "Even their women did change the natural use into that which is against nature"; and then concerning men he added, that they worked that which is unseemly by leaving the natural use of the woman. Therefore, by the phrase in question, "the natural use," it is not meant to praise conjugal connection; but thereby are denoted those flagitious deeds which are more unclean and criminal than even men's use of women, which, even if unlawful, is nevertheless natural.

8. Thomas Aquinas:
The Man Who Should Have Known Better

Feminist interpreters of Thomas Aquinas note with regret that his views on women remained disappointingly traditional; some elements in his theology, if their implications had been explored, could have resulted in a quite different evaluation of womanhood. Thomas's theology was not hampered by an anthropomorphically conceived God, for example. Rather, his names for God were abstract and nonsexual: Being Itself, the First Mover, and Pure Act. Such neutral terminology could have contributed to the development of a system not biased toward "maleness."[1] Other elements in Thomas's thought also might have encouraged a view more affirmative of women. Thomas believed that woman, like man, was created directly by God (rather than through the mediation of angels, as others had posited);[2] she, too, was in God's "image." But, for the most part, such themes were not prominent enough in Thomas's writings to shape a more enlightened evaluation of women. When we ask why the more liberal implications of his theology did not triumph, we are thrown back on such explanations as Thomas's acceptance of Aristotelian biological theories about maleness, femaleness, and reproduction.[3] The historian Eleanor Commo McLaughlin sums up the problem in this way:

> Although the medieval centuries saw some amelioration of the patristic sexual pessimism in admitting a more positive view of Christian marriage, ultimately our medieval commentators deepened the androcentric and antifemale character of the tradition under the influence of a strongly patriarchal Germanic society and

with the scientific support of the wholly androcentric Aristotelian biology. Aristotle's intellectualistic definition of human nature combined with the inherited ascetic tradition to further strengthen the limitation of the female human being to the auxiliary and instrumental role of sexual procreation, defining the woman as a misbegotten and wholly subordinate creature, hedged about with fear and loathing as an embodiment of the sensuality that threatens the purity of male mind and spirit. By giving a "scientific" basis to the earlier patristic attitudes, the Middle Ages guaranteed the survival of this antifemale anthropology long after rigorist ascetic attitudes had ceased to dominate Western society.[4]

Before we discuss Aquinas's theology regarding sexual issues, a few words about his life are appropriate. As a younger son born into a large family, Thomas was presented by his parents as an oblate at the Italian monastery of Monte Cassino in 1230, when he was only five years old. Thomas's life span of half a century was taken up with study, teaching, and religious duties: he joined the Dominican order in 1244. His literary production was immense. Although a number of multivolumed treatises remain (such as the *Summa Theologica*, from which our selections are taken), no letters have been preserved to provide us with clues concerning his personal life and interests. As far as we know, he never had any associations with women; unlike earlier church fathers, such as Augustine, he reveals nothing which suggests he had experienced a torrid youth. Psychohistorians will have difficulty unearthing much material on which to base an explanation of Thomas's character.

Thomas's traditional bias, then, cannot be linked to any dramatic or unpleasant incidents with females in his earlier life. His male-centeredness seems to have rested much more on the intellectual framework within which his theology took shape: Aristotelianism. His acceptance of Aristotelian biological theories, for example, did nothing to advance the cause of women. Aristotle had defined the female as a "misbegotten male," the result of a defective conception;[5] perfect humanity was humanity in its male form.[6] To be fair to Thomas, we must emphasize that he qualified Aristotle's definition in a way which mitigated its harshness. For one thing, Thomas as a Christian affirmed the biblical story that it was God who created woman—and God, for Thomas, was not a Being prone to make mistakes. Rather, God had a specific purpose in mind when he made the female: she was to be a useful partner in procreation. Besides, females are not conceived simply due to a defective male force; a variety of neutral and natural factors, such as the weather, could also determine femaleness, as Aristotle himself had admitted.[7] Perhaps the strongest indication Thomas gives that the production of woman was not an unhappy error is his speculation regarding the reproductive process in Eden had the first couple not sinned: the sex of the fetus would have been determined by the will of the parents, and females, he asserts, would have been born in equal numbers to males.[8] Such a view suggests that Thomas believed females had a rightful place in God's universe. Looked at from *his* standpoint, Thomas is struggling to defend God's creation of woman against those who fancied she was expendable; feminist hearts, nonetheless, are not warmed by his attempt. Critics quickly point out his affirmation of woman's individual defectiveness (even if she *is* needed to perpetuate the species).[9] Moreover, Thomas justifies the creation of females on the grounds that even the lesser grades of perfection of human nature contribute to the completeness of the world.[10] Women are not apt to feel flattered by Thomas's defense of their existence, especially when they recall that the latter argument (even defects contribute to the fullness of God's universe) was one traditionally used to explain the presence of evil in a world created and governed by an omnipotent and benevolent deity.

In addition, Thomas's use of the Aristotelian categories of form and matter, actuality and potentiality, as they were applied to the concepts of maleness and femaleness, resulted in a further depreciation of women. For Aristotle, form and matter were "the metaphysical constitutive elements of bodies";[11] matter was not to be understood as a particular physical entity, but rather as an abstract principle of potentiality. Form, on the other hand, was the determining principle which shaped matter, gave it definition. In human beings, for example, the form is the rational soul, the particular characteristic which makes us human. In discussing conception, Aristotle had postulated that the male supplied the form for the process and the female the matter;[12] the matter, contributed by the woman, "lacks soul,"[13] which deficiency is corrected by the male. Thomas accepts Aristotle's analysis but qualifies it somewhat. As a Christian, Thomas wishes to assert that it is God alone who is the author of all souls, and it is he who infuses them into the developing fetus. The male force "prepares" the matter contributed by the female so that it is ready to accept the soul,[14] but the man himself does not donate the soul which the fetus receives. Thomas's explanation deprives men of the right to claim that they are the ones who endow their offspring with "humanity." But women might unhappily note that in the Aristotelian hierarchy of values, it is still loftier to be a shaper than a mere provider of matter—and for Thomas,[15] as for Aristotle, the woman contributes nothing but the matter.

Thomas does think that matter has some influence over the quality of soul which can be infused; if the matter is "better disposed," souls with a higher capacity for intellection are put into it.[16] At first glance this assertion appears to grant women a more important role as the contributors of matter. All the same, we are left with some doubts which Thomas does not here resolve: would not the higher quality of matter, receiving a more intelligent soul, result in the production of a male child, whereas inferior matter, given a soul more in accordance with *its* value, develop into a girl child? Such an interpretation would be in accordance with Thomas's assertion that although both men and women were granted rational souls by God, woman's was weakened by being associated with a feeble female body; the soul in a female is often unable to "keep a firm grip on things" and hence falls into various sins, due to its relation with female physicality.[17] This lowly role for women in the reproductive process appears even more discouraging when we recall that conception and birth are the two unique "helps" which wives can give their husbands; for any other tasks, another man would be better suited.[18] Even in the sex act itself, the husband has the "more noble" part, activity, whereas the wife exhibits the passive receptivity of womanhood.[19]

Woman's fragility of mind and will, Thomas thought, had serious consequences in human history. It was her weakness which led the serpent to approach Eve first and trick her so easily; Adam, more intellectually alert, would at least have been able to spot the temptation. Although the man was at fault, the woman's sin was greater.[20] Thomas links woman's subjection to the male to her inferior reason. Even at creation, before the Fall, Eve was subordinated to Adam. She did not yet experience the harsh subjection she would suffer later as a penalty for her sin, but even in the innocence of Eden, she knew the subjugation "whereby the superior makes use of his subjects for their own benefit and good." Order would not have been maintained unless some (in this case, women) were destined to be "governed by others wiser than themselves," for in the male, "the discretion of reason predominates."[21]

Woman's weakness and subjection are also the reasons Thomas gives for her exclusion from the priesthood. The problem for him is not simply that the church has forbidden the ordination of women;[22] the difficulty lies much deeper. Ordination simply does not "take" if it is performed on a woman. Even if she were to undergo an ordination ceremony, it would be to no avail; her subjection to the male prevents her from receiving holy orders, for she does not have "eminence of degree." Thomas acknowledges that women past and present have exerted political rulership, but he is not willing to admit them to the priestly care of minds and souls.[23] Likewise, he does not deny that women have received spiritual gifts such as prophecy—in fact, some women exhibit spiritual gifts to a greater degree than men, but these endowments do not make them fit candidates for clerical office.[24] Thomas's views have heavily influenced the Catholic church's exclusion of women from the priesthood.

To these traditional attitudes, derived in part from the Aristotelian estimate of woman's mental and physical defectiveness, Thomas added the androcentric inheritance from biblical and patristic Christianity. The New Testament contributed metaphors to the discussion of male and female status which affirmed male superiority anew and gave it religious sanction. Ephesians 5, for example, had described man's relation to woman as one analogous to Christ's with the church. Thomas adopts the image,[25] and adds

that Eve's creation from Adam's rib was symbolic of the church's
derivation from Christ (the water and blood which flowed from
his side on the cross represent the church's sacraments).[26] Thomas
also used the Genesis 2 story to justify male supremacy. Adam
was made first, said Thomas, to mirror the biblical description of
God as Lord of the universe; just as God rules over all creation,
so Adam stands as the head of the whole human race, which
includes Eve in addition to the rest of mankind.[27]

Moreover, we suspect that the asceticism rampant in the early
Christian tradition also worked against Thomas's appreciation
of women. Since the only irreplaceable function women fulfill
is childbearing, and children are the products of sexual intercourse, women's status gets tied by implication to the evaluation
placed on the sexual act. Married intercourse is not itself evil.
Thomas, following Augustine, argues that even if the first couple
had remained innocent, sexual intercourse would have taken place
in Eden.[28] However, there would have been several differences had
the Fall not occurred. Since Eve's sin, women must forfeit their
virginity, suffer "corruption," in order to engage in intercourse;
their bodies are injured and they lose their original condition
of wholeness. In Eden, on the other hand, defloration would
not have been needed for intercourse to take place.[29] Likewise,
there would have been no lust associated with sex.[30] However,
at this point Thomas takes a step beyond Augustine. Not only
would the couple have felt pleasure, asserts Thomas; the pleasure
would have been an even greater one, because it would have been
rational[31]—a view which he derived from his teacher, Albertus
Magnus. The controlled manner in which Thomas pictures Edenic
sex contrasts sharply with the state of affairs in the post-Fall
world, in which the man, raging with lust, embraces his mate too
ardently, sinfully forgetting that she is to be treated as a wife,
not as "just another woman."[32] Thomas ultimately cannot pry
himself loose from the attitudes toward coitus which have plagued
much of Christian history. Thomas reveals his true estimate of the
sexual act when he writes that in intercourse man "becomes flesh
and nothing more."[33] This evaluation stands at the opposite pole
from that of a thinker we will consider later in this volume,[34]

John Humphrey Noyes, who saw in the "amative function of sex" (the expression of the love relation) its highest meaning.

In another section of the *Summa Theologica* not printed below, Thomas sets forth his theory of natural law. This theory is worthy of brief notice here because it remains to this day the chief theological argument of Catholicism for its prohibition of contraception. The concept of natural law was one which originated in classical Greek philosophy; in early Christianity, the "natural" acquired further significance as a moral injunction. God as the creator of nature, it was held, had established certain values and standards for human life; when we contravene them, we defy not only our "natures" but God himself.

Thomas gave more systematic expression to the concept of natural law. He defined it as rational mankind's participation in God's eternal law.[35] Because man has been endowed with reason, he can reflect on the various inclinations implanted within him by God and see what God intended their purposes to be.[36] The desire for sexual intercourse, for example, is one which man shares with the animals. But because man, unlike the animals, is rational, he can understand that intercourse has as its "end" the birth of offspring.[37] The church has always taught that humans need not be totally governed by our "lower" inclinations. We can exert our wills and refrain from engaging in sexual relations altogether, if we so choose. However, if we decide to marry and engage in sexual relations, we must allow sexual desire to lead to the goal God had intended—conception. Any attempt to thwart the "purpose" of intercourse is a grave evil. Without doubt, a reinterpretation of natural law insofar as it relates to sexuality will have to be undertaken before the Vatican modifies its stand on contraception.[39]

In these various ways, Thomas's views have contributed to the continuation of woman's secondary status—despite the fact, as we have pointed out, that there were elements in his theology which could have encouraged him to break free from the earlier tradition more dramatically than he did. His thought had the potential for development in other directions, as Mary Daly has noted. Her conclusion is that Thomas's "outdated exegesis and biology" led him astray.[40] Feminists, indeed, might not be so eager to assign to Thomas the title long ago accorded him by the church: "the angelic doctor."

One last note: Thomas's literary method may strike the reader as strange, even impenetrable; it was, however, a common one in the medieval scholarly tradition. For each problem, Thomas raises the question and gives the objections to it first. The objections represent both imaginary arguments, and, more frequently, positions actually espoused by philosophers and theologians of the past or of Thomas's own day. After the objection, Thomas inserts a (usually brief) "on the contrary," to indicate to the reader that there is another point of view. He then launches into the "I answer that," which is his own response to the former arguments. Lastly, he replies to each individual objection specifically. Thomas does not just inform the reader of his own opinions; his staggering erudition also makes available to us the variety of approaches medieval thinkers might have taken to certain problems. The technique for deciphering Thomistic texts may appear complicated at first, but patient readers will learn—with some practice—to appreciate the order and beauty of Thomas's structure.

Summa Theologica

PART 1, QUESTION 92
THE PRODUCTION OF THE WOMAN
(In Four Articles)

We must next consider the production of the woman. Under this head there are four points of inquiry: (1) Whether the woman should have been made in that first production of things? (2) Whether the woman should have been made from man? (3) Whether of man's rib? (4) Whether the woman was made immediately by God?

From Thomas Aquinas, Summa Theologica, ed. Fathers of the English Dominican Province (London: Burns, Oates and Washbourne, Ltd., 1914).

FIRST ARTICLE
WHETHER THE WOMAN SHOULD HAVE BEEN MADE IN THE FIRST PRODUCTION OF THINGS?

We proceed thus to the First Article:

Objection 1. It would seem that the woman should not have been made in the first production of things. For the Philosopher says (*De Gener. Animal. 2. 3*), that the *female is a misbegotten male*. But nothing misbegotten or defective should have been in the first production of things. Therefore woman should not have been made at that first production.

Objection 2. Further, subjection and limitation were a result of sin, for to the woman was it said after sin (Gen 3.16): *Thou shalt be under the man's power;* and Gregory says that, *Where there is no sin, there is no inequality.* But woman is naturally of less strength and dignity than man; *for the agent is always more honourable than the patient,* as Augustine says (Gen. ad lit. 12. 16). Therefore woman should not have been made in the first production of things before sin.

Objection 3. Further, occasions of sin should be cut off. But God foresaw that the woman would be an occasion of sin to man. Therefore He should not have made woman.

On the contrary, It is written (Gen. 2. 18): *It is not good for man to be alone; let us make him helper like to himself.*

I answer that, It was necessary for woman to be made, as the Scripture says, as a *helper* to man not, indeed, as a helpmate in other works, as some say, since man can be more efficiently helped by another man in other works; but as a helper in the work of generation. This can be made clear if we observe the mode of generation carried out in various living things. Some living things do not possess in themselves the power of generation, but are generated by some other specific agent, such as some plants and animals by the influence of the heavenly bodies, from some fitting matter and not from seed; others possess the active and passive generative power together; as we see in plants which are generated from seed; for the noblest vital function in plants is generation. Wherefore we observe that in these the active power of generation invariably accompanies the passive power. Among perfect animals the active power of generation belongs to the male sex, and the passive power to the female. And as among animals there is a vital operation nobler than generation, to which their life is principally directed; therefore the male sex is not found in continual union with the female in perfect animals, but only at the time of coition; so that we may consider that by this means the male and female are one, as in plants they are always united; although in some cases one of them preponderates, and in some the other. But man is yet further ordered to a still nobler vital action, and that is intellectual operation. Therefore there was greater reason for the distinction of these two forces in man; so that the female should be produced separately from the male; although they are carnally united for generation. Therefore directly after the formation of woman, it was said: *And they shall be two in one flesh* (Gen. 2. 24).

Reply Objection 1. As regards the individual nature, woman is defective and misbegotten, for the active force in the male seed tends to the production of a perfect likeness in the masculine sex; while the production of woman comes from defect in the active force or from some material indisposition, or even from some external influence; such as that of a south wind, which is moist, as the Philosopher observes (*De Gener. Animal. 4. 2*). On the other hand, as regards human nature in general, woman is not misbegotten, but is included in nature's intention as directed to the work of generation. Now the general intention of nature depends on God, Who is the universal Author of nature. Therefore, in producing nature, God formed not only the male but also the female.

Reply Objection 2. Subjection is twofold. One is servile, by virtue of which a superior makes use of a subject for his own benefit; and this kind of subjection began after sin. There is another kind of subjection, which is called economic or civil, whereby the superior makes use of his subjects for their own benefit and good; and this kind of subjection existed even before sin. For good order would have been wanting in the human family if some were not governed by others wiser than themselves. So by such a kind of subjection woman is naturally subject to man, because in man the discretion of reason predominates. Nor is inequality among men excluded by the state of innocence, as we shall prove (Q. 96, A. 3).

Reply Objection 3. If God had deprived the world of all those things which proved an occasion of sin, the universe would have been imperfect. Nor was it fitting for the common good to be destroyed in order that individual evil might be avoided; especially as God is so powerful that He can direct any evil to a good end.

SECOND ARTICLE
WHETHER WOMAN SHOULD HAVE BEEN MADE FROM MAN?

We proceed thus to the Second Article: . . .

I answer that, When all things were first formed, it was more suitable for the woman to be made from the man than (for the female to be from the male) in other animals. First, in order thus to give the first man a certain dignity consisting in this, that as God is the principle of the whole universe, so the first man, in likeness to God, was the principle of the whole human race. Wherefore Paul says that *God made the whole human race from one* (Acts 17:26). Secondly, that man might love woman all the more, and cleave to her more closely, knowing her to be fashioned from himself. Hence it is written (Gen. 2:23, 24): *She was taken out of man, wherefore a man shall leave father and mother, and shall cleave to his wife.* This was most necessary as regards the human race, in which the male and female live together for life; which is not the case with other animals. Thirdly, because, as the Philosopher says (*Ethic.* 8. 12), the human male and female are united, not only for generation, as with other animals, but also for the purpose of domestic life, in which each has his or her particular duty, and in which the man is the head of the woman. Wherefore it was suitable for the woman to be made out of man, as out of her principle. Fourthly, there is a sacramental reason for this. For by this is signified that the Church takes her origin from Christ. Wherefore the Apostle says (Eph. 5:32): *This is a great sacrament; but I speak in Christ and in the Church.* . . .

THIRD ARTICLE
WHETHER THE WOMAN WAS FITTINGLY MADE FROM THE RIB OF MAN?

We proceed thus to the Third Article: . . .

I answer that, It was right for the woman to be made from a rib of man. First, to signify the social union of man and woman, for the woman should neither use *authority* over men, and so she was not made from his head; nor was it right for her to be subject to man's contempt as his slave, and so she was not made from his feet. Secondly, for the sacramental signification; for from the side of Christ sleeping on the Cross the Sacraments flowed—namely, blood and water—on which the Church was established. . . .

FOURTH ARTICLE
WHETHER THE WOMAN WAS FORMED IMMEDIATELY BY GOD?

We proceed thus to the Fourth Article: . . .

Objection 2. Further, Augustine (*De Trin.* 3. 4) says that corporeal things are governed by God through the angels. But the woman's body was formed from corporeal matter. Therefore it was made through the ministry of the angels, and not immediately by God. . . .

I answer that, As was said above (A. 2, ad 2), the natural generation of every species is from some determinate matter. Now the matter whence man is naturally begotten is the human semen of man or woman. Wherefore from any other matter an individual of the human species cannot naturally be generated. Now God alone, the Author of nature, can produce an effect into existence outside the ordinary course of nature. Therefore God alone could produce either a man from the slime of the earth, or a woman from the rib of man. . . .

Reply Objection 2. As Augustine says (*Gen. ad lit,* 9. 15), we do not know whether the angels were employed by God in the formation of the woman; but it is certain that, as the body of man was not formed by the angels from the slime of the earth, so neither was the body of the woman formed by them from the man's rib.

PART 1, QUESTION 98
OF THE PRESERVATION OF THE SPECIES

(In Two Articles)

We next consider what belongs to the preservation of the species; and, first, of generation; secondly, of the state of the offspring. Under the first head there are two points of inquiry: (1) Whether in the state of innocence there would have been generation? (2) Whether generation would have been through coition?

FIRST ARTICLE
WHETHER IN THE STATE OF INNOCENCE GENERATION EXISTED?

We proceed thus to the First Article: . . .

I answer that, In the state of innocence there would have been generation of offspring for the multiplication of the human race; otherwise man's sin would have been very necessary, for such a great blessing to be its result. We must, therefore, observe that man, by his nature, is established, as it were, midway between corruptible and incorruptible creatures, his soul being naturally incorruptible, while his body is naturally corruptible. We must also observe that nature's purpose appears to be different as regards corruptible and incorruptible things. For that seems to be the direct purpose of nature, which is invariable and perpetual; while what is only for a time is seemingly not the chief purpose of nature, but, as it were, subordinate to something else; otherwise, when it ceased to exist, nature's purpose would become void.

Therefore, since in things corruptible none is everlasting and permanent except the species, it follows that the chief purpose of nature is the the good of the species; for the preservation of which natural generation is ordained. On the other hand, incorruptible substances survive, not only in the species, but also in the individual; wherefore even the individuals are included in the chief purpose of nature.

Hence it belongs to man to beget offspring, on the part of the naturally corruptible body. But on the part of the soul, which is incorruptible, it is fitting that the multitude of individuals should be the direct purpose of nature, or rather of the Author of nature, Who alone is the Creator of the human soul. Wherefore, to provide for the multiplication of the human race, He established the begetting of offspring even in the state of innocence. . . .

SECOND ARTICLE

WHETHER IN THE STATE OF INNOCENCE THERE WOULD HAVE BEEN GENERATION BY COITION?

We proceed thus to the Second Article:

Objection 1. It would seem that generation by coition would not have existed in the state of innocence. For, as Damascene says (*De Fid. Orth.* 2. 2: 4. 25), the first man in the terrestrial Paradise was *like an angel.* But in the future state of the resurrection, when men will be like to the angels, *they shall neither marry nor be married,* as it is written Matt. 22:30. Therefore neither in Paradise would there have been generation by coition.

Objection 2. Further, our first parents were created at the age of perfect development. Therefore, if generation by coition had existed before sin, they would have had intercourse while still in Paradise: which was not the case according to Scripture (Gen. 4:1).

Objection 3. Further, in carnal intercourse, more than at any other time, man becomes like the beasts, on account of the vehement delight which he takes therein; whence continency is praiseworthy, whereby man refrains from such pleasures. But man is compared to beasts by reason of sin, according to Psalm 48:13: *Man, when he was in honour, did not understand; he is compared to senseless beasts, and is become like to them.* Therefore, before sin, there would have been no such intercourse of man and woman.

Objection 4. Further, in the state of innocence there would have been no corruption. But virginal integrity is corrupted by intercourse. Therefore there would have been no such thing in the state of innocence.

On the contrary, God made man and woman before sin (Gen. 1 and 2). But nothing is void in God's works. Therefore, even if man had not sinned, there would have been such intercourse, to which the distinction of sex is ordained. Moreover, we are told that woman was made to be a help to man (Gen. 2:18, 20). But she was not fitted to help man except in generation, because another man would have proved a more effective help in anything else. Therefore there would have been such generation also in the state of innocence.

I answer that, Some of the earlier doctors, considering the nature of concupiscence as regards generation in our present state, concluded that in the state of innocence generation would not have been effected in the same way. Thus Gregory of Nyssa says (*De Hom. Opif.* 17) that in Paradise the human race would have been multiplied by some other means, as the angels were multiplied without coition by the operation of the Divine Power. He adds that God made man male and female before sin, because He foreknew the mode of generation which would take place after sin, which He foresaw. But this is unreasonable. For what is natural to man was neither acquired nor forfeited by sin. Now it is clear that generation by coition is natural to man by reason of his animal life, which he possessed even before sin, as above explained (Q. 17, A. 3), just as it is natural to other perfect animals, as the corporeal members make it clear. So we cannot allow that these members would not have had a natural use, as other members had, before sin.

Thus, as regards generation by coition, there are, in the present state of life, two things to be considered. One, which comes from nature, is the union of man and woman; for in every act of generation there is an active and a passive principle. Wherefore, since wherever there is distinction of sex, the active principle is male and the passive is female; the order of nature demands that for the purpose of generation there should be concurrence of male and female. The second thing to be observed is a certain deformity of excessive concupiscence, which in the state of innocence would not have existed, when the lower powers were entirely subject to reason. Wherefore Augustine says (*De Civ. Dei* 14. 26): *We must be far from supposing that offspring could not be begotten without concupiscence. All the bodily members would have been equally moved by the will, without ardent or wanton incentive, with calmness of soul and body.*

Reply Objection 1. In Paradise man would have been like an angel in his spirituality of mind, yet with an animal life in his body. After the resurrection man will be like an angel, spiritualized in soul and body. Wherefore there is no parallel.

Reply Objection 2. As Augustine says (*Gen. ad lit.* 9. 4), our first parents did not come together in Paradise, because on account of sin they were ejected from Paradise shortly after the creation of the woman; or because, having received the general Divine command relative to generation, they awaited the special command relative to the time.

Reply Objection 3. Beasts are without reason. In this way man becomes, as it were, like them in coition, because he cannot moderate concupiscence. In the state of innocence nothing of this kind would have happened that was not regulated by reason, not because delight of sense was less, as some say (rather indeed would sensible delight have been the greater in proportion to the greater purity of nature and the greater sensibility of the body), but because the force of concupiscence would not have so inordinately thrown itself into such pleasure, being curbed by reason, whose place it is not to lessen sensual pleasure, but to prevent the force of concupiscence from cleaving to it immoderately. By *immoderately* I mean going beyond the bounds of reasons, as a sober person does not take less pleasure in food taken in moderation than the glutton, but his concupiscence lingers less in such pleasures. This is what Augustine means by the words quoted, which do not exclude intensity of pleasure from the state of innocence, but the ardour of desire and restlessness of the mind. Therefore continence would not have been praiseworthy in the state of innocence, whereas it is praiseworthy in our present state, not because it removes fecundity, but because it excludes inordinate desire. In that state fecundity would have been without lust.

Reply Objection 4. As Augustine says (*De Civ. Dei* 14. 26): In *that state intercourse would have been without prejudice to virginal integrity; this would have remained intact, as it does in the menses. And just as in giving birth the mother was then relieved, not by groans of pain, but by the instigations of maturity; so in conceiving, the union was one, not of lustful desire, but of deliberate action.* . . .

PART 1, QUESTION 99 OF THE CONDITION OF THE OFFSPRING AS TO BODY

SECOND ARTICLE
WHETHER, IN THE PRIMITIVE STATE, WOMEN WOULD HAVE BEEN BORN?

We proceed thus to the Second Article:

Objection 1. It would seem that in the primitive state woman would not have been born. For the Philosopher says (*De Gener. Animal.* 2. 3) that woman is a *misbegotten male*, as though she were a product outside the purpose of nature. But in that state nothing would have been unnatural in human generation. Therefore in that state women would not have been born.

Objection 2. Further, every agent produces its like, unless prevented by insufficient power or ineptness of matter; thus a small fire cannot burn green wood. But in generation the active force is in the male. Since, therefore, in the state of innocence man's active force was not subject to defect, nor was there inept matter on the part of the woman, it seems that males would always have been born.

Objection 3. Further, in the state of innocence generation is ordered to the multiplication of the human race. But the race would have been sufficiently multiplied by the first man and woman, from the fact that they would have lived for ever. Therefore, in the state of innocence, there was no need for woman to be born.

On the contrary, nature's process in generation would have been in harmony with the manner in which it was established by God. But God established male and female in human nature, as it is written (Gen. 1 and 2). Therefore also in the state of innocence male and female would have been born.

I answer that, Nothing belonging to the completeness of human nature would have been lacking in the state of innocence. And as different grades belong to the perfection of the universe, so also diversity of sex belongs to the perfection of human nature. Therefore in the state of innocence, both sexes would have been begotten.

Reply Objection 1. Woman is said to be a *misbegotten male*, as being a product outside the purpose of nature considered in the individual case: but not against the purpose of universal nature, as above explained (Q. 92., A. 1, *ad* 2).

Reply Objection 2. The generation of woman is not occasioned either by a defect of the active force or by inept matter, as the objection supposes; but sometimes by an extrinsic accidental cause; thus the Philosopher says (*De Animal. Histor.* 6. 19): *The northern wind favours the generation of males, and the southern wind that of females:* sometimes also by some impression in the soul (of the parents) which may easily have some effect on the body (of the child). Especially was this the case in the state of innocence, when the body was more subject to the soul; so that by the mere will of the parent the sex of the offspring might be diversified.

Reply Objection 3. The offspring would have been begotten to an animal life, as to the use of food and generation. Hence it was fitting that all should generate, and not only the first parents. From this it seems to follow that males and females would have been in equal number.

PART 3 SUPPLEMENT, QUESTION 39
OF THE IMPEDIMENTS TO THIS SACRAMENT
(In Six Articles)

FIRST ARTICLE
WHETHER THE FEMALE SEX IS AN IMPEDIMENT TO
RECEIVING ORDERS?

We proceed thus to the First Article:

Objection 1. It would seem that the female sex is no impediment to receiving Orders. For the office of prophet is greater than the office of priest, since a prophet stands midway between God and priests, just as the priest does between God and people. Now the office of prophet was sometimes granted to women, as may be gathered from 4 Kings 22:14. Therefore the office of priest also may be competent to them.

Objection 2. Further, Just as Order pertains to a kind of pre-eminence, so does a position of authority as well as martyrdom and the religious state. Now authority is entrusted to women in the New Testament, as in the case of abbesses, and in the Old Testament, as in the case of Debbora, who judged Israel (Judg. 2). Moreover martyrdom and the religious life are also befitting to them. Therefore the Orders of the Church are also competent to them.

Objection 3. Further, The power of Orders is founded in the soul. But sex is not in the soul. Therefore difference in sex makes no difference to the reception of Orders.

On the contrary, It is said (1 Tim. 2:12): *I suffer not a woman to teach (in the Church),* * nor to use authority over the man.*

Further, The crown is required previous to receiving Orders, albeit not for the validity of the sacrament. But the crown or tonsure is not befitting to women according to 1 Corinthians 11. Neither therefore is the receiving of Orders.

I answer that, Certain things are required in the recipient of a sacrament as being requisite for the validity of the sacrament, and if such things be lacking, one can receive neither the sacrament nor the reality of the sacrament. Other things, however, are required, not for the validity of the sacrament, but for its lawfulness, as being congruous to the sacrament; and without these one receives the sacrament, but not the reality of the sacrament. Accordingly we must say that the male sex is required for receiving Orders not only in the second, but also in the first way. Wherefore even though a woman were made the object of all that is done in conferring Orders, she would not receive Orders, for since a sacrament is a sign, not only the thing, but the signification of the thing, is required in all sacramental action; thus it was stated above (Q. 32, A. 2) that in Extreme Unction it is necessary to have a sick man, in order to signify the need of healing. Accordingly, since it is not possible in the female sex to signify eminence of degree, for a woman is in the state of subjection, it follows that she cannot receive the sacrament of Order. Some, however, have asserted that

---

* The words in parenthesis are from 1 Corinthian 14:34, *Let women keep silence in the churches.*

the male sex is necessary for the lawfulness and not for the validity of the sacrament, because even in the Decretals (cap. *Mulieres*, dist. 32; ca. *Diaconissam*, 27, qu. 1) mention is made of deaconesses and priestesses. But *deaconess* there denotes a woman who shares in some act of a deacon, namely who reads the homilies in the Church; and *priestess* (*presbytera*) means a widow, for the word *presbyter* means elder.

Reply Objection 1. Prophecy is not a sacrament but a gift of God. Wherefore there it is not the signification, but only the thing which is necessary. And since in matters pertaining to the soul woman does not differ from man as to the thing (for sometimes a woman is found to be better than many men as regards the soul), it follows that she can receive the gift of prophecy and the like, but not the sacrament of Orders.

And thereby appears the *Reply* to the *Second* and *Third* *Objections*. However, as to abbesses, it is said that they have not ordinary authority, but delegated as it were, on account of the danger of men and women living together. But Debbora exercised authority in temporal not in priestly matters, even as now woman may have temporal power. . . .

PART 3 SUPPLEMENT, QUESTION 49 OF THE MARRIAGE GOODS

SIXTH ARTICLE
WHETHER IT IS A MORTAL SIN FOR A MAN TO HAVE KNOWLEDGE OF HIS WIFE, WITH THE INTENTION NOT OF A MARRIAGE GOOD BUT MERELY OF PLEASURE?

We proceed thus to the Sixth Article:

Objection 1. It would seem that whenever a man has knowledge of his wife, with the intention not of a marriage good but merely of pleasure, he commits a mortal sin. For according to Jerome (*Comment. in Eph.* 5:25), as quoted in the text (4. *Sent.* D. 31), *the pleasure taken in the embraces of a wanton is damnable in a husband*. Now nothing but mortal sin is said to be damnable. Therefore it is always a mortal sin to have knowledge of one's wife for mere pleasure.

Objection 2. Further, Consent to pleasure is a mortal sin, as stated in the Second Book (2 *Sent. D.* 24). Now whoever knows his wife for the sake of pleasure consents to the pleasure. Therefore he sins mortally.

Objection 3. Further, Whoever fails to refer the use of a creature to God enjoys a creature, and this is a mortal sin. But whoever uses his wife for mere pleasure does not refer that use to God. Therefore he sins mortally.

Objection 4. Further, No one should be excommunicated except for a mortal sin. Now according to the text (*loc. cit.*) a man who knows his wife for mere pleasure is debarred from entering the Church, as though he were excommunicate. Therefore every such man sins mortally.

On the contrary, As stated in the text (*loc. cit.*), according to Augustine (*Contra Jul.* 2. 10; *De Decem Chord.* 11; *Serm.* 41., *de Sanct.*), carnal intercourse of this kind is one of the daily sins, for which we say the *Our Father.* Now these are not mortal sins. Therefore, etc.

Further, It is no mortal sin to take food for mere pleasure. Therefore in like manner it is not a mortal sin for a man to use his wife merely to satisfy his desire.

I answer that, Some say that whenever pleasure is the chief motive for the marriage act it is a mortal sin; that when it is an indirect motive it is a venial sin; and that when it spurns the pleasure altogether and is displeasing, it is wholly void of venial sin; so that it would be a mortal sin to seek pleasure in this act, a venial sin to take the pleasure when offered, but that perfection requires one to detest it. But this is impossible, since according to the Philosopher (*Ethic.* 10. 3, 4) the same judgment applies to pleasure as to action, because pleasure in a good action is good, and in an evil action, evil; wherefore, as the marriage act is not evil in itself, neither will it be always a mortal sin to seek pleasure therein. Consequently the right answer to this question is that if pleasure be sought in such a way as to exclude the honesty of marriage, so that, to wit, it is not as a wife but as a woman that a man treats his wife, and that he is ready to use her in the same way if she were not his wife, it is a mortal sin; wherefore such a man is said to be too ardent a lover of his wife, because his ardour carries him away from the goods of marriage, so that it would not be sought in another than his wife, it is a venial sin.

Reply Objection 1. A man seeks wanton pleasure in his wife when he sees no more in her than he would in a wanton.

Reply Objection 2. Consent to the pleasure of the intercourse that is a mortal sin is itself a mortal sin; but such is not the consent to the marriage act.

Reply Objection 3. Although he does not actually refer the pleasure to God, he does not place his will's last end therein; otherwise he would seek it anywhere indifferently. Hence it does not follow that he enjoys a creature; but he uses a creature actually for his own sake, and himself habitually, though not actually, for God's sake.

Reply Objection 4. The reason for this statement is not that man deserves to be excommunicated for this sin, but because he renders himself unfit for spiritual things, since in that act he becomes flesh and nothing more. . . .

PART 3 SUPPLEMENT, QUESTION 64 OF THE THINGS ANNEXED TO MARRIAGE, AND FIRST OF THE PAYMENT OF THE MARRIAGE DEBT

FIFTH ARTICLE
WHETHER HUSBAND AND WIFE ARE EQUAL IN THE MARRIAGE ACT?

We proceed thus to the Fifth Article:

Objection 1. It would seem that husband and wife are not equal in the marriage act. For according to Augustine (*Gen. ad lit.* 12.) the agent is more noble than the patient. But in the marriage act the husband is as agent and the wife as patient. Therefore they are not equal in that act.

Objection 2. Further, The wife is not bound to pay her husband the debt without being asked; whereas he is so bound, as stated above (AA. 1, 2). Therefore they are not equal in the marriage act.

Objection 3. Further, The woman was made on the man's account in reference to marriage, according to Gen. 2:18, *Let us*

make him a help like unto himself. But that on account of which another thing is, is always the principal. Therefore, etc.

Objection 4. Further, Marriage is chiefly directed to the marriage act. But in marriage *the husband is the head of the wife* (Eph. 5:23). Therefore they are not equal in the aforesaid act.

On the contrary, It is written (1 Cor. 7:4): *The husband . . . hath not power of his own body,* and the same is said of the wife. Therefore they are equal in the marriage act.

Further, Marriage is a relation of equiparence, since it is a kind of union, as stated above (Q. 44., AA. 1, 3). Therefore husband and wife are equal in the marriage act.

I answer that, Equality is twofold, of quantity and of proportion. Equality of quantity is that which is observed between two quantities of the same measure, for instance a thing two cubits long and another two cubits in length. But equality of proportion is that which is observed between two proportions of the same kind as double to double. Accordingly, speaking of the first equality, husband and wife are not equal in marriage; neither as regards the marriage act, wherein the more noble part is due to the husband, nor as regards the household management, wherein the wife is ruled and the husband rules. But with reference to the second kind of equality, they are equal in both matters, because just as in both the marriage act and in the management of the household the husband is bound to the wife in all things pertaining to the husband, so is the wife bound to the husband in all things pertaining to the wife. It is in this sense that it is stated in the text (4 *Sent.* D. 32) that they are equal in paying and demanding the debt.

Reply Objection 1. Although it is more noble to be active than passive, there is the same proportion between patient and passivity as between agent and activity; and accordingly there is equality of proportion between them.

Reply Objection 2. This is accidental. For the husband having the more noble part in the marriage act, it is natural that he should be less ashamed than the wife to ask for the debt. Hence it is that the wife is not bound to pay the debt to her husband without being asked, whereas the husband is bound to pay it to the wife.

Reply Objection 3. This proves that they are not equal absolutely, but not that they are not equal in proportion.

Reply Objection 4. Although the head is the principal member, yet just as the members are bound to the head in their own respective capacities, so is the head in its own capacity bound to the members: and thus there is equality of proportion between them.

9. Dame Julian of Norwich and Margery Kempe: Divine Motherhood and Human Sisterhood

One of the most startling developments in history is the "proto-feminism" of the late Middle Ages (1200–1500). It is startling because at the same time that Thomas Aquinas is asserting the inferiority of women to men, Dante is affirming their superiority. (It is Beatrice who mediates to Dante the vision of God and who teaches him the true love that constitutes the heart of late medieval devotion.)[1] Or again, it is startling because in the very moment when vast numbers of women are being accused of witchcraft because of confessing to experiencing sexual relations with Satan, there are also women mystics who are revered for their experiences of being mystically married to Jesus or to God the Father.[2] Or again, it is startling because in the same moment when nominalist theologians are teaching the absoluteness of God's patriarchal will and his predestinating power, there are also mystical theologians who are teaching the maternity of God and stressing that His maternal love keeps us always in grace so that we shall never be lost to sin.[3]

The period of 1200–1500 is, therefore, a time of extreme social and intellectual unrest. Contradictory developments are simultaneously going on. Hence, in this volume there are four texts from the period, each of which illustrates a very different thing. Thomas Aquinas illustrates the new scientific theology which, drawing on Aristotle, explains that Christ could only be male; Julian of Norwich illustrates the new mystical theology which describes the Motherhood of God and speaks of "Christ our Mother;" the *Malleus Maleficarum* illustrates the new superstitious demonology which persecuted women for having sexual intercourse with Satan;

and Margery Kempe, who wrote the first autobiography in the English language, illustrates the new woman who assertively dominates her husband on the basis of her experience of being married not to him, but to God. (Margery actually experienced this marriage with God and wore, thereafter, a wedding ring inscribed "Jesus Christ is my love.")[4]

Two larger and more diffuse religiosocial movements also contributed to the development of feminist themes in this age: courtly love and Marian devotion.

There is today considerable disagreement among scholars about the phenomenon called "courtly love" in the late Middle Ages.[5] The troubadours of the thirteenth and fourteenth centuries disseminated this new theory of love and romantic practice which idealized women and urged men to devote themselves to the service of women for the sake of love (not sex!) alone. There are some similarities betwen this and the love mysticism of Bernard of Clairvaux which emphasized the Song of Songs as a model of the relation between God and the soul.[6] Yet there is considerable scholarly doubt today about the degree to which courtly love was actually practiced in society, and there is now evidence to suggest that the few documents we have may not be typical. Hence, there is some reluctance to accept without qualification the traditional view that courtly love

is a reaction against the generally humiliating position in mediaeval society and the theology of marriage that reflected the historical development of this social situation. . . . The consequences of this generally low view of women in the Middle Ages for the theology of marriage are in striking contrast to the exaltation of women and of sexual desire in the literature of courtly love.[7]

Though there is scholarly disagreement about the extent of the influence of courtly love in the late Middle Ages, there is no such disagreement about the development and influence of Marian devotion during this time. In the late Middle Ages, there is a surge of devotion to Mary and it takes a significantly new form.[8] In this period, devotion focuses especially on Mary as our *spiritual mother* (based especially on the Johannine text where Christ says to his disciple, "Behold thy mother" [John 19:27]). Before the twelfth century, Mary was important as the Mother of God (*theotokos*), but not as our mother.[9] This meant that we were not related to God through her, but were related to God through the male figure Jesus Christ. Her status was not mediatorial or archetypal for our faith. But in the late Middle Ages, this changed. Now the figure of Mary is moved to the mediatorial and archetypal position in our lives, for she is conceived now to be not merely Mother of God, but our mother as well. Because we relate to God through her, our experience of God fuses with her and this is a way of "feminizing" God and faith. In fact, once this feminizing of the God-experience has taken place, there emerge theologians who speak about the "Motherhood of God" and "Christ our Mother." (See the selection from Julian below.) Such a theological development could not have taken place without the new forms of Marian devotion.

To illustrate the "protofeminism" of the late Middle Ages, we have chosen texts from Dame Julian of Norwich (1342–1416, or before 1423) and Margery Kempe (c. 1373–post 1439). Dame Julian was an extraordinarily subtle and orthodox theologian, whose single book *Revelations of Divine Love* recounts sixteen visions she had together with her intellectual interpretations of them. Though orthodox, she was also original; and her thoughts about "Christ our Mother" and "the Motherhood of God" are taken from this work.[10] It would be a mistake, however, to think that these ideas dominate her book. It contains, in fact, so much that one must simply read the whole of it to grasp the subtlety of her mind. In making this point, we respect Dame Julian's final warning to readers of her *Revelations*:

> And beware thou take not one thing after thy affection and liking, and leave another: for that is the condition of a heretic. But take everything with other, and truly understand [that] all is according to holy Scripture and grounded in the same.[11]

Dame Julian was an anchorite, that is, a nun who lived alone. Her cell, however, was a room attached to the side of a church in Norwich, England. It had a window opening into the church itself so that she could participate in the liturgy, and it had a window opening outwards so that she could receive visitors, speak with them, and give counsel. One of her visitors was Margery Kempe, a woman of forty who visited Julian when the latter was over seventy.[12] Margery needed counsel and support. After almost twenty years of marriage and fourteen children, Margery had begun to have visions of Christ and she felt compelled to break off sexual relations with her husband and to live alone—preparatory to going on a pilgrimage by foot to Jerusalem. If there were anyone more unlike Julian than Margery, it is hard to imagine who that person would be. Julian's modern editor suggests that she rebuked Margery by saying "to her fanatical contemporary," "When God visiteth a creature with tears of Contrition, Devotion and Contemplation, he may and ought to believe that the Holy Ghost is in his soul."[13] For an editor to call Margery "fanatical" does her an injustice. Margery's problem was that she was so in love with Christ that whenever she heard preaching of his crucifixion, she broke out in tears. When a visiting preacher complained, "I would this woman were out of the church; she annoyeth the people," Margery's friends defended her, saying "Sir, hold her excused. She cannot withstand it."[14]

In any case, Julian gave Margery real support—confirming that her emotional outbursts were not against the Spirit, but were a sign of the Spirit's indwelling. And, from Margery's text, we see that she and Julian spoke of the full range of things Margery had experienced and proposed to undertake—and received sisterly confirmation and support. Students may be interested in comparing Julian's actual speech to Margery, in the selection below, with the single line selected by the editor mentioned above for the sake of putting down this "fanatic."

Following her interviews with Julian, Margery left her husband and made several pilgrimages: the Holy Land and Italy (1414–1415), the pilgrim site of Santiago de Compostela in Portugal (1417–1418), and Norway and Danzig (1433–1434).[15] From 1425–1431 she nursed and cared for her husband while he was bedridden up to the time of his death. Christ told her, after John had fallen and injured himself,

I bid you now keep him for love of me, for he has for some time fulfilled your will and mine, both. And he has made your body free to me, so that you could serve me, and live chaste and clean; so I want you now to be free to help him at his need in my name.[16]

In the course of these pilgrimages, Margery pursued with zeal all opportunities to meet with theologians and to discuss with them her experiences. Visiting Constance in 1414–15, when the Council was being held, she met an English friar who was also a papal legate and "gave him details of her revelations and her constant fear of diabolical delusions."[17] In this encounter, and in others, she received support and confirmation. But it occasionally happened that she was accused of heresy—a charge closely connected with that of witchcraft.

In the next section of this volume, we shall study the *Malleus Maleficarum* and see the extent to which it is directed against women who claim to have relations with supernatural beings. Margery is exactly such a woman, and it is not surprising that she came occasionally under suspicion as she wandered about on her pilgrimages, preoccupied with religious matters (her fellow pilgrims thought she was too "serious"), and perhaps occasionally even teaching or preaching. Near Hull, for example, she was accused of Lollardism (the heresy associated with Wycliffe). She was then taken under escort to the Archbishop of York to be judged. Some shouted at her, "Burn this false heretic." Others pleaded with her: "Damsel, forsake this life that thou hast, and go and spin and card as other women do, and suffer not so much shame and woe."[18]

When she arrived at the court where the Archbishop of York was seated, his first words were, "What, woman, art thou come again: I would fain be delivered of thee." And then he turned to the court and told them that he had previously tried Margery and "found no default in her. Furthermore, sirs, I have, since that time, spoken with good men who hold her to be a perfect woman, and a good woman."[19]

Though these incidents may amuse us today, we should not take them lightly. It is exactly women like Margery Kempe who were accused of witchcraft and burned to death for less than she had done. It was only the testimony of "good men" who saved her and—given Margery's relatively high social standing and constant caution to check out her experiences with persons holding ecclesiastical authority—her own prudence. Many women were not as fortunate or as clever as she.

In the selection that follows, we see illustrated three closely related concerns which form the pattern of Margery's life: her freedom from a sexual relation with her husband which eventuated in a new kind of loving friendship with him, the support she received in this from her spiritual sister Julian of Norwich, and, finally, the new marriage that she made with her heavenly lover.

It would have been some kind of adultery if Christ had taken Margery for his own while she was still wed to her husband. By a carefully executed scheme of divine manipulation, Margery follows Christ's lead and strikes a bargain with her husband: he wants her to have sexual intercourse with him again as they used to before she started being so religious; he wants her to eat and drink with him on Fridays as they used to before Christ ordered her to take up the meatless Friday fast; and he wants her to pay off all their debts before she begins her pilgrimage to the Holy Land. (Margery was of a higher social standing than her husband and owned certain business interests.)

Under instruction from Christ, Margery trades desires with her husband. If he will agree to a perpetual oath of celibacy with her, then she, having now been freed by Christ from the command to observe meatless Fridays, will join her husband at the feast. (And she also agrees to pay off the debts—perhaps suggesting that independent incomes gives women some power in a relation!) Later, after Christ "slays" John's sexual passion for Margery, they mutually enter into a pact of chastity before the bishop, thereafter living out their life together, as Margery says, "in great gladness of spirit." In fact, Margery and John's relationship deepen when the possessive aspects of sexual relating is no longer a bone of contention between them. Margery says that the new John "was ready when all others failed, and went with her where our Lord would send her."

Margery's marriage to Christ comes as no surprise to a student of the mystical tradition. Other strong women such as Angela of Fogligno, Catherine of Siena, and Teresa of Avila—the latter two both "doctors" of the Church—have experienced a marriage to

Christ.[20] The discovery of these medieval women mystics is the possibility of having a sexualized relation with God, a discovery which only women in love with Jesus could have made. Once the discovery was made, however, its implications began to be tentatively explored as well for males in love with Jesus (Johann von Staupitz, John of the Cross).

The Revelations of Divine Love

When I was thirty years and a half, God sent me a bodily sickness; in which I lay three days and three nights. And on the fourth night I received all the rites of Holy Church, and thought not to have lived till day. I understood in my reason, and by the pains I felt, that I was going to die. Thus I endured until day; and by then, my body, as regards feeling, was dead from the middle downwards.

My curate was sent for to be present at my end. He set the cross before my face, and said: "I have brought the image of thy saviour; look thereupon, and comfort thee therewith."

And in this time, suddenly I saw the red blood running down from under the garland, hot and fresh, plenteous and life-like, just as it was in the time that the garland of thorns was pressed down on his blessed head. Even so I conceived truly that it was himself, God and man, the same that suffered for me, who showed it to me —without any intermediary.

In the same showing, suddenly the Trinity filled full my heart with the utmost joy. Thus I understood it shall be in heaven without end unto all that come thither. For the Trinity is God, and God is the Trinity. The Trinity is our Maker. The Trinity is our Keeper. The Trinity is our everlasting Lover. (Chap. 3–4 passim.)

And then I saw that God rejoices that he is our Father; and God rejoices that he is our Mother; and God rejoices that he is our true Spouse, and that our soul is his beloved wife. And Christ rejoices that he is our Brother; and Jesus rejoices that he is our Saviour. These are five high joys.

From Julian of Norwich, *The Revelations of Divine Love*, trans. James Walsh (New York: Harper & Bros., 1961).

And thus, in our making, God almighty is our kindly Father; and God all-wisdom is our kindly Mother, with the love and goodness of the Holy Ghost; which is all one God, one Lord. And in the knitting and the oneing he is our very true Spouse, and we his loved wife and his fair maiden. With which wife he was never displeased; for he says: "I love thee, and thou lovest me, and our love shall never be parted in two."

I beheld the working of all the blessed Trinity. In which beholding I saw and understood these three properties: the property of the Fatherhood, and the property of the Motherhood, and the property of the Lordship—in one God. In our Father almighty we have our keeping and our bliss, in respect of the substance of our kind, which is applied to us by our creation, from without-beginning. And in the second Person (i.e., of the Trinity) in understanding the wisdom, we have our keeping in respect of our sensuality, our restoring and our saving. For he is our Mother, Brother and Saviour. And in our good Lord the Holy Ghost we have our rewarding and our enrichment for our living and our travail; which, of his high, plenteous grace, and in his marvellous courtesy, endlessly surpasses all that we desire.

And furthermore, I saw that the second Person, who is our Mother substantially—the same very dear Person is now become our Mother sensually. For of God's making we are double: that is to say, substantial and sensual. Our substance is that higher part which we have in our Father, God almighty. And the second Person of the Trinity is our Mother in kind, in our substantial making—in whom we are grounded and rooted; and he is our Mother of mercy in taking our sensuality. And thus "our Mother" means for us different manners of his working, in whom our parts are kept unseparated. For in our Mother Christ, we have profit and increase; and in mercy he re-forms and restores us: and by the power of his passion, his death and his uprising, oned us to our substance. Thus our Mother in mercy works to all his beloved children who are docile and obedient to him.

Thus Jesus Christ, who does good against evil, is our very Mother. We have our being of him, there, where the ground of Motherhood begins; with all the sweet keeping of love that endlessly follows. As truly as God is our Father, so truly is God our Mother.

And he showed me that in these sweet words: "I it am: the might and the goodness of the Fatherhood. I it am: the wisdom and the kindness of Motherhood. I it am: the light and the grace that is all blessed love. I it am, the Trinity."

Thus is Jesus our true Mother in kind, of our first making; and he is our true Mother in grace by his taking of our made kind. All the fair working and all the sweet offices for our kind of most dear Motherhood are appropriated to the second Person. For in him we have this godly will whole and secure without end, both in kind and in grace, of his own proper goodness. I understand three types of beholding of Motherhood in God.

The first is the ground of making of our kind. The second is the taking of our kind—and there begins the Motherhood of grace. The third is Motherhood in working. And therein is a forth-spreading, by the same grace, of a length and breadth, of a height and a deepness without end. All is one love.

Our kind Mother, our gracious Mother—for he would all wholly become our Mother in all things—he made the ground of his work to be full low and full mildly in the Maiden's womb. That is to say: our high God, the sovereign Wisdom of all, in this lowly place he arrayed him and made him all ready; in our poor flesh, himself to do the service and office of Motherhood, in all things.

The mother's service is nearest, readiest and surest; nearest, for it is most like us; readiest, for it is most of love; surest, for it is most of truth. This office no one might nor could ever do to the full, except he alone. We know that all our mothers bear us to pain and to dying; a strange thing, that! But our true Mother Jesus, he alone bears us to joy and to endless living; blessed may he be! Thus he sustains us within him, in love and in travail to the full time in which he willed to suffer the sharpest throes and most grievous pains that ever were, or ever shall be; and he died at the last. Yet all this might not fully satisfy his marvellous love. And that he showed in these high overpassing words of love: "If I could suffer more, I would suffer more." He could no more die, but he would not cease working.

Wherefore it behove him to feed us; for the very dear love of motherhood made him our debtor. The mother can give her child to suck of her milk. But our precious Mother Jesus, he can feed us with himself; and does, full courteously and tenderly, with the Blessed Sacrament, that is the precious food of true life.

The mother can lay her child tenderly to her breast. But our tender Mother Jesus can lead us, as he usually does, to his blessed breast, by his sweet open side; and show us there, in part, the Godhead and the joys of heaven, with a ghostly* sureness of endless bliss.

This fair lovely word "Mother," it is so sweet and so kind in itself, that it cannot truly be said to any nor of any, but to him and of him who is very Mother of life and of all. To the property of Motherhood belongs kind love, wisdom and knowing; and it is God. For though it is true that our bodily forthbringing is but little, lowly and simple in comparison with our ghostly forthbringing; yet it is he that does the first in the creatures by whom it is done. The kind loving mother understands and knows the need of her child. She keeps it full tenderly, as the kind and condition of motherhood will. And ever as it waxes in age and in stature, she changes her way of working, but not her love. And when it comes to a more advanced age, she permits it to be chastised, for the breaking down of vices, and to make the child receive virtues and grace. This work, with all that is fair and good, our Lord does it, in those by whom it is done.

Thus he is our Mother like us by the working of grace in the lower part, for the sake of the higher. And he wills that we know it. For he wills to have all our love fastened to him. And in this I saw that all the debts that we owe, by God's bidding, to fatherhood and motherhood is fulfilled in true loving of God.

Although an earthly mother may possibly allow her child to perish, our heavenly Mother Jesus can never allow us who are his children to perish. For he is almighty, all-wisdom and all-love: and so is none but he. Blessed may he be! But oftentimes, when our falling and our wretchedness is showed to us, we are so sore adread, and so greatly ashamed of ourselves, that we scarcely know where to put ourselves. Yet even then our courteous Mother wills not

* ghostly=spiritual.

that we flee away; nothing could be more displeasing to him. Rather, he wills us to behave as a child. For when a child is distressed and afraid, it runs hastily to the mother. And if it can do nothing else, it cries to the mother for help, with all its might. So will he have us behave as the meek child, saying this: "My kind Mother, my gracious Mother, my most dear Mother, have mercy on me. I have made myself foul and unlike to thee; and I cannot or may not amend it but with thy help and grace." The sweet gracious hands of our Mother are ready and diligent about us. (Chap. 52, 58, 59, 60, 61 passim.)

The Book of Margery Kempe, 1426

Then this creature[21] was bidden by Our Lord to go to an anchoress in Norwich, named Dame Jelyan [Julian of Norwich], and so she did, and showed her the grace that God put into her soul, of compunction, contrition, sweetness and devotion, compassion with holy meditation and high contemplation, and full many holy speeches and dalliance that Our Lord spoke to her soul; and many wonderful revelations, which she showed to the anchoress to find out if there were any deceit in them, for the anchoress was expert in such things and could give good counsel.

The anchoress, hearing the marvellous goodness of Our Lord, highly thanked God with all her heart for his visitation, counselling this creature to be obedient to the will of Our Lord God and to fulfil with all her might whatever he put into her soul, if it were not against the worship of God, and profit of her fellow Christians, for if it were, then it were not the moving of a good spirit, but rather of an evil spirit. Said she: "The Holy Ghost never moves contrary to charity, for if he did, he would be contrary to his own self for he is all charity. Also he moves a soul to all chasteness, for chaste livers are called the temple of the Holy Ghost, and the Holy Ghost makes a soul stable and steadfast in the right faith, and the right belief. And a double person in soul is ever unstable and unsteadfast

From Margery Kempe, The Book of Margery Kempe, ed. W. Butler-Bowen (London: Jonathan Cape, 1936).

in all his ways. One who is ever doubting is like the flood of the sea which is moved and born about with the wind, and that person is not likely to receive the gifts of God." "Any creature that has these tokens may steadfastly believe that the Holy Ghost dwells in his soul. And much more when God visits a creature with tears of contrition, devotion, and compassion, he may and ought to believe that the Holy Ghost is in his soul. Saint Paul says that the Holy Ghost asks for us with mourning and weeping unspeakable, that is to say, he makes us to ask and pray with mourning and weeping so plenteously that the tears may not be numbered. No evil spirit may give these tokens, for Saint Jerome says that tears torment the devil more than do the pains of hell. God and the devil are ever at odds and they shall never dwell together in one place, and the devil has no power in a person's soul. Holy Writ says that the soul of a rightful person is the seat of God, and so I trust, sister, that you be. I pray God grant you perseverance. Set all your trust in God and fear not the language of the world, for the more despite, shame and reproof that you have in the world, the more is your merit in the sight of God. Patience is necessary to you, for in that you shall keep your soul."

Much was the holy dalliance that the anchoress and this creature had by communing in the love of Our Lord Jesus Christ the many days that they were together. (Chap. 18.)

It befell on a Friday on Midsummer Eve in right hot weather, as this creature was coming from York-ward carrying a bottle with beer in her hand, and her husband a cake in his bosom, that he asked his wife this question:

"Margery, if there came a man with a sword, who would strike off my head, unless I should commune naturally with you as I have done before,[22] tell me on your conscience—for you say you will not lie—whether you would suffer my head to be smitten off, or whether you would allow me to meddle with you again, as I did at one time?"

"Alas sir," said she, "why raise this matter, when we have been chaste these eight weeks?"

"For I will know your heart."

And then she said with great sorrow: "Forsooth, I would rather see you being slain, than that we should turn again to our un-cleanness."

And he replied: "You are no good wife."

Then she asked: "I pray you, suffer me to make a vow of chastity at what bishop's hand God wills."

"Nay," he said, "that I will not grant you, for now may I use you without deadly sin, and then I might not do so." Then she said to him: "If it be the will of the Holy Ghost to fulfil what I have said, I pray God that you may consent thereto; and if it be not the will of the Holy Ghost, I pray God you never consent to it."

Then they went forth towards Bridlington in right hot weather, the creature having great sorrow and dread for her chastity. As they came by a cross, her husband sat down under the cross, calling his wife to him and saying these words unto her: "Margery, grant me my desire, and I shall grant you your desire. My first desire is that we shall still lie together in bed as we have done before; the second, that you shall pay my debts before you go to Jerusalem; and the third, that you shall eat and drink with me on Fridays as you used to do."

"Nay, sir," said she, "to break the Friday, I will never grant you while I live."[23]

"Well," said he, "then I shall meddle with you again."

She prayed him that he would give her leave to say her prayers, and he granted it kindly. Then she knelt down beside a cross in the field and prayed in this manner, with a great abundance of tears:

"Lord God, thou knowest all things. Thou knowest what sorrow I have had to be chaste in my body to thee all these three years, and now might I have my will, and dare not for love of thee. For if I should break that manner of fasting which thou commandest me to keep on the Friday, without meat or drink, I should now have my desire. But, Blessed Lord, thou knowest that I will not contravene thy will, and much now is my sorrow unless I find comfort in thee. Now, Blessed Jesus, make thy will known to me unworthy, that I may follow it thereafter and fulfil it with all my might."

Then Our Lord Jesus Christ with great sweetness spoke to her, commanding her to go again to her husband, and pray him to grant her what she desired:

"And he shall have what he desires. For, my dearworthy daughter, this was the cause that I bade thee fast, so that thou shouldst the sooner obtain and get thy desire, and now it is granted to thee. I will no longer that thou fast. Therefore I bid thee in the Name of Jesus, eat and drink as thy husband doth." Then this creature thanked Our Lord Jesus Christ for his grace and goodness, and rose up and went to her husband, saying to him: "Sir, if it please you, you shall grant me my desire, and you shall have your desire. Grant me that you will not come into my bed, and I grant you to requite your debts before I go to Jerusalem. Make my body free to God so that you never make challenge to me, by asking any debt of matrimony. After this day, while you live, I will eat and drink on the Friday at your bidding."

Then said her husband: "As free may your body be to God as it has been to me."

This creature thanked God, greatly rejoicing that she had her desire, praying her husband that they should say three "Our Fathers" in worship of the Trinity for the great grace he had granted them. And so they did, kneeling under a cross, and afterwards they ate and drank together in great gladness of spirit. This was on a Friday on Midsummer's Eve. (Chap. 11.)

10. The *Malleus Maleficarum*: The Woman as Witch

The *Malleus Maleficarum*, or *Hammer Against Witches*, was published in 1486 as a handbook for inquisitors. It is the selection in this book which is most revealing of male hatred and fear of women, "heavily laden with sexual paranoia and prurience."[1] The historical circumstances occasioning such a brutal outburst against women are still disputed, but the character and object of the attack are not. The ratio of women to men accused of witchcraft ranged anywhere from 20–1 to 100–1.[2] In some cases almost the entire female population of a village was killed. For example, Trevor-Roper reports that "in twenty-two villages 368 witches were burnt between 1587 and 1593, and two villages, in 1585, were left with only one female inhabitant apiece."[3]

It is hard for us to imagine the immensity of the victimization. Estimates range from a low of 50,000 deaths to a high of over a million.[4] Not merely in numbers of those killed, but also the systematic character of their selection and persecution resembles the modern destruction of the Jews. Yet it is significant that no major historian focuses specifically on this fact: that the victims of the witchcraft persecution were primarily women. Why?

The persecution of witches began in the thirteenth century and continued for 500 years, being waged with special ferocity between 1500 and 1700. Before the thirteenth century, Christian theologians and bishops had explicitly opposed belief in witches.[5] Belief in night-flying and witch's metamorphosis was explicitly condemned as "infidel" or "pagan."[6] Charlemagne decreed the death penalty for anyone who burned supposed witches.[7] So, we see that before the thirteenth century there was a well-developed body of law and religious teaching that should have served as a bulwark against the outburst that occurred. But it occurred. What happened?

There are differing theories advanced by modern historians. One school of thought running from the Brothers Grimm to the English Margaret Murray, affirmed that there were genuine witch cults which continued the practice of pre-Christian rites.[8] Other historians such as Hugh Trevor-Roper and Norman Cohn argue that there were no such witch-cults and that the persecution was based on an ideology which extracted through the torture of its victims the confirmatory evidence it desired.[9] But why should such a persecution break out as it did and when it did? And why should its special victims be women?

Hugh Trevor-Roper asserts that the cause of the witchcraft persecution was a major social upheaval. In its expansive period, in the thirteenth century, the "feudal society of Christian Europe came into conflict with social groups which it could not assimilate, and whose defense of their own identity was seen, at first, as 'heresy.' "[10] These groups included the Albigensians and the Vaudois, groups which dwelt in remote mountainous regions of France and Switzerland. Both these groups adhered to dualistic religions of good and evil. To the Christian outsiders, it was as if they worshiped the Devil.[11]

At first there was only local and sporadic persecution of these "strangers." But in the fourteenth century, the Black Death broke out in Europe and there was the Hundred Year's War in France. Thus, says Trevor-Roper, "every spectacular episode increased the power of the myth. Like the Jew, the witch became the stereotype of the incurable nonconformist; and in the declining Middle Ages, the two were joined as scapegoats for the ills of society."[12]

By the end of the fifteenth century, Trevor-Roper believes, a whole doctrine of witchcraft had been developed together with a technique of systematic persecution. The Dominican inquisitors Heinrich Institor (Kraemer) and Jakob Sprenger compiled and published the mammoth encyclopedia of demonology from which our selection is taken: the *Malleus Maleficarum*. Two years earlier, in

1484, they had solicited a bull from Pope Innocent VIII which deplored witchcraft and authorized the two Dominicans to extirpate it.[13] They published this bull along with the *Malleus*, and this set in motion a period of persecution on a grand scale that was to last for two hundred years.

What is most striking about the *Malleus* is its preoccupation with sexual functions and its vicious attack on women in general. Sprenger and Kraemer believed that women were particularly susceptible to witchcraft because they were lightminded, fickle, feeble in intelligence, quick to waver in faith, and were cursed with an almost insatiable sexual desire so that they lusted for intercourse with the Devil.[14] Men, for their part, were instructed to praise God for preserving them from this terrible curse, symbolized by the fact that God had come to earth as a member of the male sex, thus giving it a sort of immunity to such evil.[15]

Witches were thought to have special powers over the sexual and reproductive functions. Moreover, they also were believed to have a dampening effect upon male potency, though the authors of the *Malleus* hedge on the point whether witches actually had the power to undermine male sexual capacity (to the point of removing their genital organs) or whether such problems were the result of a bewitching delusion or "glamour," as they called it.[16] The authors gave a theological rationale for their overwhelming stress on venereal functions: God permitted witches "more power over this act, by which the first sin was disseminated, than over other human actions."[17]

In another section of the treatise, not included in our selections, the inquisitors detailed the correct procedures to be followed in witchcraft trials and warned against the wiles witches would use to escape detection or to get judges under their power. Various tortures, including the ingenious witch's chair, were used to extract confessions, and the use of torture produced a large number of spurious confessions which confirmed, to the inquisitors, the truth the *Malleus Maleficarum* taught. In this way, the theory produced its own evidence.

Because of the *Malleus*, the persecution of witches became an important part of the larger social unrest of the sixteenth and seventeenth centuries, claiming its thousands of victims—especially women. There may have been pagan practices still continuing in the mountains of Europe, as Margaret Murray contends. But it is only the vast social upheavals that can explain why the persecution of witches occurred when it did. Says Trevor-Roper, "When a 'great fear' takes hold of a society, that society looks naturally to the stereotype of the enemy in its midst; and once the witch had become the stereotype, witchcraft would be the universal accusation."[18]

It is conclusions such as these that leads Norman Cohn in his *Europe's Inner Demons* finally to direct us to "psychohistory" for an explanation of witchcraft; for although we may grant Trevor-Roper's thesis that social upheavals tend to create scapegoats, this in itself does not explain the particular group that is chosen as the scapegoat. Cohn suggests that the psychological reason witches were singled out for persecution is because of

> unconscious resentment against Christianity as too strict a religion, against Christ as too stern a taskmaster. Psychologically it is altogether plausible that such an unconscious hatred would find an outlet in an obsession with the overwhelming power of Christ's great antagonist, Satan, and especially in fantasies of erotic debauches with Him.[19]

The problem with Cohn's theory is that it overlooks the fact that the scapegoat is not "Satan," it is *women*. Women are the persecuted ones, but to read Cohn's book one would never note this omnipresent fact. And when Cohn goes on to say, "It is not at all surprising that the tension between conscious beliefs and ideals on the one hand, and unconscious desires and restraints on the other, should lead some frustrated or neurotic women to imagine that they had given themselves, body and soul, to the Devil or to a subordinate demon,"[20] he sounds like Sprenger and Kraemer themselves! All these men and their theories about frustrated, neurotic women! Just who is scapegoating whom?

The most obvious fact of the great witchcraft persecution is that *men were persecuting women*, primarily because of anxiety about women's sexual powers. It is not repressed resentment against Christ, but repressed resentment against women that broke forth in this difficult period of social upheaval and change. Part of that social upheaval included the Black Plague and religious reformation; part of it included the development of commercial civilization and the emergence of a new status for women as the equals of men. (See the selections from Margery Kempe and John Milton in this volume.) Richardson relates the emergence of witchcraft especially to anxiety about the new status of women, arguing that "the exaggerated authority of the male over the female in the patriarchal system also was a defense against unconscious anxieties about the sexual power of women" and that this anxiety "was first objectified and then catharsized in the figure of the Witch."[21] This proposal at least explains why women were chosen as the scapegoats during this period when the older civilization was completely breaking down.

Trevor-Roper asserts that the theory of witchcraft was based on the belief that there is a Kingdom of Satan that parallels, and is in conflict with, the Kingdom of God. Witch persecution could only cease, he argues, once this belief had been discredited. Hence, he explains the cessation of the persecution of witches as the consequence of the scientific concept of nature, which was developed in the eighteenth century.[22] An alternative to Trevor-Roper's theory is to argue that if the persecution of witches was rooted in male anxiety about the sexual power of women, an anxiety that burst forth in persecution as the old patriarchal culture was disintegrating, then the witch-craze would end only as women attained a new status and men began to find themselves relatively secure with it. That is the view of the editors of this volume, and it should be noted that it is more consistent with Trevor-Roper's own explanation of the origins of the witch hunt being in social upheaval—for, to be consistent, he should see the end of the witch hunts in the creation of a new social order.

But, whatever may have been the external factors that led to the breakdown of Western society in the late Middle Ages, the *Malleus Maleficarum* is an unsurpassed revelation of the primal anxiety about women that lurks in the heart of every man. The only comparable documents we have are the great Greek myths that preserve traces of male fear of the power and evil of women.

Malleus Maleficarum

PART 1, QUESTION 6

CONCERNING WITCHES WHO COPULATE WITH DEVILS

WHY IT IS THAT WOMEN ARE CHIEFLY ADDICTED TO
EVIL SUPERSTITIONS

There is also, concerning witches who copulate with devils, much difficulty in considering the methods by which such abominations are consummated. On the part of the devil: first, of what element the body is made that he assumes; secondly, whether the act is always accompanied by the injection of semen received from another; thirdly, as to time and place, whether he commits this act more frequently at one time than at another; fourthly, whether the act is invisible to any who may be standing by. And on the part of the women, it has to be inquired whether only they who were themselves conceived in this filthy manner are often visited by devils; or secondly, whether it is those who were offered to devils by midwives at the time of their birth; and thirdly, whether the actual venereal delectation of such is of a weaker sort. But we cannot here reply to all these questions, both because we are only engaged in a general study, and because in the second part of this work they are all singly explained by their operations, as will appear in the fourth chapter, where mention is made of each separate method. Therefore let us now chiefly consider women; and first, why this kind of perfidy is found more in so fragile a sex than in men. And our inquiry will first be general, as to the general conditions of women; secondly, particular, as to which sort of women are found to be given to superstition and witchcraft; and thirdly, specifically with regard to midwives, who surpass all others in wickedness.

WHY SUPERSTITION IS CHIEFLY FOUND IN WOMEN

As for the first question, why a greater number of witches is found in the fragile feminine sex than among men; it is indeed a fact that

From J. Sprenger and H. Kramer, *Malleus Maleficarum*, trans. Montague Summers (London: The Pushkin Press, 1948).

it were idle to contradict, since it is accredited by actual experience, apart from the verbal testimony of credible witnesses. And without in any way detracting from a sex in which God has always taken great glory that His might should be spread abroad, let us say that various men have assigned various reasons for this fact, which nevertheless agree in principle. Wherefore it is good, for the admonition of women, to speak of this matter; and it has often been proved by experience that they are eager to hear of it, so long as it is set forth with discretion. . . .

. . . Since women are feebler both in mind and body, it is not surprising that they should come under the spell of witchcraft. For as regards intellect, or the understanding of spiritual things, they seem to be of a different nature from men; a fact which is vouched for by the logic of the authorities, backed by various examples from the Scriptures. Terence says: Women are intellectually like children. And Lactantius (*Institutiones*,3: No woman understood philosophy except Temeste. And *Proverbs* 11, as it were describing a woman, says: As a jewel of gold in a swine's snout, so is a fair woman which is without discretion.

But the natural reason is that she is more carnal than a man, as is clear from her many carnal abominations. And it should be noted that there was a defect in the formation of the first woman, since she was formed from a bent rib, that is, a rib of the breast, which is bent as it were in a contrary direction to a man. And since through this defect she is an imperfect animal, she always deceives. For Cato says: When a woman weeps she weaves snares. And again: When a woman weeps she labours to deceive a man. And this is shown by Samson's wife, who coaxed him to tell her the riddle he had propounded to the Philistines, and told them the answer, and so deceived him. And it is clear in the case of the first woman that she had little faith; for when the serpent asked why they did not eat of every tree in Paradise, she answered: Of every tree, etc.—lest perchance we die. Thereby she showed that she doubted, and had little faith in the word of God. And all this is indicated by the etymology of the word; for *Femina* comes from *Fe* and *Minus*, since she is ever weaker to hold and preserve the faith. And this as regards faith is of her very nature;

although both by grace and nature faith never failed in the Blessed Virgin, even at the time of Christ's Passion, when it failed in all men.

Therefore a wicked woman is by her nature quicker to waver in her faith, and consequently quicker to adjure the faith, which is the root of witchcraft. . . .

If we inquire, we find that nearly all the kingdoms of the world have been overthrown by women. Troy, which was a prosperous kingdom, for the rape of one woman, Helen, destroyed, and many thousands of Greeks slain. The kingdom of the Jews suffered much misfortune and destruction through the accursed Jezebel, and her daughter Athaliah, queen of Judah, who caused her son's sons to be killed, that on their death she might reign herself; yet each of them was slain. The kingdom of the Romans endured much evil through Cleopatra, Queen of Egypt, that worst of women. And so with others. Therefore it is no wonder if the world now suffers through the malice of women.

And now let us examine the carnal desires of the body itself, whence has arisen unconscionable harm to human life. Justly may we say with Cato of Utica: If the world could be rid of women, we should not be without God in our intercourse. For truly, without the wickedness of women, to say nothing of witchcraft, the world would still remain proof against innumerable dangers. Hear what Valerius said to Rufinus: You do not know that woman is the Chimaera, but it is good that you should know it; for that monster was of three forms; its face was that of a radiant and noble lion, it had the filthy belly of a goat, and it was armed with the virulent tail of a viper. And he means that a woman is beautiful to look upon, contaminating to the touch, and deadly to keep.

Let us consider another property of hers, the voice. For as she is a liar by nature, so in her speech she stings while she delights us. Wherefore her voice is like the song of the Sirens, who with their sweet melody entice the passers-by and kill them. For they kill them by emptying their purses, consuming their strength, and causing them to forsake God. Again Valerius says to Rufinus: When she speaks it is a delight which flavours the sin; the flower of love is a rose, because under its blossom there are hidden many thorns. See Proverbs 5:3–4: Her mouth is smoother than oil; that is, her speech is afterwards as bitter as absinthium. [Her throat is smoother than oil. But her end is as bitter as wormwood.]

Let us consider also her gait, posture, and habit, in which is vanity of vanities. There is no man in the world who studies so hard to please the good God as even an ordinary woman studies by by her vanities to please men. An example of this is to be found in the life of Pelagia, a worldly woman who was wont to go about Antioch attired and adorned most extravagantly. A holy father, named Nonnus, saw her and began to weep, saying to his companions that never in all his life had he used such diligence to please God; and much more he added to this effect, which is preserved in his orations.

It is this which is lamented in Ecclesiastes 7, and which the Church even now laments on account of the great multitude of witches. And I have found a woman more bitter than death, who is the hunter's snare, and her heart is a net, and her hands are bands. He that pleaseth God shall escape from her; but he that is a sinner shall be caught by her. More bitter than death, that is, than the devil: Apocalypse 6:8, His name was Death. For though the devil tempted Eve to sin, yet Eve seduced Adam. And as the sin of Eve would not have brought death to our soul and body unless the sin had afterwards passed on to Adam, to which he was tempted by Eve, not by the devil, therefore she is more bitter than death.

More bitter than death, again, because that is natural and destroys only the body; but the sin which rose from woman destroys the soul by depriving it of grace, and delivers the body up to the punishment for sin.

More bitter than death, again, because bodily death is an open and terrible enemy, but woman is a wheedling and secret enemy.

And that she is more perilous than a snare does not speak of the snare of hunters, but of devils. For men are caught not only through their carnal desires, when they see and hear women: for S. Bernard says: Their face is a burning wind and their voice the hissing of serpents: but they also cast wicked spells on countless men and animals. And when it is said that her heart is a net, it speaks of the inscrutable malice which reigns in their hearts. And her hands are as bands for binding; for when they place their hands on a creature to bewitch it, then with the help of the devil they perform their design.

To conclude. All witchcraft comes from carnal lust, which is in women insatiable. See Proverb 30: There are three things that are never satisfied, yea, a fourth thing which says not, It is enough; that is, the mouth of the womb. Wherefore for the sake of fulfilling their lusts they consort even with devils. More such reasons could be brought forward, but to the understanding it is sufficiently clear that it is no matter for wonder that there are more women than men found infected with the heresy of witchcraft. And in consequence of this, it is better called the heresy of witches than of wizards, since the name is taken from the more powerful party. And blessed be the Highest Who has so far preserved the male sex from so great a crime: for since He was willing to be born and to suffer for us, therefore He has granted to men this privilege.

WHAT SORT OF WOMEN ARE FOUND TO BE ABOVE ALL OTHERS SUPERSTITIOUS AND WITCHES

As to our second inquiry, what sort of women more than others are found to be superstitious and infected with witchcraft; it must be said, as was shown in the preceding inquiry, that three general vices appear to have special dominion over wicked women, namely, infidelity, ambition, and lust. Therefore they are more than others inclined towards witchcraft, who more than others are given to these vices. Again, since of these three vices the last chiefly predominates, women being insatiable etc., it follows that those among ambitious women are more deeply infected who are more hot to satisfy their filthy lusts; and such are adulteresses, fornicatresses, and the concubines of the Great.

Now there are, as it is said in the Papal Bull, seven methods by which they infect with witchcraft the venereal act and the conception of the womb: First, by inclining the minds of men to inordinate passion; second, by obstructing their generative force; third, by removing the members accommodated to that act; fourth, by changing men into beasts by their magic art; fifth, by destroying the generative force in women; sixth, by procuring abortion; seventh, by offering children to devils, besides other animals and fruits of the earth with which they work much harm. And all these will be considered later; but for the present let us give our minds to the injuries towards men.

And first concerning those who are bewitched into an inordinate love or hatred, this is a matter of a sort that it is difficult to discuss before the general intelligence. Yet it must be granted that it is a fact. For S. Thomas (4:34), treating of obstructions caused by witches, shows that God allows the devil greater power against men's venereal acts than against their other actions; and gives this reason, that this is likely to be so, since those women are chiefly apt to be witches who are most disposed to such acts. For he says that, since the first corruption of sin by which man became the slave of the devil came to us through the act of generation, therefore greater power is allowed by God to the devil in this act than in all others. Also the power of witches is more apparent in serpents, as it is said, than in other animals, because through the means of a serpent the devil tempted woman. For this reason also, as is shown afterwards, although matrimony is a work of God, as being instituted by Him, yet it is sometimes wrecked by the work of the devil: not indeed through main force, since then he might be thought stronger than God, by causing some temporary or permanent impediment in the conjugal act.

And touching this we may say what is known by experience; that these women satisfy their filthy lusts not only in themselves, but even in the mighty ones of the age, of whatever state and condition; causing by all sorts of witchcraft the death of their souls through the excessive infatuation of carnal love, in such a way that for no shame or persuasion can they desist from such acts. And through such men, since the witches will not permit any harm to come to them either from themselves or from others once they have them in their power, there arises the great danger of the time, namely, the extermination of the Faith. And in this way do witches every day increase.

And would that this were not true according to experience. But indeed such hatred is aroused by witchcraft between those joined in the sacrament of matrimony, and such freezing up of the generative forces, that men are unable to perform the necessary action for begetting offsprings. . . .

QUESTION VIII
WHETHER WITCHES CAN HEBETATE THE POWERS OF GENERATION OR OBSTRUCT THE VENEREAL ACT.

And as to this, Peter of Palude (3. 34) notes five methods. For he says that the devil, being a spirit, has power over a corporeal creature to cause or prevent a local motion. Therefore he can prevent bodies from approaching each other, either directly or indirectly, by interposing himself in some bodily shape. In this way it happened to the young man who was betrothed to an idol and nevertheless married a young maiden, and was consequently unable to copulate with her. Secondly, he can excite a man to that act, or freeze his desire for it, by the virture of secret things of which he best knows the power. Thirdly, he can so disturb a man's perception and imagination as to make the woman appear loathsome to him: since he can, as has been said, influence the imagination. Fourthly, he can directly prevent the erection of that member which is adapted to fructification, just as he can prevent a local motion. Fifthly, he can prevent the flow of the vital essence to the members in which lies the motive power; by closing as it were the seminary ducts, so that it does not descend to the generative channels, or falls back from them, or does not project from them, or in any of many ways fails in its function. . . .

PART 2, QUESTION 1, CHAPTERS 6 AND 7

HOW WITCHES IMPEDE AND PREVENT THE POWER OF PROCREATION

Concerning the method by which they obstruct the procreant function both in men and animals, and in both sexes, the reader may consult that which has been written already on the questions,

Whether devils can through witches turn the minds of men to love or hatred. There, after the solutions of the arguments, a specific declaration is made relating to the method by which, with God's permission, they can obstruct the procreant function.

But it must be noted that such obstruction is caused both intrinsically and extrinsically. Intrinsically they cause it in two ways. First, when they directly prevent the erection of the member which is accommodated to fructification. And this need not seem impossible, when it is considered that they are able to vitiate the natural use of any member. Secondly, when they prevent the flow of the vital essences to the members in which resides the motive force, closing up the seminal ducts so that it does not reach the generative vessels, or so that it cannot be ejaculated, or is fruitlessly spilled.

Extrinsically they cause it at times by means of images, or by the eating of herbs; sometimes by other external means, such as cocks' testicles. But it must not be thought that it is by the virtue of these things that a man is made impotent, but by the occult power of devils' illusions witches by this means procure such impotence, namely, that they cause a man to be unable to copulate, or a woman to conceive.

And the reason for this is that God allows them more power over this act, by which the first sin was disseminated, than over other human actions. Similarly they have more power over serpents, which are the most subject to the influence of incantations, than over other animals. Wherefore it has often been found by us and other Inquisitors that they have caused this obstruction by means of serpents or some such things.

For a certain wizard who had been arrested confessed that for many years he had by witchcraft brought sterility upon all the men and animals which inhabited a certain house. Moreover, Nider tells of a wizard named Stadlin who was taken in the diocese of Lausanne, and confessed that in certain house where a man and his wife were living, he had by his witchcraft successively killed in the woman's womb seven children, so that for many years the woman always miscarried. And that, in the same way, he had caused that all the pregnant cattle and animals of the house were during those years unable to give birth to any live issue. And when he was questioned as to how he had done this, and what manner of charge should be preferred against him, he discovered his crime, saying: I put a serpent under the threshold of the outer door of the house; and if this is removed, fecundity will be restored to the inhabitants. And it was as he said; for though the serpent was not found, having been reduced to dust, the whole piece of ground was removed, and in the same year fecundity was restored to the wife and to all the animals.

Another instance occurred hardly four years ago in Reichshofen. There was a most notorious witch, who could at all times and by a mere touch bewitch women and cause an abortion. Now the wife of a certain nobleman in that place had become pregnant and had engaged a midwife to take care of her, and had been warned by the midwife not to go out of the castle, and above all to be careful not to hold any speech or conversation with that witch. After some weeks, unmindful of that warning, she went out of the castle to visit some women who were met together on some festive occasion; and when she had sat down for a little, the witch came, and, as if for the purpose of saluting her, placed both her hands on her stomach; and suddenly she felt the child moving in pain. Frightened by this, she returned home and told the midwife what had happened. Then the midwife exclaimed: "Alas! you have already lost your child." And so it proved when her time came; for she gave birth, not to an entire abortion, but little by little to separate fragments of its head and feet and hands. And this great affliction was permitted by God to punish her husband, whose duty it was to bring witches to justice and avenge their injuries to the Creator.

And there was in the town of Mersburg in the diocese of Constance a certain young man who was bewitched in such a way that he could never perform the carnal act with any woman except one. And many have heard him tell that he had often wished to refuse that woman, and take flight to other lands; but that hitherto he had been compelled to rise up in the night and to come very quickly back, sometimes over land, and sometimes through the air as if he were flying. . . .

And what, then, is to be thought of those witches who in this way sometimes collect male organs in great numbers, as many as twenty or thirty members together, and put them in a bird's nest, or shut them up in a box, where they move themselves like living members, and eat oats and corn, as has been seen by many and is a matter of common report? It is to be said that it is all done by devil's work and illusion, for the senses of those who see them are deluded in the way we have said. For a certain man tells that, when he had lost his member, he approached a known witch to ask her to restore it to him. She told the afflicted man to climb a tree, and that he might take which he liked out of a nest in which there were several members. And when he tried to take a big one, the witch said: You must not take that one; adding, because it belonged to a parish priest.

All these things are caused by devils through an illusion or glamour, in the manner we have said, by confusing the organ of vision by transmuting the mental images in the imaginative faculty. And it must not be said that these members which are shown are devils in assumed members, just as they sometimes appear to witches and men in assumed aerial bodies, and converse with them. And the reason is that they effect this thing by an easier method, namely, by drawing out an inner mental image from the repository of the memory, and impressing it on the imagination.

11. Luther and the Protestant Reformation: From Nun to Parson's Wife

The Protestant Reformation, Roland Bainton held, exerted a "greater influence on the family than on the political and economic spheres."[1] With the course of time, a new concept of the family and home emerged in Protestantism[2] and Luther was no doubt the seminal figure in this revolution. Although he was not the first of the Reformers to marry, his writings on the subject and the family life into which he so bravely plunged in middle age[3] prepared the way for the Protestant idea of the family for generations to come.

It may seem paradoxical to some that Luther, who stripped marriage of the sacramental status it had been accorded in Catholicism, also revolted against what he considered to be the church's denigration of marriage and exaltation of celibacy.[4] He openly advocated that monks and nuns should forsake the cloister once they understood that they were living contrary to God's word. When his advice was heeded, Luther found himself in the unaccustomed role of marriage broker for the displaced nuns and eventually as the husband of one of them, Katherine von Bora. Luther's protest against the Catholic church, however, should not be viewed primarily as an attempt to correct its ceremonies and practices;[5] there were deeper theological motives behind Luther's break with Catholicism which stemmed from his personal religious experience of God's gracious forgiveness of sinful mankind as that came to be expressed in the doctrine of justification by faith.

Luther thought that the Catholicism of his day had not stressed sufficiently that God through Jesus Christ has accomplished our salvation for us. We do not "earn" favor with God by the performance of religious "works" such as buying letters of indulgence, going on pilgrimages, or offering masses. All of us are unworthy sinners who have no righteousness of our own to offer God. Paul's words about God's justifying activity (for example, in Romans 3:23) were interpreted by Luther to mean that God had forgiven us, despite the fact that we did not deserve forgiveness and from an outward point of view might still appear to be wallowing in the mud of sin. Luther dismissed the whole Catholic understanding of merit as a distortion of the central truth of the Christian faith. No monk or nun might presume that he or she was more righteous in the eyes of God than was a layperson; the doctrine of justification by faith was a great leveler of persons. In fact, Luther argued from 1520 on that many objections could be raised against the practice of taking monastic vows, which in his opinion were non-scriptural and destroyed the freedom of a Christian.[6]

The Estate of Marriage was written in 1522 when Luther was still an inexperienced bachelor, while his Lectures on Genesis date from 1535–1536, a decade after his marriage. In both treatises, Luther's argument proceeds from biblical grounds. He points out that God's command is to "reproduce and multiply," in contrast to what he considered the unwarranted practice in Catholicism of taking vows of celibacy If God has made marriage an ordinance, everyone has the duty to marry except those truly rare persons who have the gift of celibacy or those with bodily defects which would prevent them from performing the sexual act. All the misogynist propaganda from the pagan and Christian traditions should be discounted. Luther capped his argument for marriage by warning that failure to marry early could lead to all sorts of evils—fornication, "secret sins" (presumably masturbation), and downright physical ill health.

Did Luther's new estimate of marriage as an "estate" commanded by God entail a higher position for women? The evidence is not unambiguous. Despite Luther's disapproval of the invectives against women and marriage found in earlier writings, his notion that women's real talent lies in childbearing is hardly revolutionary.

Much of his thinking on the topic of women appears to be that of traditional Christianity: through Eve's sin, women became subject to men and now serve as a "medicine" or "antidote" for the male when his sexual desires press upon him. Her subjection means that she cannot teach or rule and must continue to be "named" by the man she marries in much the same way as Adam named Eve, along with the animals.

On the other hand, Luther acknowledged that men were extremely dependent upon women, not just for the bearing of children, but in many spheres of life. Without women, he wrote, "the home, cities, economic life and government would virtually disappear."[7] Moreover, he admitted that the wife has certain rights to sexual relations and children, and if the husband cannot provide her with these, she may, as a last resort, turn to bigamy.[8] And Luther's depiction of the father engaged in some of the less pleasant aspects of childcare—washing the diapers, for example— mitigates the impression we elsewhere receive of the patriarchally oriented family.

Whatever Luther's theoretical opinions on male-female relations and marriage may have been, the *Table Talk* suggests that he and Katy were a happy and devoted couple. Luther was genuinely comforted by Katy[9] and rejoiced to see her pigtails on the pillow next to him;[10] probably it would not be amiss to guess that she enjoyed his presence as well.

However, in the shift from nun to wife, many women actually lost personal status, for women in the convent often had considerably more power than they could have had in the secular world as wives and mothers.[11] When the women religious heeded Luther's words and gave their hands in marriage, they relinquished roles as leaders of spiritual life and lost the confirming experience of sisterhood found in monastic communities. For some few women, however, the Protestant Reformation opened up an increased possibility for exercising both a spiritual and a social influence on the world. The marriage of Martin Luther and Katherine von Bora was exemplary for generations of Protestant ministerial households, especially in Germany. These households became the cultural, intellectual, and social centers of their communities, providing models of human life which could be emulated by others. In these families, the wife and husband were partners. The woman, like Katherine Luther, was invested not only with the handling of traditional domestic tasks, but also was given responsibility for administering a program of personal counseling, intellectual discussion, and artistic activity, especially music.

Although these ministers' wives were hardly the independent professional women we admire today, they were the first of the nonaristocratic women to have an acknowledged position in secular life. It is true that they held that position by virtue of their relationship with their husbands; nonetheless, their role required some fundamental change in the traditional notion of a wife as having purely domestic status.

The Estate of Marriage

Jesus. How I dread preaching on the estate of Marriage! I am reluctant to do it because I am afraid if I once get really involved in the subject it will make a lot of work for me and for others. The shameful confusion wrought by the accursed papal law has occasioned so much distress, and the lax authority of both the spiritual and the temporal swords has given rise to so many dreadful abuses and false situations, that I would much prefer neither to look into the matter nor to hear of it. But timidity is no help in an emergency; I must proceed. I must try to instruct poor bewildered consciences, and take up the matter boldly. This sermon is divided into three parts.

Part 1. In the first part we shall consider which persons may enter into marriage with one another. In order to proceed aright let us direct our attention to Genesis 1:27, "So God created man . . . male and female he created them." From this passage we may be assured that God divided mankind into two classes, namely, male and female, or a he and a she. This was so pleasing

From Martin Luther, "The Estate of Marriage," *Luther's Works,* vol. 45, *The Christian in Society* 2, ed. Walther I. Brandt. (Philadelphia: Muhlenberg Press, 1962).

to him that he himself called it a good creation (Gen. 1:31). Therefore, each one of us must have the kind of body God has created for us. I cannot make myself a woman, nor can you make yourself a man; we do not have that power. But we are exactly as he created us: I a man and you a woman. Moreover, he wills to have his excellent handiwork honored as his divine creation, and not despised. The man is not to despise or scoff at the woman or her body, nor the woman the man. But each should honor the other's image and body as a divine and good creation that is well-pleasing unto God himself.

In the second place, after God had made man and woman he blessed them and said to them, "Be fruitful and multiply" (Gen. 1:28). From this passage we may be assured that man and woman should and must come together in order to multiply. Now this [ordinance] is just as inflexible as the first, and no more to be despised and made fun of than the other, since God gives it his blessing and does something over and above the act of creation. Hence as it is not within my power not to be a man, so it is not my prerogative to be without a woman. Again, as it is not in your power not to be a woman, so it is not your prerogative to be without a man. For it is not a matter of free choice or decision but a natural and necessary thing, that whatever is a man must have a woman and whatever is a woman must have a man.

For this word which God speaks, "Be fruitful and multiply," is not a command. It is more than a command, namely, a divine ordinance [Werk] which it is not our prerogative to hinder or ignore. Rather, it is just as necessary as the fact that I am a man, and more necessary than sleeping and waking, eating and drinking, and emptying the bowels and bladder. It is a nature and disposition just as innate as the organs involved in it. Therefore, just as God does not command anyone to be a man or a woman but creates them the way they have to be, so he does not command them to multiply but creates them so that they have to multiply. And wherever men try to resist this, it remains irresistible nonetheless and goes its way through fornication, adultery, and secret sins, for this is a matter of nature and not of choice.

In the third place, from this ordinance of creation God has

himself exempted three categories of men, saying in Matthew 19:12, "There are eunuchs who have been so from birth, and there are eunuchs who have been made eunuchs by men, and there are eunuchs who have made themselves eunuchs for the sake of the kingdom of heaven." Apart from these three groups, let no man presume to be without a spouse. And whoever does not fall within one of these categories should not consider anything except the estate of marriage. Otherwise it is simply impossible for you to remain righteous. For the Word of God which created you and said, "Be fruitful and multiply," abides and rules within you; you can by no means ignore it, or you will be bound to commit heinous sins without end. . . .

From this you can now see the extent of the validity of all cloister vows. No vow of any youth or maiden is valid before God, except that of a person in one of the three categories which God alone has himself excepted. Therefore, priests, monks, and nuns are duty-bound to forsake their vows whenever they find that God's ordinance to produce seed and to multiply is powerful and strong within them. They have no power by any authority, law, command, or vow to hinder this which God has created within them. If they do hinder it, however, you may be sure that they will not remain pure but inevitably besmirch themselves with secret sins or fornication. For they are simply incapable of resisting the word and ordinance of God within them. Matters will take their course as God has ordained.

As to the first category, which Christ calls "eunuchs who have been so from birth," these are the ones whom men call impotent, who are by nature not equipped to produce seed and multiply because they are physically frigid or weak or have some other bodily deficiency which makes them unfit for the estate of marriage. Such cases occur among both men and woman. These we need not take into account, for God has himself exempted them and so formed them that the blessing of being able to multiply has not come to them. The injunction, "Be fruitful and multiply," does not apply to them; just as when God creates a person crippled or blind, that person is not obligated to walk or see, because he cannot.

I once wrote down some advice concerning such persons for

those who hear confession. It related to those cases where a husband or wife comes and wants to learn what he should do: his spouse is unable to fulfill the conjugal duty, yet he cannot get along without it because he finds that God's ordinance to multiply is still in force within him. Here they have accused me of teaching that when a husband is unable to satisfy his wife's sexual desire she should run to somebody else. Let the topsy-turvy liars spread their lies. The words of Christ and his apostles were turned upside down; should they not also turn my words topsy-turvy? To whose detriment it will be they shall surely find out.

What I said was this: if a woman who is fit for marriage has a husband who is not, and she is unable openly to take unto herself another—and unwilling, too, to do anything dishonorable—since the pope in such a case demands without cause abundant testimony and evidence, she should say to her husband, "Look, my dear husband, you are unable to fulfill your conjugal duty toward me; you have cheated me out of my maidenhood and even imperiled my honor and my soul's salvation; in the sight of God there is no real marriage between us. Grant me the privilege of contracting a secret marriage with your brother or closest relative, and you retain the title of husband so that your property will not fall to strangers. Consent to being betrayed voluntarily by me, as you have betrayed me without my consent."

I stated further that the husband is obligated to consent to such an arrangement and thus to provide for her the conjugal duty and children, and that if he refuses to do so she should secretly flee from him to some other country and there contract a marriage. I gave this advice at a time when I was still timid. However, I should like now to give sounder advice in the matter, and take a firmer grip on the wool of a man who thus makes a fool of his wife. The same principle would apply if the circumstances were reversed, although this happens less frequently in the case of wives than of husbands. It will not do to lead one's fellow-man around by the nose so wantonly in matters of such great import involving his body, goods, honor, and salvation. He has to be told to make it right. . . .

The third category consists of those spiritually rich and exalted persons, bridled by the grace of God, who are equipped for marriage by nature and physical capacity and nevertheless voluntarily remain celibate. These put it this way, "I could marry if I wish, I am capable of it. But it does not attract me. I would rather work on the kingdom of heaven, i.e., the gospel, and beget spiritual children." Such persons are rare, not one in a thousand, for they are a special miracle of God. No one should venture on such a life unless he be especially called by God, like Jeremiah (16:2), or unless he finds God's grace to be so powerful within him that the divine injunction. "Be fruitful and multiply," has no place in him. . . .

Part 3. In the third part, in order that we may say something about the estate of marriage which will be conducive toward the soul's salvation, we shall now consider how to live a Christian and godly life in that estate. . . .

What we would speak most of is the fact that the estate of marriage has universally fallen into such awful disrepute. There are many pagan books which treat of nothing but the depravity of womankind and the unhappiness of the estate of marriage, such that some have thought that even if Wisdom itself were a woman one should not marry. A Roman official was once supposed to encourage young men to take wives (because the country was in need of a large population on account of its incessant wars). Among other things he said to them, "My dear young men, if we could only live without women we would be spared a great deal of annoyance; but since we cannot do without them, take to yourselves wives," etc. He was criticized by some on the ground that his words were ill-considered and would only serve to discourage the young men. Others, on the contrary, said that because Metellus was a brave man he had spoken rightly, for an honorable man should speak the truth without fear or hypocrisy.

So they concluded that woman is a necessary evil, and that no household can be without such an evil. These are the words of blind heathen, who are ignorant of the fact that man and woman are God's creation. They blaspheme his work, as if man and woman just came into being spontaneously! I imagine that if women were to write books they would say exactly the same thing about men. What they have failed to set down in writing, however, they express with their grumbling and complaining whenever they get together.

Every day one encounters parents who forget their former misery because, like the mouse, they have now had their fill. They deter their children from marriage but entice them into priesthood and nunnery, citing the trials and troubles of married life. Thus do they bring their own children home to the devil, as we daily observe; they provide them with ease for the body and hell for the soul.

Since God had to suffer such disdain of his work from the pagans, he therefore also gave them their reward, of which Paul writes in Romans 1:24–28, and allowed them to fall into immorality and a stream of uncleanness until they henceforth carnally abused not women but boys and dumb beasts. Even their women carnally abused themselves and each other. Because they blasphemed the work of God, he gave them up to a base mind, of which the books of the pagans are full, most shamelessly crammed full. . . .

Now observe that when that clever harlot, our natural reason (which the pagans followed in trying to be most clever), takes a look at married life, she turn up her nose and says, "Alas, must I rock the baby, wash its diapers, make its bed, smell its stench, stay up nights with it, take care of it when it cries, heal its rashes and sores, and on top of that care for my wife, provide for her, labor at my trade, take care of this and take care of that, do this and do that, endure this and endure that, and whatever else of bitterness and drudgery married life involves? What, should I make such a prisoner of myself? O you poor, wretched fellow, have you take a wife? Fie, fie upon such wretchedness and bitterness! It is better to remain free and lead a peaceful, carefree life; I will become a priest or a nun and compel my children to do likewise."

What then does Christian faith say to this? It opens its eyes, looks upon all these insignificant, distasteful, and despised duties in the spirit, and is aware that they are all adorned with divine approval as with the costliest gold and jewels. It says, "O God, because I am certain that thou hast created me as a man and hast from my body begotten this child, I also know for a certainty that it meets with thy perfect pleasure. I confess to thee that I am not worthy to rock the little babe or wash its diapers, or to be entrusted with the care of the child and its mother. How is it that I, without any merit, have come to this distinction of being certain that I am serving thy most precious will? O how gladly will I do so, though the duties should be even more insignificant and despised. Neither frost nor heat, neither drudgery nor labor, will distress or dissuade me, for I am certain that it is thus pleasing in thy sight."

A wife too should regard her duties in the same light, as she suckles the child, rocks and bathes it, and cares for it in other ways; and as she busies herself with other duties and renders help and obedience to her husband. These are truly golden and noble works. This is also how to comfort and encourage a woman in the pangs of childbirth, not by repeating St. Margaret legends and other silly old wives' tales but by speaking thus, "Dear Grete, remember that you are a woman, and that this work of God in you is pleasing to him. Trust joyfully in his will, and let him have his way with you. Work with all your might to bring forth the child. Should it mean your death, then depart happily, for you will die in a noble deed and in subservience to God. If you were not a woman you should now wish to be one for the sake of this very work alone, that you might thus gloriously suffer and even die in the performance of God's work and will. For here you have the word of God, who so created you and implanted within you this extremity." Tell me, is not this indeed, as Solomon says (Prov. 18:22), "to obtain favor from the Lord," even in the midst of such extremity?

Now you tell me, when a father goes ahead and washes diapers or performs some other mean task for his child, and someone ridicules him as an effeminate fool—though that father is acting in the spirit just described and in Christian faith—my dear fellow you tell me, which of the two is most keenly ridiculing the other? God, with all his angels and creatures, is smiling—not because that father is washing diapers, but because he is doing so in Christian faith. Those who sneer at him and see only the task but not the faith are ridiculing God with all his creatures, as the biggest fool on earth. Indeed, they are only ridiculing themselves; with all their cleverness they are nothing but devil's fools.

St. Cyprian, that great and admirable man and holy martyr, wrote that one should kiss the newborn infant, even before it is baptized, in honor of the hands of God here engaged in a brand new deed. What do you suppose he would have said about a baptized infant? There was a true Christian, who correctly recognized and regarded God's work and creature. Therefore, I say that all nuns and monks who lack faith, and who trust in their own chastity and in their order, are not worthy of rocking a baptized child or preparing its pap, even if it were the child of a harlot. This is because their order and manner of life has no word of God as its warrant. They cannot boast that what they do is pleasing in God's sight, as can the woman in childbirth, even if her child is born out of wedlock. . . .

I therefore pass over the good or evil which experience offers, and confine myself to such good as Scripture and truth ascribe to marriage. It is no slight boon that in wedlock fornication and unchastity are checked and eliminated. This in itself is so great a good that it alone should be enough to induce men to marry forthwith, and for many reasons.

The first reason is that fornication destroys not only the soul but also body, property, honor, and family as well. For we see how licentious and wicked life not only brings great disgrace but is also a spendthrift life, more costly than wedlock, and that illicit partners necessarily occasion greater suffering for one another than do married folk. Beyond that it consumes the body, corrupts flesh and blood, nature, and physical constitution. Through such a variety of evil consequences God takes a rigid position, as though he would actually drive people away from fornication and into marriage. However, few are thereby convinced or converted. . . .

The estate of marriage, however, redounds to the benefit not alone of the body, property, honor, and soul of an individual, but also to the benefit of whole cities and countries, in that they remain exempt from the plagues imposed by God. We know only too well that the most terrible plagues* have befallen lands and

* Luther probably was referring to syphilis

people because of fornication. This was the sin cited as the reason why the world was drowned in the Deluge (Gen. 6:1–13), and Sodom and Gomorrah were buried in flames (Gen. 19:1–24). Scripture also cites many other plagues, even in the case of holy men such as David (2 Sam. 11–12), Solomon (1 Kings 11:1–13), and Samson (Judg. 16:1–2). We see before our very eyes that God even now sends more new plagues. . . .

Physicians are not amiss when they say: If this natural function is forcibly restrained it necessarily strikes into the flesh and blood and becomes a poison, whence the body becomes unhealthy, enervated, sweaty, and foul-smelling. That which should have issued in fruitfulness and propagation has to be absorbed within the body itself. Unless there is terrific hunger or immense labor or the supreme grace, the body cannot take it; it necessarily becomes unhealthy and sickly. Hence, we see how weak and sickly barren women are. Those who are fruitful, however, are healthier, cleanlier and happier. And even if they bear themselves weary—or ultimately bear themselves out—that does not hurt. Let them bear themselves out. This is the purpose for which they exist. It is better to have a brief life with good health than a long life in ill health.

But the greatest good in married life, that which makes all suffering and labor worth while, is that God grants offspring and commands that they be brought up to worship and serve him. In all the world this is the noblest and most precious work, because to God there can be nothing dearer than the salvation of souls. Now since we are all duty-bound to suffer death, if need be, that we might bring a single soul to God, you can see how rich the estate of marriage is in good works. God has entrusted to its bosom souls begotten of its own body, on whom it can lavish all manner of Christian works. Most certainly father and mother are apostles, bishops, and priests to their children, for it is they who make them acquainted with the gospel. In short, there is no greater or nobler authority on earth than that of parents over their children, for this authority is both spiritual and temporal. Whoever teaches the gospel to another is truly his apostle and bishop. Mitre and staff and great estates indeed produce idols, but teaching the gospel produces apostles and bishops. See therefore how good and great is God's work and ordinance! . . .

To sum the matter up: whoever finds himself unsuited to the celibate life should see to it right away that he has something to do and to work at; then let him strike out in God's name and get married. A young man should marry at the age of twenty at the latest, a young woman at fifteen to eighteen; that's when they are still in good health and best suited for marriage. Let God worry about how they and their children are to be fed. God makes children; he will surely also feed them. Should he fail to exalt you and them here on earth, then take satisfaction in the fact that he has granted you a Christian marriage, and know that he will exalt you there; and be thankful to him for his gifts and favors.

With all this extolling of married life, however, I have not meant to ascribe to nature a condition of sinlessness. On the contrary, I say that flesh and blood, corrupted through Adam, is conceived and born in sin, as Psalm 51:5 says. Intercourse is never without sin; but God excuses it by his grace because the estate of marriage is his work, and he preserves in and through the sin all that good which he has implanted and blessed in marriage.

Lectures on Genesis

Genesis 2:18: *The Lord God also said: It is not good that man is alone; I shall make him a help which should be before him.*

We have the church established by the Word and a distinct form of worship. There was no need of civil government, since nature was unimpaired and without sin. Now also the household is set up. For God makes a husband of lonely Adam and joins him to a wife, who was needed to bring about the increase of the human race. Just as we pointed out above in connection with the creation of man that Adam was created in accordance with a well-considered counsel, so here, too, we perceive that Eve is being

From Martin Luther, *Lectures on Genesis, Luther's Works*, vol. 1, ed. Jaroslav Pelikan (St. Louis: Concordia Publishing House, 1958).

created according to a definite plan. Thus here once more Moses points out that man is a unique creature and that he is suited to be a partaker of divinity and of immortality. For man is a more excellent creature than heaven and earth and everything that is in them.

But Moses wanted to point out in a special way that the other part of humanity, the woman, was created by a unique counsel of God in order to show that this sex, too, is suited for the kind of life which Adam was expecting and that this sex was to be useful for procreation. Hence it follows that if the woman had not been deceived by the serpent and had not sinned, she would have been the equal of Adam in all respects. For the punishment, that she is now subjected to the man, was imposed on her after sin and because of sin, just as the other hardships and dangers were: travail, pain, and countless other vexations. Therefore Eve was not like the woman of today; her state was far better and more excellent, and she was in no respect inferior to Adam, whether you count the qualities of the body or those of the mind. . . .

Today, after our nature has become corrupted by sin, woman is needed not only to secure increase but also for companionship and for protection. The management of the household must have the ministration of the dear ladies. In addition—and this is lamentable—woman is also necessary as an antidote against sin. And so, in the case of the woman, we must think not only of the managing of the household which she does, but also of the medicine which she is. In this respect Paul says (1 Cor. 7:2): "Because of fornication let each one have his own wife." And the Master of the Sentences declares learnedly that matrimony was established in Paradise as a duty, but after sin also as an antidote. Therefore we are compelled to make use of this sex in order to avoid sin. It is almost shameful to say this, but nevertheless it is true. For there are very few who marry solely as a matter of duty. . . .

Therefore was this fall not a terrible thing? For truly in all nature there was no activity more excellent and more admirable than procreation. After the proclamation of the name of God it is the most important activity Adam and Eve in the state of innocence could carry on—as free from sin in doing this as they were in praising God. Although this activity, like the other wretched remnants of the first state, continues in nature until now, how horribly marred it has become! In honor husband and wife are joined in public before the congregation; but when they are alone, they come together with a feeling of the utmost shame. I am not speaking now about the hideousness inherent in our flesh, namely, the bestial desire and lust. All these are clear indications of original sin. . . .

. . . However, it is a great favor that God has preserved woman for us—against our will and wish, as it were—both for procreation and also as a medicine against the sin of fornication. In Paradise woman would have been a help for a duty only. But now she is also, and for the greater part at that, an antidote and a medicine; we can hardly speak of her without a feeling of shame, and surely we cannot make use of her without shame. The reason is sin. In Paradise that union would have taken place without any bashfulness, as an activity created and blessed by God. It would have been accompanied by a noble delight, such as there was at that time in eating and drinking. Now, alas, it is so hideous and frightful a pleasure that physicians compare it with epilepsy or falling sickness. Thus an actual disease is linked with the very activity of procreation. We are in the state of sin and of death; therefore we also undergo this punishment, that we cannot make use of woman without the horrible passion of lust and, so to speak, without epilepsy. . . .

Genesis 2:23: *This one will be called Woman, because she has been taken from the man.*

And now, just as through the Holy Spirit Adam had an understanding of past events which he had not seen, and glorified God and praised Him for the creation of his mate, so now he prophesies regarding the future when he says that she must be called "Woman." We are altogether unable to imitate the nicety of the Hebrew language. אִישׁ denotes a man. But he says that Eve must be called אִשָּׁה, as though for "wife" you would say "she-man" from man, a heroic woman who performs manly acts.

Moreover, this designation carries with it a wonderful and

pleasing description of marriage, in which, as the jurist also says, the wife shines by reason of her husband's rays. Whatever the husband has, this the wife has and possesses in its entirety. Their partnership involves not only their means but children, food, bed, and dwelling; their purposes, too, are the same. The result is that the husband differs from the wife in no other respect than in sex; otherwise the woman is altogether a man. Whatever the man has in the home and is, this the woman has and is; she differs only in sex and in something that Paul mentions 1 Timothy 2:13, namely, that she is a woman by origin, because the woman came from the man and not the man from the woman.

Also of this fellowship we observe some remnants today, although pitiable ones, if we look back to the first beginning. For if the wife is honorable, virtuous, and pious, she shares in all the cares, endeavors, duties, and functions of her husband. With this end in view she was created in the beginning; and for this reason she is called woman, or, if we were able to say so in Latin, a "she-man." Thus she differs only in sex from the head of the household, inasmuch as she was taken from the flesh of the man. Although this can be said only of Eve, who was created in this manner, nevertheless in Matthew 19:5 Christ applies it to all wives when He says that husband and wife are one flesh. In this way, although your wife has not been made from your bones, nevertheless, because she is your wife, she is the mistress of the house just as you are its master, except that the wife was made subject to the man by the Law which was given after sin. This punishment is similar to the others which dulled those glorious conditions of Paradise of which this text informs us. Moses is not speaking of the wretched life which married people now live but of the innocence in Paradise. There the management would have been equally divided, just as Adam prophesies here that Eve must be called "she-man," or "virago" because she performs similar activities in the home. Now the sweat of the face is imposed upon man, and woman is given the command that she should be under her husband. Yet there remain remnants, like dregs, of the dominion, so that even now the wife can be called "virago" because she has a share in the property. . . .

Genesis 3:16: *But to the woman He said: I will greatly multiply your sorrow when you are pregnant. In pain you will bear children, and you will be under your husband's power; and he will rule over you.*

The second part of the curse has to do with cohabitation. If Eve had not sinned, she would not only have given birth without pain, but her union with her husband would have been just as honorable as it is honorable today to eat or converse with one's wife at the table. Rearing children would also have been very easy and would have abounded in joy. These benefits have been lost through sin, and there have followed those familiar evils of pain and work which are connected with gestation, birth, and nurturing. Just as a pretty girl, without any inconvenience, nay, even with great pleasure and some pride, wears on her head a beautiful wreath woven with flowers, so, if she had not sinned, Eve would have carried her child in her womb without any inconvenience and with great joy. Now there is also added to those sorrows of gestation and birth that Eve has been placed under the power of her husband, she who previously was very free and, as the sharer of all gifts of God, was in no respect inferior to her husband.

This punishment, too, springs from original sin; and the woman bears it just as unwillingly as she bears those pains and inconveniences that have been placed upon her flesh. The rule remains with the husband, and the wife is compelled to obey him by God's command. He rules the home and the state, wages wars, defends his possessions, tills the soil, builds, plants, etc. The woman, on the other hand, is like a nail driven into the wall. She sits at home, and for this reason Paul, in Titus 2:5, calls her an οἰκουργός. The pagans have depicted Venus as standing on a seashell; for just as the snail carried its house with it, so the wife should stay at home and look after the affairs of the household, as one who has been deprived of the ability of administering those affairs that are outside and that concern the state. She does not go beyond her most personal duties.

If Eve had persisted in the truth, she would not only not have been subjected to the rule of her husband, but she herself would also have been a partner in the rule which is now entirely the concern of males. Women are generally disinclined to put up with this burden, and they naturally seek to gain what they have lost through sin. If they are unable to do more, they at least indicate their impatience by grumbling. However, they cannot perform the functions of men, teach, rule, etc. In procreation and in feeding and nurturing their offspring they are masters. In this way Eve is punished; but, as I said in the beginning, it is a gladsome punishment if you consider the hope of eternal life and the honor of motherhood which have been left her. . . .

Genesis 3:20: *And Adam called the name of his wife Eve, because she was the mother of all the living.*

We heard above that the punishment of being under her husband's power was inflicted on the woman. An indication of that power is given here. It is not God who gives her a name; it is Adam, as the lord of Eve, just as he had previously given names to the animals as creatures put under him. No animal thought out a name for itself; all were assigned their names and received the prestige and honor of a name from their lord Adam. Similarly even today, when a woman marries a man, she loses the name of her family and is called by the name of her husband. It would be unnatural if a husband wanted to be called by his wife's name. This is an indication and a confirmation of the punishment or subjection which the woman incurred through her sin. Likewise, if the husband changes his place of residence, the woman is compelled to follow him as her lord. So manifold are the traces in nature which remind us of sin and of our misfortune. . . .

12. John Milton:
The Puritan Transformation of Marriage

John Milton (1608–1674) represents the Puritan tradition in this volume. The great contribution of the Puritans was to combine "the romantic love relation and the marriage relation" thereby creating "the new social institution of romantic marriage."[1] The Puritans transformed the traditional conception of marriage, making conversation, companionship, and love a higher value than sexual relation and procreation. The most important proponent of this innovation was John Milton who "hailed wedded love in a spirit like our own," but who was also "too far ahead of his own time, and died in a world that seemed increasingly to scorn the ideals he believed in."[2]

Milton is best known for his great epic poems *Paradise Lost* and *Paradise Regained*, which he completed towards the end of his life. But in his middle years, he was an active polemicist for social reform, promoting especially freedom of the press and more liberal grounds for divorce. Arthur Barker argues that Milton's general commitment to liberalism, that is, to freedom as the primary social value, led him to promote both of these causes.[3] Other scholars propose, rather, that Milton's views of divorce are only special pleadings for his own interests, since his first marriage began very unhappily.[4] John Halkett points out that if Milton had argued for divorce on the grounds of desertion, he probably could have won his case. But he did not and Halkett concludes that "we must assume that whatever personal involvement there is in the tracts lies in Milton's convictions about the nature of marriage. . . . His experience may have helped to shape those convictions, but it is inaccurate to read the tracts as largely personal documents."[5]

The Doctrine and Discipline of Divorce is the selection from Milton included in this volume. The treatise was submitted to the synod convened by Parliament in 1643. It is the first treatise on divorce written in English and is, therefore, more important for how it poses the problems than for how it resolves them. It excited so much controversy that Milton revised and enlarged it, publishing a second edition the following year. He also published, shortly afterwards, three more technical treatises on divorce: *The Judgment of Martin Bucer concerning Divorce*, the *Tetrachordon*, and the *Colasterion*.[6] These four documents are known as Milton's divorce tracts.

The key to Milton's conception of marriage is that he regards it, first of all, as a spiritual relationship rather than as a sexual relationship. It proceeds "from the mind rather than the body."[7] The chief purpose of this relation, according to Milton, is to provide conversation and companionship to relieve human loneliness rather than to provide a partner to relieve sexual lust. Hence, Milton believes that marriage was instituted by God before the Fall when he saw that it was not good for man to be alone. From this viewpoint, Milton disagrees with the older Christian tradition which held that God instituted marriage after the fall as a dike against sin and a remedy for sexual lust, a position advocated by St. Paul.

The goal of marriage, according to Milton, is love, that is, a relationship of sharing which conduces to happiness and mutual help. But this love presupposes a certain compatibility of persons and temperaments. Where such compatibility is absent (and it is natural that it sometimes be absent, for temperaments differ through no fault of their own), then no true marriage can exist even if there be a sexual relation. In fact, Milton argues that a sexual relation between two incompatible persons makes them more aware of their separateness and increases the feeling of loneliness, making things worse than if there had been no sex at all. Hence, Milton regards loveless sex as antimarital, for it increases, rather than decreases, the distance between people and their sense of locked-in-selfness and despair.

Milton concludes by arguing against the entire Christian tradition to that point, asserting that God himself has given a law that requires persons to divorce wherever there is "uncleanness" (Deut. 24:1). Milton interprets this uncleanness to mean the "unfitness of mind" which "hinders the solace and perfect society of the married couple, and what hinders that more than the unfitness and defectiveness of an unconjugal mind."[8] This teaching of scripture is absolute, says Milton, and not even Christ can revoke it. Divorce, therefore, is not merely allowed to an unhappily married couple; it is commanded to them as a moral obligation. To continue in an unhappy marriage, says Milton, is against the purpose of marriage itself. In the selection below, we shall see how he argues this point.

How radical Milton's view of marriage are can also be seen from his judgment regarding adultery. Adultery is usually regarded as the worst offense agains marriage and, in the Christian tradition, is often the only permissible ground for divorce. But Milton does not regard adultery as the most serious problem. The worst problem, says Milton, is "idolatry," by which he means a rejection of the spiritual companionship, or godly society, which is the main purpose of marriage itself. He says,

> Now whether Idolatry or Adultery be the greatest violation of marriage, if any demand, let him thus consider that among Christian Writers touching matrimony, there be three chief ends thereof agreed on; Godly society, next civil [society], and thirdly, that of the marriage-bed. Of these the first in name to be the highest and most excellent, no baptiz'd man can deny; nor that Idolatry smites directly against this prime end, nor that such as the violated end is, such is the violation: but he who affirms adultery to be the highest breach, affirms the bed to be the highest of marriage, which in truth is a gross and boorish opinion.[9]

From a feminist perspective, Milton's understanding of marriage must be regarded as a real advance beyond the traditional viewpoint which made the slaking of male lust and female procreation into the primary purpose. Milton's view of marriage is built on the idea of spiritual reciprocity wherein men and women are each fully human and images of one another. The woman is not here downgraded to the role of childbearer and confined to the domestic sphere. Marriage here attains a new dignity and, with this, women attain a new dignity, too.

However, this is to put the best face on the matter; for when we inquire more carefully into what Milton means by the "idolatry" that is a greater violation of marriage than even adultery, we discover his patriarchalism. Idolatry, according to Milton, is loving another Lord than one's own Lord, thereby rejecting the proper hierarchy of society. The proper hierarchy of marriage, according to Milton, is that the wife should be subject to her husband for the two are created "hee for God only, shee for God in him." If the wife disobeys her husband and has a will that is not subject to his, then, says Milton, this is a greater wrong to marriage that even adultery. This is the "unconjugal mind" and "uncleanness" for which a man must divorce his wife.

By the very line of argument, we also see that Milton will deny that a woman can divorce her husband for idolatry, for he is not supposed to be subordinate to her. (Uncleanness does not apply to men!) In fact, even if the husband were to be an unbeliever, Milton would deny that this constitutes grounds for divorce. Here, he simply adopts the old text of St. Paul counseling the woman to be patient and kind, hoping to change her husband's heart by her good behavior. As a wife, she is to have no independent will or life of her own.

From the feminist viewpoint, Milton is a mixture of promising new beginnings that are then immediately compromised by traditional patriarchal prejudices. His view of marriage leads towards the greater equality and freedom we affirm today; but the combination of Milton's hierarchical viewpoint together with his Protestant insistence upon the necessity of marriage for everyone drives women into a greater subordination to men. At least in the Catholic spiritual tradition, there is an emphasis upon two things which Milton has lost: the notion of a *direct* relation of married women to God rather than one mediated by their husbands, and the possibility of celibacy as an alternative to marriage. These two factors gave women like Margery Kempe a power vis-à-vis the marriage relation that Milton's wives have lost.[11]

Whatever one decides about Milton, he is an original and

towering mind, wrestling to bring together the best that he knows and unafraid of theological and moral innovation. For example, Milton very carefully rejects the traditional interpretation which blamed Eve for the fall of the human race. While it is true that his Eve falls first, she falls because Adam had unwisely exposed her to temptation. According to Milton, the human race does not fall with Eve's sin, but falls when Adam decides he cannot live without Eve and therefore decides freely and fully to sin. When Eve explains that she has tasted the fatal fruit, Adam is already making up his mind to join her in sin and death, saying

> Some cursed fraud
> Of enemy hath beguiled thee, yet unknown,
> And me with thee hath ruined, for with thee
> Certain my resolution is to die.
> . . . I feel
> The link of nature draw me; flesh of flesh,
> Bone of my bone thou art, and from thy state
> Mine never shall be parted, bliss or woe.[12]

Here we see that Adam is moved by the conception of romantic love in marriage, which is precisely the Puritan contribution to the Christian doctrine of marriage. Even further, though Adam's responsibility for the fall is decidedly patriarchal, Milton does give to Eve the initiating role in human redemption. It is she who first achieves contrition, and Adam's following her lead is a weak "me, too."

Milton's attitude towards the role of women is both tantalizingly liberal and destructively patriarchal, at one and the same time. He blames Adam for the fall of the human race, certainly an improvement over the older misogynistic view that held Eve had seduced Adam. But Adam's responsibility for the species derives precisely from Milton's making him paternally responsible for Eve's welfare as well as for his own. Milton's positions are a discordant medley of new and of old.

[A modern paraphrase of John Milton's text]

The Doctrine and Discipline of Divorce
Revised for the Benefit of Both Sexes

Book I
Preface

People are responsible for their own miseries as well as for most of the evils which they attribute to God's activity. Of particular concern is the absurdity of the canonical decrees about divorce.

What is more suited to the solace and delight of a person than marriage? Yet the misinterpretation of some Scriptures, especially those Old Testament texts which allow divorce, has often changed the blessing of matrimony into a mutual grief, or at least into a depressing captivity from which there is no redemption. These misinterpretations run to both extremes: too much freedom to divorce or too great severity against it.

God taught us why he instituted marriage. He expressly implied that its purpose was to be the fitting and happy companionship of man with woman, to comfort and refresh him against the evil of solitary life. The purpose of procreation was not mentioned until later, as a secondary end in dignity even if not in necessity. Yet the practice now is that once two persons have been wedded in church and experienced sexual intercourse, they are obliged forever to live together even though they may have been mistaken in marrying in the first place. Whether because of error or deception, it may turn out that their dispositions, thoughts, or constitutions prevent them from living happily together or being a remedy against loneliness. Yet in such cases, the present law prohibiting divorce forces them, as long as they are not frigid or impotent, to live together in their unspeakable weariness and to despair of ever having the kind of companionship for which God primarily intended marriage.

What a calamity this is! The Writer of Ecclesiastes would sigh out, "What a sore evil is this under the sun!"

The cause of this awful situation is the canon law, whose adherents do not charitably consult the Interpreter and Guide of our faith, but rely instead on the literal interpretation of the text. They are doubtlessly inspired by the Devil to make marriage become so insupportable that some persons do not dare to marry and some others, who do, become weary of it and begin to live licentiously. For many years, in fact, the theologians of the Church despised marriage as a defilement of the flesh, forbidding it altogether to priests and seeking to dissuade widows and widowers from remarrying. For example, look at the writings of Tertullian and Jerome.

CHAPTER I

My position. Proved from the Old Testament.

It is my intention, if at all possible, to remove the canonists' oppression which has resulted from a literal interpretation of Scripture. That interpretation has not only disturbed the peaceful estate of domestic society, but it has also over-burdened, if not overwhelmed, many Christians by leaving them without helpful pastoral care. My argumentation will involve advocating a position which replies to Scriptural as well as rational objections.

My position is that an unfitness for marriage, or a psychological incompatibility which would appear to be incapable of reconciliation, is a greater reason for divorce than natural frigidity, for it interferes with the main purpose of marriage, that is, solace and peace. Such grounds for divorce are especially forceful where no children are involved and if there is mutual consent.

This I conclude from the law in Deuteronomy 24:1, "When a man has taken a wife and married her, and it comes to pass that she find no favor in his eyes because he has found some uncleanness in her, let him write her a bill of divorce, give it to her hand, and send her out of his house . . ." Christ himself teaches that this law shall never be abrogated until the end of the world.

The cause of divorce mentioned in Deuteronomy is "some uncleanness." The Hebrew word means "nakedness of ought" or "lacking what is fitting," which all reputable interpreters understand as referring to the mind as well as to the body. What greater nakedness or unfitness is there than that lack or defect of conjugal mind which hinders the solace and peace of the married couple? My view of divorce is in perfect agreement with that described in the best sense of the law of Moses. Even in the Old

Testament, the cause of divorce is a matter of pure charity and is plainly moral; moreover, it is invoked more now than ever before and is, therefore, certainly lawful. If such was God's gracious law under the Old Covenant, how much more so will it be God's intention under the Covenant of Grace to spare his servants their misery and grief and grant them, instead, remedy and relief.

CHAPTER II

The first reason of this law of divorce is grounded on the primary reason of matrimony: no covenant ever creates obligations that contradict the purpose for which it is made.

Good sense and fairness require that no law or covenant should tend to undermine the very institution it is supposed to preserve. This holds for God's Covenant with man and for covenants between human beings. Hence, the law of marriage should not perpetually bind innocent individuals who have made a mistake in their choice of each other as marriage partners. When nothing but a false understanding of God's law keeps partners together, then the force of the law works against God's express purpose for establishing that law. For God's chief end in creating woman to be joined to man is expressed in his own words. It is this expression which tells us what constitutes a true marriage. "It is not good," said God, "for man to be alone. I will create a companion for him." The meaning of these words is clear. It is God's intention that a just and happy companionship be the chief and most noble end of marriage. Nothing in these words indicates the necessity of sexual union, but rather these words indicate that marriage is to prevent loneliness in a man's life. On this point Fagius, Calvin, Pareus, and Rivetus are in total agreement. Indeed it shows both God's blessing and man's excellence that the comfort and satisfaction of the mind is given priority over the sensual satisfaction of the body. To honor this higher purpose is the true sanctity of marriage.

It is thus with all generous married persons. When minds and hearts are united, some lack of sexual satisfaction can be borne much more easily. But if the situation is reversed, and there is sexual satisfaction but no spiritual union, then the delight of the body will quickly become unsavory. In such cases the loneliness of man which God had intended marriage to prevent increases in a way much worse than in the loneliest single life.

In single life the absence of a companion trains a man to be self-sufficient or to seek out a mate. But in the situation of the unhappily married man, he is faced continually by his mistaken hopes, and has no remedy for them. For men inclined to depression this must be a daily suffering like unto that endured by those condemned to death.

It is unthinkable that by one mistake so noble a creature as man should be imprisoned by marriage in the very loneliness that he sought to escape through marriage. It is evident that if marriage with a given woman not only does not lessen a man's loneliness, but even increases it, and in the increasing leads to a personal dejection and diminishment of family life, then that marriage is not a true marriage.

In such a situation the wronged spouse does the courageous thing in claiming the right to seek true companionship, rather than trying to find compensation in loose living, or in allowing his vital strength to be drained away by his efforts to cope with such a burden. It was in view of just such a situation that the mercy of the Law of Moses (which commands men to divorce) was practiced.

CHAPTER III

Concerning the ignorance and evil of Canon Law which provides for the right of the body in marriage, but does not provide for the sufferings of the mind and heart.

How preposterous that Canon Law should have been so careful to provide against eventualities of sexual impediment without also providing against impediments in that union of minds and hearts which is so essential to the most sacred end of marriage. If the sensual union of bodies is not possible then, according to Canon Law, the marriage is not a real one. Yet, according to Canon Law the inability to achieve union of minds and hearts in an agreeable companionship is to be endured no matter what the consequences of this suffering may be. Wisdom and love, weighing the intent of God's own institution, would see that an individual imprisoned in loneliness deserves to be freed, even more than does the individual who can not find relief in marriage for his sexual desires.

In the marriage ceremony, we read that we should not enter into marriage just to satisfy our sexual appetites, like brute beasts who are without understanding. But Canon Law is written as though only the satisfaction of the sexual appetite is to be considered, for that Law asserts that if sexual union is impossible, the marriage is annulled.

CHAPTER IV

Marriage, according to the words of our Saviour, is not first the remedy of lust, but rather the fulfillment of conjugal love and companionship.

St. Paul says, "It is better to marry than to burn." Marriage is ordained to remedy man's burning, but exactly what kind of burning? Certainly not the mere bodily impulses toward sensual satisfaction. God does not concern himself principally with such matters. What is this burning then but the desire which God gave to Adam in Paradise before he committed the sin of incontinence. God saw it was not good that man be left alone to experience that burning desire to be united with another, body and soul, in the loving society of wedlock. If this union was so important before the fall when man was perfect in himself, how much more important is it now, after the fall, for man to have an intimate helpmate, a true marriage partner?

A man who has made the mistake of choosing an incompatible spouse, remains more alone than before his marriage and suffers a burning much harder to bear than that of the body's passions. This burning, which cannot be brought under control by physical discipline, is a pure longing for love and companionship, a longing stronger than death itself. This is the true spiritual burning which marriage is ordained to remedy, a burning which can not be extinguished in those men who have made the choice of an incompatible marriage partner.

Chapter IX

Adultery is not the greatest breach of matrimony. There are other violations that are just as important.

In order to determine whether idolatry or adultery be the greatest violation of marriage, let us consider the three chief ends of marriage agreed upon among Christian authors. These ends are: first, spiritual union; second, civil union; and third, the union of the marriage-bed. No baptized man could deny that the first of these ends is the most excellent, nor could he deny that idolatry strikes at the very heart of this primary end.

He who claims that adultery is the greatest breach, claims that the marriage-bed is the greatest good of marriage. And those crude men who believe such a thing, as common as they are, are as far from the light of civility, philosophy, and Scripture as they could possibly be.

It is beyond question that the noblest end of marriage is the help it gives in the pursuit of a holy life. But if the needs of the individual are considered in the light of the three ends of matrimony ordained by God, then the most important is the one that the individual most sought to fulfill through marrying. And a marriage is most broken when it fails to achieve that for which it was undertaken, that is, the attainment of spiritual union, or civil union, or sexual union. That law which recognizes only the last and least noble of those unions is perverse, and as cold as the sexual frigidity of which alone it is mindful.

Now let me return to my first point. There I indicated that incompatibility of minds and hearts is a just cause for divorce. First, because it opposes the purpose of marriage as God instituted it, and keeps marriage from satisfying the pure and spiritual desires that God kindled in man to be the bond of wedlock. Second, that it leads many to enter into adulterous relations, as the heart seeks elsewhere the consolations it had hoped to find at home in marriage. Or else it leads to a man's denying God as he finds himself in a trying situation, bound there by a mistaken notion of God's Law. What is actually binding him is not God, but man's unrighteous ignorance. While such a prohibition against divorce safeguards outward formalities, the inward reality is one in which religious faith dies because a man is compelled to remain married.

CHAPTER XIII

Concerning the ninth reason about marriage. Where genuine relationship is not present, there is no true matrimony. Marriage is to be compared with all the other covenants and vows which can be broken for a good of man. Marriage is the Sacrament of the Papists, and unfit marriage is the Idol of the Protestants.

Ninthly, I suppose everyone would agree that marriage is a human society, and that all genuine relationships must proceed from the mind rather than the body. If the mind cannot find in marriage the companionship that it so reasonably and humanly desires, then marriage is not a human relationship but a contractual formality. In wisdom and fairness such marriages should be dissolved.

But, it is often argued that marriage is more than human since it is the covenant of God (Proverbs 2:17). Therefore, man cannot dissolve it. I answer that if marriage be more than human, so much more does it indicate that the most important union is that of minds and hearts, rather than bodies. The greatest breach of that covenant is the absence of a union of minds and hearts, not the absence of bodily union, for the body has the least importance in a covenant which is more than human. Thus, the above reason for dissolving the marriage still holds good.

13. Ann Lee: The Messiah as Woman

Ann Lee (1736–1784), like Jesus, left no books or written documents which testify to herself. Her life was one of revolt against the "mystery of iniquity," whether it manifested itself in customary sexual relationships, tedious religious practices, or militarism. She was a pioneer in "opening the Gospel," first in England and later in America. She mothered her communal United Society of Believers in Christ's Second Appearing by means of miraculous healings, discernment of spirits, and through an example of hard work, productive industry, and frontier common sense. Her "children" left records and eyewitness accounts of her life and sayings, just as Jesus' followers wrote the Gospels.[1]

Ann was born to poverty in Manchester, England. As a young adult, she worked as an assistant in the clothing industry and as a cook; she had no education and could not write her own name. At age twenty-two, she came under the influence of Jane and James Wardley, a husband and wife team of "Shaking Quakers" carrying on the charismatic tradition of the Cevenol prophets who had fled from France. At age twenty-six, she married Abraham Standerin, a blacksmith and perfectly ordinary sort of fellow who was never able to comprehend his wife's strange ways during the thirteen years of their ever-worsening marriage until they were finally separated. Ann bore and buried four infants; the deliveries were difficult and the last one nearly took her life. She understood the death of her children as God's judgment against her "concupiscence." Passing through a time of bone-racking asceticism, she denied herself "every gratification of a carnal nature." Finally, she says, "My soul broke forth to God, which I felt as sensibly as ever a woman did a child, when she was delivered of it."

After a short but difficult time in prison as a result of religious persecution of the Shakers for their boisterous faith in 1773–1774, Ann issued the revelation that she had seen a "grand vision of the very transgression of the first man and woman in the Garden of Eden, the cause wherein all mankind was lost and separated from God." Sexual intercourse had been the first and continued to be the original sin, the source of all the world's wrongs—war, slavery, poverty, disease, inequality of men and women. The "ugly serpent" of sex was to be made extinct through repentance and a life of simple chastity. In place of carnal marriage, Ann had now experienced a marriage with Christ:

> I feel him present with me, as sensibly as I feel my hands together! I have been walking in fine vallies with Christ, as with a lover. I am married to the Lord Jesus Christ. He is my head and my husband, and I have no other! I have walked, hand in hand, with him in heaven. I feel the blood of Christ running through my soul and body, washing me; Him do I acknowledge, as my head and Lord.[2]

Similarly, Ann taught, anyone who wanted to be married should marry the Lord.

Ann and a few faithful followers "opened the Gospel" in America in 1774; they settled finally at Niskeyuna, near Albany, New York. From their frontier plantation, Mother Ann and the sisters and brethren went out on preaching missions to New England or welcomed seekers to their tidy, well-provisioned commune. There the newcomers were personally chastised for their lust and attachment to this world until they were moved to repent their fallen nature and vowed to enter upon a life of sinless perfection. Perhaps the greatest charm of the movement was the wildly free and entrancing singing and dancing which was the daily fare at worship among the Shakers, punctuating their hard work and giving release to their otherwise pent-up energies.[3]

The new world proved as hostile to them as had the old. Because of their pacifism, they were mistaken for British Loyalists during the War of Independence. They were brutally handled, whipped and beaten in some instances, and a perverse investigation of Mother's Ann's person was undertaken by the curious crowd on such occasions to see if she really were a woman. But the distinctly individualistic self-discipline of their style of life stood them in good stead as well against the impatience of young American religious and political zealots as it had against the constabulary of old England.

The novelties of Shaker productiveness extended beyond packaging garden seeds, making brooms, and inventing the washing machine. Ann Lee stood, to be sure, in an ancient theological tradition of charismatic women who, in their marriage to Christ, expressed their womanhood in a revolutionary manner. Like Ann, her English contemporary, Joanna Southcott, a servant girl from Devonshire, also eschewed sexual relations as the sin of the First Parents in the Garden, identified with the "woman clothed with the sun" (Rev. 12), and allowed herself to be called "Mother" as the redemptrix of the race.[4] But Ann's and the Shakers' further extension of these ideas expanded Christian theology to perceive the dimension of femaleness within God. Like the Christian Gnostics of the primitive Church before her and like Mary Baker Eddy, the foundress of Christian Science, after her, Ann knew that God, in whose image both sexes of humanity were created, must also therefore be both male and female. Whereas Jesus Christ had been the incarnation of the Logos-Word or male principle within Godhead, Mother Ann was now the incarnation of the promised Comforter, the Holy Spirit, or female principle within Godhead.

The effect of this kind of theology has been not only the enrichment of American life through the production of the longest-lived and sturdiest of communistic experiments but also to provide a theoretical foundation for the understanding of the full equality of males and females in the language of of eighteenth- and nineteenth-century Christian Biblicism. The contrast between the liberation of women according to the biblical mythology of Ann Lee and the Shakers and that according to the economic mythology of the *Communist Manifesto* of Marx and Engels, issued in England in 1848 while the Shakers were at the height of their influence in America, is significant.[5] Both communistic movements understood, each in its own terms, that equality of the sexes could come about only as a result of terminating the exploitation of women through their sexuality.[6]

The selections that follow are from nineteenth-century Shaker writings which sought to preserve eye-witness testimonies of Ann Lee's life and her teachings. The first section records memories of her character and way of dealing with people. The second section presents her key teachings regarding the importance of the female principle and her criticism of the exclusively "mannish" character of traditional Christianity. For example, Ann Lee taught that God is both a mother and a father; hence the work of redemption must be fulfilled by two Messiahs—the male Jesus and the female Ann Lee. The Shakers were very aware that their founder's contribution to Christianity "exceeded that of the times of Origen, Luther, and Calvin." What she taught, they believed, was "startling, and important to mankind":

> 1st. Because she was a woman. 2d. Because she was an inspired woman. 3d. Because she enlarged the scope of religious experience. 4th. Because she unfolded a principle, an idea which no man, not even Jesus, had announced, or, perhaps, surmised.[7]

The final sections of our reading are descriptions of Shaker communal life—"true brotherly and sisterly love and *angelic* affection between the sexes"[8]—and worship. Some of the songs, whose words are given below, present the new teaching regarding "the Dual Christ" and "Our Father-Mother God." Academic society tends to exaggerate the influence of rational theology and to underestimate the influence of communal living, songs, and simple repeated prayer in forming people's attitudes and behavior. One of the editors [HR] therefore wishes to add his own experience at this point. Out of my childhood, the most important religious memory I have is my bedtime prayer, a copy of which was also framed and hanging on the wall:

> Father-Mother God
> Loving Me
> Guard me while I sleep
> Guide my little feet up to Thee.

This prayer, by Mary Baker Eddy, the founder of Christian Science, had an extraordinary influence on my thoughts and feelings—both then and now. I knew that not only was God *both* a Father and a Mother (and therefore like something more than any one thing I experienced around me), but also that my mother and my father—and some mysterious relation between them—was the way God was present in the world. I am convinced that this early experience and teaching concerning the divine androgyny as a norm by which every human being, male or female, is to live has shaped all of my mature theological reflection. The way that religion is presented in prayer and song, especially in the archetypally crucial periods of childhood, traveling, and illness, are decisive for all else in the religious sphere.

Mother Ann Lee
And the Shakers

(Sources indicated after each selection.)

Ezekiel Stevens of Canterbury, related the following: . . . In the early part of the year 1781, a large assembly of the Believers were gathered at Watervliet. . . . Mother [Ann Lee] was at that time under great sufferings of soul. She came forth with a very powerful gift of God and reproved the people for their hardness of heart, and unbelief in the Second Appearance of Christ. "Especially ye men and brethren, I upbraid you for your unbelief and hardness of heart," said she. She spake of the unbelieving Jews, in Christ's first appearance, and, added she, "Even his own disciples, after he arose from the dead, though he had often told them that he should rise the third day, believed it not. They would not believe that he had risen because he appeared, first, to a woman! So great was their unbelief that the words of Mary seemed to them like idle tales! His appearing first, to a woman, showed that his Second Appearing would be in a woman." So great was the manifestation of the power of God in Mother at this time, that many were unable to abide in her presence, her words were like flames of fire, and her voice like peals of thunder.

Reported by Eunice Goodrich:

Samuel Fitch believed the gospel, being at Watervliet, and having received a great manifestation of light and understanding, he said to Mother Ann, "Christ is called the Second Adam, and thou art the Second Eve." She answered, "Flesh and blood has not revealed it unto thee, Samuel; but God has" (cf. Matt. 16:16–17).

Reported by Samuel Fitch:

Morell Baker, Senr., visited the Church at Watervliet in 1784. . . . He said to her, "Thou art the Bride, the Lamb's wife!" She answered, "Thou hast rightly said, for so I am. Christ is my husband. I now see many souls who have left the body and have come to hear the gospel! I now hear the hosts of heaven singing praises to God."

Reported by Morell Baker, Senr.:

The same year . . . Mother Ann appeared clothed in majesty, and her visage was exceedingly glorious. She spake with great power, saying, "I am married to the Lord Jesus Christ! He is my head and my husband, and I have no other! I have walked hand in hand with him in Heaven! I have seen the Patriarchs, Prophets and Apostles; I have conversed with them, and I know them."

Ann Lee, seventeen hundred and seventy years after Jesus, began her practical era. . . . As her birth is chronicled in the midst of a modern civilization, which exceeded that of the times of Origen, Luther, and Calvin, so is her religious development, more than their's, startling, and important to mankind. The reasons are: 1st. Because she was a woman. 2d. Because she was an inspired woman. 3d. Because she enlarged the scope of religious experience. 4th. Because she unfolded a principle, an idea which no man, not even Jesus, had announced, or, perhaps, surmised!

From *Testimonies of the Life, Character, Revelations and Doctrines of Mother Ann Lee* (Albany: Weed, Parsons and Company, Printers, 1888), pp. 268–273, 161–165.

Abraham, Issac, Jesus, Paul, and other inspired persons were illuminated, on many integral principles, but never sufficiently to perceive the plenitude of woman's nature, and the equality of her destiny. They had a God of almighty force; of infinite intelligence; of inconstant temper; of love for the lovely; of hate for the hateful; with a heaven for his friends; with a hell for his enemies (Jesus was excepted in this). But, in the outreaching of these minds toward a comprehension and presentation of their God, you will detect a one-sided dependence, confessed; a short sighted obligation and responsibility, and a semi-civilized acknowledgment of the Divine personality and character. It was all *manish!* God was a "Male" God, and woman was supplemental. Paul, therefore, *permitted* the women "to speak," in meeting, with *certain insulting restrictions and by-laws affixed.* The Jews kept women in the back ground, if not in the tented kitchen; and nowhere does their God disapprobate the custom. . . .

Ann Lee's crime was, *she was a woman, with a claim upon mankind by Heaven's inspiration.* Her sin, was unpardonable! Gracious Heavens! A Woman inspired?! What a blemish on the masculine fraternity! "God of *masculine* quantities infinite. The eternally isolated "male" of the Prophets and Apostles, down with this ambitious Venus in religion! Scare her fanatical followers, and confound the people who listen at her meetings!" But she would not "down" at their bidding! The "Male" God of the churches lived as complacently and essentially in this "Female" incarnation, as in the expanded universe. . . . Ann Lee demonstrated the idea, the impersonal principle . . . that, qualitatively and quantitatively, the celestial stream set just as surely through woman's soul, as through man's fertilizing, and equalizing the sexual hemispheres as they flow. She broke down the partition wall which custom had built between the woman spirit and its celestial Fountain Source. . . .

But it is the central Principle, the idea of Ann Lee, for which we now reverently inquire. That principle in brief is this: God is dual—Male and Female—Father and Mother! Hindoo teachers obtained a golden glimpse of this impersonal truth. Forming and destroying principles—male and female energies and laws were perceived and taught by early inhabitants. But not one person, from god Brahma to President Buchanan has done what Ann Lee did, for this world-revolutionizing idea! She centrifugated it in a thousand different forms of expression. It took wings in her spirit. Better than the Virgin Mary's sainted position in the ethical temple, is the simple announcement that *God is as much woman as man*—a oneness, composed of two individual equal halves—love and wisdom, absolute, and balanced eternally.

When the foundation of man's redemption was laid by the work of Christ's first appearing, the way began also to be prepared for his second appearing, to make a final end of sin, and to bring in everlasting righteousness. For, although the foundation was laid, yet there could be no complete redemption from sin, until the revelation of Christ, for its final destruction, should be made where sin first took its seat.

As sin first took its seat in the woman, and thence entered the human race, and as Christ in taking upon him the nature of fallen man, in Jesus, to purify and redeem him, made his first appearing in the line of the male only; therefore the mystery of iniquity or *man of sin* was not fully revealed, nor the mystery of God finished, in Christ's first appearing.

And therefore, it was also necessary, that Christ should make his second appearing in the line of the female, and that in one who was conceived in sin, and lost in the fulness of man's fall; because in the woman the root of sin was first planted, and its final destruction must begin where its foundation was first laid, and from whence it first entered the human race.

Therefore, in the fulness of time, according to the unchangeable purpose of God, that same Spirit and word of power, which created man at the beginning—which spake by all the Prophets—which dwelt in the man Jesus—which was given to the Apostles and true witnesses as the holy Spirit and word of promise, which groaned in them, waiting for the day of redemption—and which

Andrew Jackson Davis, "Ann Lee," in Giles B. Avery, *Sketches of Shakers and Shakerism* (Albany: Weed, Parsons, and Company, Printers,-1884).

was spoken of in the language of prophecy, as "a woman travailing with child, and pain to be delivered" (cf. Rev. 12:2,) was revealed in a woman.

And that woman, in whom was manifested that Spirit and word of power, who was anointed and chosen of God, to reveal the mystery of iniquity, to stand as the first in her order, to accomplish the purpose of God, in the restoration of that which was lost by the transgression of the first woman, and to finish the work of man's final redemption, was ANN LEE.

As a chosen vessel, appointed by Divine wisdom, she, by her faithful obedience to that same anointing, became the temple of the Holy Spirit, and the second heir with Jesus, in the covenant and promise of eternal life. And by her sufferings and travail for a lost world, and her union and subjection to Christ Jesus, her Lord and Head, she became the *first born of many sisters*, and the true MOTHER *of all living* in the new creation. . . .

And in this covenant, both male and female, as brethren and sisters in the family of Christ, jointly united by the bond of love, find each their correspondent relation to the first cause of their existence, through the joint parentage of their redemption.

Then the man who was called Jesus, and the woman who was called Ann, are verily the two first visible foundation pillars of the Church of Christ—the two anointed ones—the two first heirs of promise, between whom the covenant of eternal life is established —the first Father and Mother of all the children of regeneration— the two first visible Parents in the work of redemption—and in whom was revealed the invisible joint Parentage in the new creation, for the increase of that seed through which "all the families of the earth shall be blessed" (cf. Gen. 12:3).

As it is not possible that there can be any offspring or increase in the human family, without a natural mother, so neither is it possible that there can be any offspring, or any increase in the family of Christ, without a spiritual Mother. Not the existence of male and female in the man alone, but all creation, in both the animal and vegetable kingdoms, the fishes that swim in the seas, the birds that fly in the air, yea, the very herbs and flowers of the field, all demonstrate and establish this fact, namely: That all living creation is supported and advanced through the female order. And that therefore the female is the crowning glory, and perfects the creative works of God. . . .

It is believed and acknowledged likewise, that Christ the second Adam is, and must be, the *Father* of all who are born again—of all the children of the second or spiritual birth; but how can these be born again, without a Mother? Can a father *beget* and also *conceive*, and *bear*, and bring forth children? There can be no such thing, either in heaven or on earth. . . . To no individual person, nor to any personages whatever, from the beginning to the end of time, can these prophetic figures be applied; save only to Christ, the quickening Spirit, and to their first born Son and Daughter, the *Lord Jesus* and *Mother Ann*, who of God are blessed forevermore—yea, *forever and ever*.

Some people suppose the opposite sexes among the Shakers never commune together; this is simply preposterous! While Shakers live, absolutely, pure virgin lives, no people in the world enjoy such a range of freedom, in the social sense, between the sexes; but it is required to be free from all that would tend to fleshly affections and actions. The power thus to live, in virgin purity and innocence, is found in the conviction that a spotless, virgin, angelic life is the order of the kingdom of Christ, and is higher, better, happier than a sensual, worldly life. Add to this, protective by-laws, which all are in honor bound to keep, thus: "One brother and one sister not allowed to work together, walk out, or ride out together alone." "Males and females not allowed to touch each other unnecessarily, nor to hold secret correspondence." "Males and females not allowed to room together." Shakers are anti-Mormon, anti-Oneidian, and anti-Nicholaitan, in faith and practice, as becomes the true followers of Christ. They do not condemn marriage, nor orderly generation, *as worldly institution*, but claim these have no place in Christ's kingdom; therefore, *relegate them to the world, where alone they belong*. In contra-

Benjamin S. Youngs and Calvin Green, *Testimony of Christ's Second Appearing*, etc., 4th ed., (Albany: Van Benthuysen, Printer, 1856), pp. 383–384, 513–515).

distinction, nevertheless, to monastics, Shakers have no cloisters
or nunneries to seclude and abnormalize the sexes, in their social
and spiritual relations, to dry up the fountain of pure life-giving
magnetism—true brotherly and sisterly love and angelic affection
between the sexes.

Giles B. Avery, *Sketches of Shakers and Shakerism*, p. 12.

The New Song

> Lo, Christ again hath come! The Prophet's purpose
> Now begins to dawn! Christ, our God reveals—
> A dual Spirit—Father—Mother—God!
> Thus, all the signs declare. First, tables two
> Mosaic Law proclaimed: then cherubs two,
> The Mercy seat adorn! . . . .
> . . . All nations to embrace,
> May all their courts now ope, their doors ajar
> Now stand, and let the Queen of glory in.
> The Dual Christ upon the cloud now sits
> Sickle in hand, to thrust, and reap the world!
> The clusters of earth's vine to gather home,
> To garner of Our Father—Mother—God. . . .

Giles B. Avery, *Sketches of Shakers and Shakerism*, p. 24.

Mother

(1)
> Let names and sects and parties
> Accost my ears no more.
> My ever blessed Mother,
> Forever I'll adore:
> Appointed by kind heaven,
> My Saviour to reveal,
> Her doctrine is confirmed
> With an eternal seal.

(2)
> She was the Lords anointed,
> To show the root of sin;
> And in its full destruction,

Her gospel did begin:
She strip'd a carnal nature,
Of all its deep disguise,
And laid it plan and naked,
Before the sinner's eyes.

(3)
"Sunk in your base corruptions,
Ye wicked and unclean!
You read your sealed Bibles,
But know not what they mean:
Confess your filthy actions,
And put your lusts away,
And live the life of JESUS:
This is the only way."

(6)
At Manchester, in England,
This blessed fire began,
And like a flame in stubble,
From house to house it ran:
A few at first receiv'd it,
And did their lusts forsake;
And soon their inward power
Brought on a mighty shake.

(14)
How much are they deceived,
Who think that Mother's dead!
She lives among her offspring,
Who just begin to spread;
And in her outward order,
There's one supplies her room,
And still the name of Mother,
Is like a sweet perfume.

E. D. Andrews, *The Gift to be Simple: Songs, Dances and Rituals of the American Shakers* (New York: Dover Publications Inc., 1940, 1962), pp. 47–51; there are sixteen stanzas to "Mother."

14. Schleiermacher and Baader: Individuality and Androgyny

The cultural movement of romanticism is represented in this volume by the great Protestant theologian Friedrich Schleiermacher (1768–1834) and the Catholic Franz von Baader (1765–1841).[1] Romanticism is a complex movement and cannot be characterized in a single way. Here we are concerned primarily with German romanticism, especially in its philosophical and religious aspects. For our purposes, it is sufficient to note that romanticism originated as a reaction against the extreme rationalism and deism of the Enlightenment. It stressed, rather, the primacy of intuitive feeling and affirmed that God is an immanent principle of life within the world.[2] In this way, the romantics opposed the rational mechanistic cosmology of the Enlightenment (God as "watch-maker"; the world is like a "watch"). They replaced it with an organic cosmology that conceived all reality to be one living being animated by a divine soul.

For these reasons, the romantics were less interested in scientific analysis than in artistic and religious strivings toward unity with the whole. Moreover, because they believed that the divine spirit which animated all things was fully present in each thing, the romantics had a very high view of individuality: they believed that each individual is a microcosm of the whole. When Alfred Lord Tennyson wrote that, from contemplating a single flower, he could "know what God and man is," he was expressing this romantic conception of individuality that regarded the individual as the embodiment of the Whole.

The implications of this viewpoint for feminists is striking: the romantics rejected the notion that sexual difference defines individuality. Rather, they argued that as a person becomes an individual microcosm of reality, he or she becomes more and more androgynous. Someone who is only male or only female is not whole. To be come whole, we must become both male and female, and to the extent that we do so we become more individual.

In fact, because the analytical rational approach to life had been traditionally associated with men, romanticism tended to glorify woman as possessing more aptitude for feeling, immediacy, unity with life, and individuality. Their very powers of empathy make women able to be more complete than men. For these reasons, Schleiermacher believes that woman possess a "higher self-awareness in immediate experience, if not in conceptual awareness" than men do.[3] His is a reverse sexism. He, with other romantics, ascribes the traditional qualities to men and women, but now judges that masculine rationality is "superintellectual" and the source of human unrest and sin.[4] Man's very rationality, says Schleiermacher, makes him more fickle and unstable than women, for women possess an inner continuity and unity. In fact, Schleiermacher even puts this criticism into the mouth of one of his female characters in *Christmas Eve*, having her tell a circle of men that they engage in "a restless striving, an indecisive, ever-changing grasping and letting go which we women are simply unable to understand."[5]

While we may take an ironic delight in this reversal (for here men are being accused of the very things that the *Malleus Maleficarum* charged against women), we should realize that this is still a sexist motif. But, in fact, the glorification of women was not the main thrust of romanticism, but was rather a polemical rhetoric used against the Enlightenment exaggeration of reason's power. The main interest, Schleiermacher says, is that men and women "become one," that is, become more like one another. So, he writes, "We see that in the development of their spiritual nature, although it [i.e., this spiritual nature] must be the same in both, men and women have different ways—to the end that here too they become one by sharing knowledge of each other."[6]

The creation of this androgynous individuality, according to

Schleiermacher, takes place primarily through the relationship of friendship and conversation. The very genre of Schleiermacher's *Christmas Eve*, the selection in this volume, makes this point.[7] It is a spirited dialogue, inspired by Plato's *Symposium*, among a group of men and women friends who are as different from one another as friends as they are as genders. In the context of friendship and conversation, there is a give-and-take wherein differences are respected such that each person may become more and more individual and, at the same time, more and more whole. Friendship, says Schleiermacher, "originates in the reciprocal completion and confirmation of individuality."[8] Love, on the other hand, originates in "a total unification of consciousness which brings forth a new image."[9] Therefore, says Schleiermacher, "procreation is bound up with love rather than with friendship, [for] love involves necessarily the merging of two personalities."[10]

On the basis of this distinction, Schleiermacher then proceeds to argue for the superiority of friendship over love, and even makes friendship the criterion of true love. He argues as follows:

> Those who from love want only the merging of personalities are effectively materialists, since they know nothing of individuality [which is a spiritual reality]. True love always leads to friendship, and therefore true love strives towards marriage, which, in the spiritual sense, is a union of love and friendship. Friendship, on the other hand, need not involve love, since friendship relates to the discursive knowledge and discourse appropriate to individuality. . . . Hence, it is easier to come to the end of love than to the end of friendship.[11]

Since friendship, especially between men and women, was understood by the romantics to be a spiritual relation which aided in the development of the individual, and because the individual was the highest value, friendship took priority for them over not only love but even ordinary marriage. Hence, Schleiermacher for years offended his friends by carrying on a relation with a married woman although she lived with her husband in an unhappy and childless marriage. Regarding this relation, Martin Redeker says,

> Schleiermacher held the view that in marriage every woman had an inalienable right to her own individuality. This romantic con-

ception of individuality was for him in agreement with the view that a marriage in which a woman is prevented by the moral unworthiness of the other partner from developing her own individuality is no longer a marriage but a subversion of mankind's holiest bonds. Therefore, he considered it his duty to dissolve such a marriage which was really no marriage.[12]

Our first selection is taken from *Christmas Eve*, a dialogue written by Schleiermacher in 1805 just two months after Eleanor Grünow had broken off their relation, mentioned above. (Hence, Schleiermacher appears in this dialogue as a lonely figure, Josef, who says of himself, "As Christ had no bride but the church . . . and yet his heart was full of heavenly love and joy, so I too seem to be born to endeavor after such a life.")[13]

The dialogue form facilitates Schleiermacher in making his essential point: that the friendship of men and women is even more important than marriage. He presents a group of friends who are gathered on Christmas eve and who discuss, among other things, how differently men, women, and children experience life. In this way, Schleiermacher is not only able to make his formal point— that wholeness of personality requires friendship and conversation among men and women—but also is able to present a model of men and women giving to and receiving from one another. The deepest teaching of *Christmas Eve* is precisely this picture of friendly intercourse among men and women (and children!). In fact, no place else in this volume do we actually see men and women speaking and interacting with one another.

In addition, Schleiermacher also advances a theory about the development of consciousness. He shows us the child, Sophie, who experiences everything with undivided immediacy and wholeness. In her, true wisdom (*sophia*) is found. According to Schleiermacher, the development of consciousness requires a splitting of this undivided consciousness, a splitting which takes place in the intellectual sphere by the emergence of reflectiveness and which takes place in the social sphere through the emergence of sexual difference. In men, reflectiveness develops by creative discontinuity with childhood; in women, however, the development takes place without creating such discontinuity. For this reason, Schleiermacher feels that women are both closer to the experience of child-hood and also to the experience of the higher consciousness wherein mature reflectiveness recombines with the child's experi-ence of immediacy. Men for Schleiermacher, are both more mature and less mature than women. They represent the middle stage in consciousness. For this reason men and women need one another for both to grow to wholeness and the highest consciousness.

When we turn from Schleiermacher's *Christmas Eve* to the Baader selection in this volume, we encounter a totally different style of thinking and writing, but the same romantic ideas. Ac-cording to Baader, God created Adam in His image to be man and woman, that is, as a whole person. Adam was originally androgy-nous, but fell out of this condition into sexual dividedness by "lusting for the woman within." Baader calls this woman within the "Celestial Virgin" and "Sophia." Here is how he understands the idea:[14]

Baader holds to the older Platonic-Augustinian view which believes that we have our life in God and that God's Wisdom illuminates our minds from within.[15] This Divine Wisdom is Sophia, and we are in God only as we have Sophia in us as the principle of inner illumination. When we "lust after Sophia" (the "Celestial Virgin," the "woman within"), we seek to objectify it and control it. We seek to rule over it rather than allowing it to rule over us. We seek an autonomous reason rather than seeking a reason which is dependent upon and illuminated by Divine Wisdom. (So, for example, Baader says that Hegel's attempt to set up an absolute science, independent from and above religion, was "lusting after Sophia.") When we separate ourselves from this "woman within," says Baader, God confirms the division we have already created in ourselves by dividing us and setting man and woman against one another. Note that for Baader, Eve, or woman, is not the "woman within" or the embodiment of the Celestial Virgin. Eve is only half of the divided original Adam. Hence Adam is not Eve's "lord," as in traditional Christianity; for both are separated from God and each other in the same way.

Though Baader's way of presenting his ideas is through esoteric symbolism and metaphor, he is arguing—both in style and content

—against the Enlightenment conception of reason and is seeking to reestablish the older doctrine of divine illumination and life in God. For example, when, in the selection that follows, Baader speaks about the "world-spirit" in Adam that "writhed up in himself" and "lusted after the Celestial Virgin," he is mocking Hegel's *Weltgeist* (world-spirit) which is a nontheistic principle of absolute reason that Hegel believed ruled the world. (Hegel had his own way with metaphors: he called Napoleon "the *Weltgeist* on horseback.") Nor should we misunderstand Baader's use of terminology from alchemy. Baader already knew what Carl Jung, in our generation, has rediscovered: that alchemy is actually a psychological symbolism concerned with describing the creative nonrational processes of life.

Since the fall, says Baader, the fully androgynous nature has been present only in the Christ. Jesus, according to Baader, is both male and female. (Mary, he says, is also male and female.) That is why the Christ has founded religion of love. Love teaches us that we can regain paradise once more, recovering our masculine-feminine completeness *through* our relation with the sexual other, *but not by stopping there.* Baader insists that even though it involves difficulty and pain, a person must grow beyond his or her distinctive sexuality. "The new [androgynous] image cannot be attained without the dissolution of the old [nonandrogynous] one."[16] Therefore, says Baader, there can be no true love unless people are willing to sacrifice their maleness and femaleness and seek to become whole and complete individuals through love. Men and women must help one another to transcend maleness and femaleness.

This means, of course, that although sexual intercourse is rightfully part of love, eventually persons must sacrifice it in order to attain to the higher kind of love which can do without sex. They can do that only by giving up everything that belongs to sexual difference in their growth to personal wholeness. This mystical androgyny has clear affinities with the Catholic tradition and can be contrasted with Schleiermacher's moral androgyny which presupposes the maintenance of sexual distinctiveness within a love-friendship where both parties participate in each other's differences and "become one by sharing knowledge of each other."[17]

In the nineteenth century, Baader exercised enormous influence. He was instrumental in getting Schelling to see that evil was something positive in the will; he introduced Goethe to the works of Jakob Boehme; and his thoughts are reflected in writings of Kierkegaard. Yet in our time he is little remembered. His fate is like that of philosophical and religious romanticism generally, and even his much more famous counterpart, Friedrich Schleiermacher, is in eclipse. They have been displaced by the new orthodoxy. Compare, for example, the ideas of Baader and Schleiermacher with the ideas of Karl Barth, also presented in this volume. Barth's theology originates in a total repudiation of Schleiermacher's thought, and a special focus of Barth's concern is to oppose every suggestion that the line between the sexes is not clear and permanent—with woman in second place in the "sequence." Adam is "A," she is "B". With these things in mind, we can appreciate how far Schleiermacher and Baader were ahead of our time!

Yet there is a renewed interest in Baader. Two volumes of his writings on sexuality and social philosophy have been recently republished.[18] To encourage this new interest, we have asked Dr. Frank Flinn to prepare the translation in this volume from Baader's "The Destructive Influence of Rational Materialism on Higher Physics, Poetry, and Art."[19] We are grateful for his contribution, which includes also material in this introduction.

Christmas Eve:
Dialogue on the Incarnation

In the meantime Sophie [eleven years old] had been mostly at the piano getting acquainted with her newly acquired treasures. Part of them she did not know, and many of those she knew she wanted to greet at once as her own possessions. At this moment

From Friedrich Schleiermacher, *Christmas Eve: Dialogue on the Incarnation*, trans. Terrence N. Tice (Richmond: John Knox Press, 1967).

she could be heard singing a choral from a cantata, her voice carrying with particular clarity the lines:

> Who gave his Son that we might ever live,
> All things to us with him shall he not give?

upon which there followed the magnificent fugue:

> If I possess but thee, I ask no more of earth or heaven.

When she had finished, she closed the keyboard and returned to the drawing room.

"Look there," exclaimed Leonhardt, when he spied her coming— "our little prophetess! Now I shall determine how far she is still under your influence." Stretching out his hand to her, he asked: "Tell me, little one, wouldn't you rather be merry than sad?"

"I do not think I am either at just this moment," she replied.

"What! not merry after receiving so many lovely presents? Ah, the solemn music must have made you feel that way! Bu you have not quite understood what I meant. What I asked, no doubt unnecessarily, was which of the two you would rather be: merry or sad?"

"Oh, that's hard to say," she responded. "I do not particularly favor one or the other. I always just like to be whatever I am at the moment."

"Now you've got me puzzled all over again, my little sphinx. What do you mean by that?"

"Well," she said, "all I know is that sometimes feelings of gladness and sorrow get strangely mixed up and fight each other; and that makes me uneasy, because I can tell, as Mother has also pointed out, that something is always wrong or out of kilter then, and so I don't like it."

"All right," he asked again, "suppose you have only one feeling or the other, is it all the same to you whether you are merry or sad?"

"Why no! For I just like to be what I am, and what I like to be is not a matter of indifference to me. Oh, Mother," she went on, turning to Ernestine, "please help! He is questioning me in such a strange way, and I don't understand at all what he is getting at. Let him ask the grownups, for they will certainly know better how to answer him."

"Actually," said Ernestine, "I don't think you will get much further with her, Leonhardt. She isn't at all accustomed to sorting out her experiences."

Ernst was smiling at him broadly. "But don't let this one attempt scare you off," he comforted. "Catechising is nonetheless a fine art, of which one can make as good use in the courts as elsewhere. And one always learns something from it, unless of course one has started off on the wrong track!"

"But isn't she going to have any feeling about this?" Leonhardt asked of Ernestine, ignoring Ernst's jesting. "I mean, doesn't she know whether she would prefer a glad state of mind to a sad one?"

"Who knows?" she rejoined. "What do you think, Sophie?"

"I really don't know, Mother. I can be satisfied in one attitude or the other, and at present I feel extraordinarily fine without being in either one. Only he makes me uneasy with his questions, because I can't make out what all I am supposed to pull together to answer them." Thereupon she softly kissed her mother's hand and retreated to the far end of the room, now dark but for the lingering glow of a few lamps, to seek the company of her Christmas presents.

"Well, this she has clearly shown us," uttered Karoline only half aloud: "what that childlike attitude is without which one cannot enter into the kingdom of God. It is simply to accept each mood and feeling for itself and to desire only to have them pure and whole."

"True," spoke Eduard, "except that she is no longer just a child, but a young girl; and therefore this is not altogether the attitude of a child."

Karoline looked over at him and went on: "What you say is true enough, but only from our point of view. Think of the complaints one hears from both young and old, even in these special days of childlike celebration, that they can no longer enjoy themselves so much as when they were children. I would just say that these surely do not arise from people who have had such a happy childhood. Only yesterday I way saying that my capacity for lively enjoyment is as great as ever it was, in fact greater. The people who heard this were astonished! And I could only marvel that they were."

"Yes," joked Leonhardt, "and the poor child herself will often be thought silly by such ogres as these, even when she has done nothing more than react with childlike joy over something requiring girlish dignity! But let it pass, my fine child, for these gainsayers are so deprived that nature has assigned them a second childhood at life's end, so that when they have reached this goal they may take one last consoling draught from the cup of joy, to close their long, doleful, dreary years."

"Surely this is more serious and tragic than funny," countered Ernst. "For me, at least, scarcely anything makes me shudder more than the vision you have just stirred up. How horrible that the great body of mankind should become unaware of the beautiful growth of a human life, and tormented with boredom, simply because they have to leave the first objects of childish delight behind but never nourish the capacity for gaining higher things! I do not know whether to say they even look upon life, or are even in attendance, for even this would seem too much for their utter incapacity to bear. And so their life would go on, until at last, out of nothing, a second childhood is born. But such a childhood is as much related to the first as a contrary old dwarf is to a lovely and winsome child, or as the wavering flicker of a dying flame is to the embracing splendor and dancing form of one newly lit."

"One thing leads me to enter an objection," spoke up Agnes. "Is it really true that our first objects of delight as children have to be dropped behind before we can attain to higher things? May there not be a way of attaining these without letting the first go? Does life begin, then, with a sheer illusion, in which there is no truth at all, nothing enduring? I wonder how I am to understand this. Think of the man who has achieved a mature awareness of himself and the world and who has found God. Obviously this does not happen without struggle and conflict. Do his joys, then, depend upon destroying not only what is evil in his life but also what is innocent and faultless? For this is how we always designate what is childlike—or, if you prefer, even what is childish. Or must time already have killed off, by I don't know what poison, the pristine joys of life? And must the transition out of the one state into the other pass, in every instance, through a 'nothing'?"

"One might indeed call it a nothing," added Ernestine thoughtfully. "And yet it seems that men, in contrast to women, tend to lead an odd, wild sort of life between childhood and their better days, a life passionate and perplexed. They will admit this themselves—one might almost say the best men will admit it most of all. On the one hand, the period looks like a continuation of childhood, whose delights also have their own impetuous and disruptive character. On the other hand, the period takes the form of a restless striving, an indecisive, ever-changing grasping and letting go which we women are simply unable to understand. In our sex, the two tendencies also fuse, but less perceptibly. The course of our entire life already lies indicated in our childhood play, except that as we grow older the higher meaning of this and that gradually becomes clear. Even when, in our own way, we come to an understanding of God and of the world, we tend to express our sublimest, tenderest feelings over and over again in those same precious trifles and with that same gentle demeanor which put us on friendly terms with the world in our childhood days."

"Thus," said Eduard, "we see that in the development of their spiritual nature, although it must be the same in both, men and women have their different ways—to the end that here too they may become one by sharing knowledge of each other. It may well be true, and it seems clearly so to me, that the contrast between the spontaneous and the reflective emerges more strongly in us men. And during the period of transition it reveals itself in that restless striving, that passionate conflict with the world and within oneself you referred to. But within the calm, graceful nature of women comes to light the continuity and inner unity of the two, the spontaneous and the reflective. With you, holy earnestness and blithesome play are effortlessly united."

"But then," Leonhardt jocularly countered, "we men, oddly enough, would be more Christian than the women! For Christianity is always speaking of a conversion, a change of heart, a new life whereby the old man is driven out. And of this, if what we have just heard is true, you women—leaving out a few Magdalenes—would have no need whatsoever."

"But Christ himself," rejoined Karoline, "was not converted. For this very reason he has always been the patron and protector of women; and whereas you men have only contended about him, we have loved and honored him. Or consider: what can you say against the notion that we have at last applied the correct interpretation to the old proverb that we women go right on being children while you men must first be turned about to become so again?"

"And to bring this matter close to home," added Eduard: "what is the celebration of Jesus' infancy but the distinct acknowledgment of the immediate union of the divine with the being of a child, by virtue of which no conversion is further needed? And remember the view Agnes has expressed on behalf of all women. She said, in effect, that from the point of birth on they already presuppose and seek for the divine presence in their children, even as the church presupposes and seeks for it in Christ."

"Yes, this very festival," said Friederike, "is the most direct proof, and the best, that our situation really is as Ernestine has described it."

"How so?" asked Leonhardt.

"Because here," she replied, "one can examine the nature of our joy in small yet neither forgotten nor unrecognizable sections of our life story, to see whether this joy has undergone any number of sudden changes. One scarcely need put the question to our conscience, for the matter speaks for itself. It is obvious enough that on the whole women and girls are the soul of these little celebrations. They fuss the most over them, but are also the most purely receptive and get the most heightened enjoyment. If these were left only to you men, they would soon go under. Through us alone do they become ongoing traditions.

"But couldn't we have religious joy for its own sake alone?" she inquired. "And wouldn't that be so if we had only made a new discovery of it later on? So one may ask. For us, however, everything fits together now just as it did in our earlier years. Already in our childhood we attributed special significance to these gifts, for example. They meant more to us than the same gifts at other times. Then, of course, it was only a dark, mysterious presentiment of what has since gradually become clearer. Yet we always most prefer it to appear in much the same shape as before. We will not let the accustomed symbol go. In fact, given the exactness with which the precious little moments of life stick in our memory, I think one could trace out, step by step, just how the higher awareness has emerged in us."

[The women now tell stories which focus on the image of the Mother and the Christchild, but develop its archetypal meaning as a symbol of spiritual growth and rebirth. After these stories, the four men present discourses on "The Meaning of Christmas." Each man presents a different theoretical viewpoint: skeptical, historical, aesthetic, philosophical. The fourth man to speak is Eduard, who picks up the Marian theme again by stressing the Johannine teaching that the Word was made flesh. What this means, says Eduard, is that we must see the divine in the finite and fleshly; we must see, as Mary did, the Christ in the child. Finally, Josef (i.e., Schleiermacher himself) joins the party and mediates between the "stories" of the women and the "discourses" of the men by extolling the speechlessness of the child, who experiences things in true immediacy. Josef's words provide the rationale and vindication of Sophie's attitudes which appear at the beginning of our reading. In Sophie, there is an immediacy of "the feeling of absolute dependence" which is Schleiermacher's definition of religion.]

Josef had come in while he was talking and, although he had very quietly entered and taken a seat, Eduard had noticed him. "By no means," he replied when Eduard addressed him. "You shall certainly be the last. I have not come to deliver a speech but to enjoy myself with you; and I must quite honestly say that it seems to me odd, almost folly even, that you should be carrying on with such exercises, however nicely you may have done them. Aha! but I already get the drift. Your evil principle is among you again: this Leonhardt, this contriving, reflective, dialectical, super-intellectual man. No doubt you have been addressing yourselves to him;

for your own selves you would surely not have needed such goings on and wouldn't have fallen into them. Yet they couldn't have been to any avail with him! And the poor women must have had to go along with it. Now just think what lovely music they could have sung for you, in which all the piety of your discourse could have dwelt far more profoundly. Or think how charmingly they might have conversed with you, out of hearts full of love and joy. Such would have eased and refreshed you differently, and better too, than you could possibly have been affected by these celebratory addresses of yours!

"For my part, today I am of no use for such things at all. For me, all forms are rigid, all speech-making too tedious and cold. Itself unbounded by speech, the subject of Christmas claims, indeed creates in me a speechless joy, and I cannot but laugh and exult like a child. Today all men are children to me, and are all the dearer on that account. The solemn wrinkles are for once smoothed away, the years and cares do not stand written on the brow. Eyes sparkle and dance again, the sign of a beautiful and serene existence within. To my good fortune, I too have become just like a child again. As a child stifles his childish pain, suppressing his sighs and holding back his tears, when something is done to arouse his childish joy, so it is with me today. The long, deep, irrepressible pain in my life is soothed as never before. I feel at home, as if born anew into the better world, in which pain and grieving have no meaning and no room any more. I look upon all things with a gladsome eye, even what has most deeply wounded me. As Christ had no bride but the church, no children but his friends, no household but the temple and the world, and yet his heart was full of heavenly love and joy, so I too seem to be born to endeavor after such a life.

"And so I have roamed about the whole evening, everywhere taking part most heartily in every little happening and amusement I have come across. I have laughed, and I have loved it all. It was one long affectionate kiss which I have given to the world, and now my enjoyment with you shall be the last impress of my lips. For you know that you are the dearest of all to me.

"Come, then, and above all bring the child if she is not yet asleep, and let me see your glories, and let us be glad and sing something religious and joyful!"

"The Destructive Influence of Rational Materialism on Higher Physics, Poetry, and Art"

The Scriptures call the breach between the first humans and God a breach of marriage. (In Old German, marriage was called a covenant and vice versa; likewise the Old and New Covenants were called the Old and New Marriages.) Secondly, ancient scholars of both the Scriptures and Nature maintained that the first sin of humanity stems from the temptation to misuse mankind's paradisaical and non-animal power of reproduction. As a result mankind lost this power. This state of circumstances required that man be broken in two and that woman be made out of man, as the second chapter of Genesis teaches. Finally, these scholars assert that Adam's false existence begins with the separation of his female child-bearing attribute.

Now we ought not to identify the female attribute with [Sophia or] the Celestial Virgin, i.e., with the *idea* or ideal of humanity, as many in the past have done. Rather, we should so interpret this notion to mean that the Celestial Virgin would abide in Adam as the eternal idea of God only so long as Adam would preserve in himself the virginal *imago Dei*. This image was intended to belong to him essentially as the creature of God. In and through the *imago Dei* Adam would bring his male and female attributes, tempered when he was created, into an actual and indissoluble union of the body, although the possibility of their dissolution was still there, just as Adam still had the possibility of becoming incarnate in an earthly body. It is in this sense that we are to understand that man and wife, as male and female attributes, were originally one body.

Since just the opposite in fact took place and since the Celestial

From Franz von Baader, "The Destructive Influence of Rational Materialism on Higher Physics, Poetry, and Art," *Sämtliche Werke*, ed. F. Hoffmann, J. Hamberger, and A. Lutterbeck (Leipzig, 1851–60), vol. 3, pp. 287ff.

Virgin withdrew from Adam, woman was made not from the Virgin but from the female element which was already dislocated, while Adam was deformed into masculinity. This deformation became actual in the second moment of sin, which Genesis symbolizes as the delight Adam and Eve took in eating the forbidden fruit.

Of this great catastrophe let me only say that in Adam the world-spirit lusted after the Celestial Virgin and that Adam allowed it to writhe up in himself. As a result, the androgyne—the natural attributes of male and female, or as the ancient alchemists would say, the two tinctures—disintegrated. The male element deteriorated into fiery wrath. The female element, which degenerated into water, had to be set in opposition in order to contain the unrestrained spread of fiery wrath in the same way that the Flood contained the world's conflagration.

In our own times man sees his sin objectified in woman; woman sees hers in man. Yet sin did not begin with woman. It was brought to an end and fulfilled in her, for from woman, Eva, comes Ave [i.e., Mary]. This is the beginning of the restoration of humanity. Androgyny is the sign of the indwelling of the Celestial Virgin, which in turn is the sign of the indwelling of the *imago Dei*. However we should not make the mistake our "mystics" do and represent the relationship between God and humanity the same as the relationship between man and woman. Rather, the former relationship is merely intimated by the latter.

Adam's appointed trial and mission was to maintain in himself the primal image of androgyny, i.e., the unity of sexual powers. If he could do that he would preserve himself as the *imago Dei*, which is neither male nor female. Thus it was necessary that Adam pass through the trial of temptation. Had he been able to extinguish the possibility of becoming male and female or of becoming animal, he would have overcome and subjected the world-spirit both within and outside himself. Only then would he have become in reality lord, king or master of the external world, since, as the saying goes, the crown belongs to the victor.

Without the concept of androgyny, the central concept of religion—the *imago Dei*—remains incomprehensible. Failure to understand this doctrine explains the lack of understanding of

Christianity in our own day. Painters and sculptors were closer to the truth when they depicted the Madonna as the central image and focus of all religious representation. We regret that theologians have not opened their minds to what artists and sculptors see, while they themselves have seldom been faithful to their own feelings about the *imago Dei*, nor have they been pure or productive in regard to them. Purity is unity of feeling, and only this is productive. Only when we behold the heavenly, androgynous and angelic nature in the Madonna, the Christos and the Angels is our male and female concupiscence fully at peace and free from every inner and outer compulsion. In these moments concupiscence becomes enraptured, elevated, and taken up into an angelic nature.

In pagan representation the focus is in direct opposition to the image of androgyny. The two sexual powers are thought of in terms of polaric opposition and inflammation. The result is the distorted image of the hermaphrodite, which imbues and enflames pagan art either overtly or covertly. The oldest image of Venus was the one of *Venus barbarata* (bearded Venus). Hence there can be little wonder that in the pagan world there is no struggle to return to androgyny as the manifestation of the integration of man and woman. Sexuality is dealt with in terms of itself and without reference to the exorcism of religious love. The latter is the sole principle of every free association and elevates the subjection and suffering connected with sexuality to the level of a free covenant. The sexual relationship, as dreamed up by pagan philosophers and naturalists, is physically and psychically the orgiastic, loveless and self-seeking conflict of either the man or the woman. Each seeks to enflame the hermaphroditic embers of doubleness inside the self and for the self. Each seeks to tear away from the other that which each needs for this self-inflammation. In loveless copulation a man and a woman seek for the liberation in a self-search. Thereby the man becomes a tool for the woman, the woman a tool for the man. Liberation from sexual instinct in the pagan world, consequently, is thought of in terms of the scorn men and women hold for each other's persons as well as their mutual hostility. . . .

Profane poetry impudently mistreats sexual love in every way possible. Sexuality is made a topic of frivolity or of sentimentality;

it is thought of in terms of rational-industrial degradation or even made diabolical. For this reason religious poetry must always keep its sights on the higher meaning of sexual love. Sexual love is no different from and no less than the substantiating covenant which two lovers have between one another before God, who is Love in all its forms. They are related in such a way that they mutually help one another to restore internally the image of the Celestial Virgin, of God and of the spiritual Body which had been lost and broken apart. Only as a covenant is sexual love conceivable as a sacrament. Only with the goal of restoration do lovers reach beyond temporal existence toward eternally true being. Something which is merely earthly and temporal cannot and should not be called a sacrament.

In a covenant of love a man should so help the woman to free herself from the unwholeness of her femininity; conversely a woman should help the man to free himself from his masculinity so that in both of the the *primal image of humanity* is once again elevated in an internal way. Thus they both become full human beings and are freed from being half-human and half-savage. (Savagery, in its deeper meaning, implies alienation from the life of God as well as estrangement from God's household.) In short, the lovers become full human beings, i.e., Christians. For the expression "to become a Christian" is synonymous with the rebirth and reacquisition of the integrity of human nature. Whoever shows me a Christian, shows me a person who is caught up, if only in a small way, in the reintegration of his or her humanity. And whoever shows me someone so caught up, shows me a Christian.

In our time it is of the utmost importance that we shed full light on the concept of Christianity as reintegrated humanity. Only a theology which presents sin as disintegration and redemption as rebirth and reintegration will be victorious over its opponents. When the Scriptures say that the old Adam must die for the new to have life, we should realize that man and woman is meant by the phrase "old Adam." The "new Adam," the one originally created in the image of God, is neither man nor woman.

15. Living in the Kingdom of God:
John Humphrey Noyes and the Oneida Community

Nineteenth-century America abounded in Utopian societies; it has been estimated that about 500 of them flourished during that period.[1] One of the most famous, the Oneida Community in upstate New York, was founded by John Humphrey Noyes (1811–1886) and remained in operation from 1849 until 1881. At its height, Oneida counted over 300 persons in its membership.[2] Noyes, who had studied theology at Andover Theological Seminary and Yale Theological School, adopted the belief of some revivalists of his day that Christianity was a religion of "perfectionism": believing Christians no longer were held captive by sin, but were members of the Kingdom of God which was in the process of establishment. Noyes, however, developed conclusions from this view which were not acceptable to the religious establishment—nor to "respectable" people in general—of the mid-nineteenth century. In the Kingdom, Noyes thought, all men and women would give their affection freely to fellow believers; no longer would they limit their loving to the traditional marriage relation, which Noyes once described as "the odious obligation of one party and the sensual recklessness of the other."[3]

Over against the Shaker conviction that sexual abstinence was necessary among those dedicated to God, Noyes formulated his idea of "complex marriage," in which all believers would be married to each other and "brotherly love" would abound. Since the world at large did not appear sufficiently advanced to renounce the exclusive ties of monogamy, Noyes endeavored to experiment with his plan at the Oneida commune. "Complex marriage" was practiced at Oneida until 1879, shortly before the breakup of the community. It is clear from Noyes's writings that he thought the arrangement was one way of implementing the biblical decrees regarding love for one's fellow humans in the Kingdom of God.

Sexual union, Noyes believed, was the chief means of demonstrating one's love for others.[4] The "amative" function of sex was the one he thought to be the most important, the one which raised humans above the level of the beasts; the procreative function, on the other hand, needed careful regulation. The latter was accomplished by the practice of "male continence," intercourse without ejaculation.[5] Noyes thought that engaging in the sex act without taking precautions of the sort he recommended to prevent the conception of unwanted children was a great evil. That "male continence" must have had considerable success is testified to by the fact that only thirty children were born to the community in the first twenty years of its existence.[6] The rigors of pregnancy and the raising of numerous children put a blight upon the lives of women, Noyes thought, and did not necessarily contribute to "amativeness" between the sexes. The method of "amative" sexual relations was taught in the Oneida community by the initiation of the younger members by older ones—not merely younger women by older men, but also younger men by older women, who thus in serving their functions as sexual initiators assumed roles traditionally considered "male."[7] (The fundamental distinction in the Oneida group was not between male and female, but between the more spiritual and the less spiritual membership.) Needless to say, these practices were not viewed with much favor by the law and periodically Noyes found himself in difficulties with the authorities, charged with adultery or statutory rape.

Noyes's great concern for women's lives was shown not just in his desire that women be relieved from excessive childbearing and time-consuming childrearing activities;[8] he wished them to enjoy sexual relations, Moreover, he encouraged them to engage in a variety of daily occupations, including some usually considered to be masculine pursuits, such as hoeing corn.[9] Noyes looked forward to the day when men and women would share their labors, with the result, he thought, that work would be much more attractive.[10] In preparation for that new order of life, Noyes encouraged the women to dress in a comfortable, free fashion (some wore a trouser costume) and to cut their hair short.[11]

The Oneida women, however, do not seem to have embraced the ideals of the suffrage movement; in fact, they were rather critical of Elizabeth Cady Stanton, Susan B. Anthony, and their associates. The Oneida females disliked the view that men and women could be considered as independent of one another, or even worse, as competitors.[12] One woman wrote in the Oneida newsletter, the *Circular*, "The grand right I ask for women is to love the men and be loved by them. That I imagine would adjust all other claims. It is but a cold, dismal right, in my opinion, to be allowed to vote, or to acquire and hold property. . . . I would rather be tyrannized over by him, than to be *independent* of him, and I would rather have no *rights* than to be separate."[13] The intention behind such a statement, of course, is to reject American individualism and the belief that relations between the sexes could be justly worked out within that framework, as was advocated by the suffrage leaders. Perhaps the females in the Oneida community felt that they had already achieved sexual equality and did not have to concern themselves with the plight of women who remained in a society which had not comprehended the new communal order of life open to Christians. Within the Oneida commune itself, however, the revolutionary view of "amativeness" pointed the way to new modes of sexual relationships for the future, if not to feminist ideals.

Bible Communism

CHAPTER 2

SHOWING THAT MARRIAGE IS NOT AN INSTITUTION OF THE KINGDOM OF HEAVEN, AND MUST GIVE PLACE TO COMMUNISM.

Proposition 5. In the kingdom of heaven, the institution of marriage which assigns the exclusive possession of one woman to one

From Oneida Community, *Bible Communism* (Philadelphia: Porcupine Press, 1972; original printing by The Office of *The Circular*, Brooklyn, 1853).

man, does not exist (Matt. 22:23–30). "In the resurrection they neither marry nor are given in marriage."

Note: Christ, in the passage referred to, does not exclude the sexual distinction, or sexual intercourse, from the heavenly state, but only the world's method of assigning the sexes to each other, which alone creates the difficulty presented in the question of the Sadducees. Their question evidently referred only to the matter of ownership. Seven men had been married to one woman, and dying successively, the question was, whose she should be in the resurrection. Suppose the question had been asked, in reference to slavery instead of marriage, thus: A man owning a slave dies and leaves him to his brother; he dying, bequeaths him to the next brother, and so seven of them in succession own this slave; now whose slave shall he be in the resurrection? This, evidently, is the amount of the Sadducees' question, and Christ's answer is as though he had said that in the resurrection there are neither slaves nor slaveholders. It is nullification of the idea of marriage ownership. Can any thing more be made of it? To assume from this passage a nullification of the sexual relation, as the Shakers and others do, is as absurd as it would be to assume that because there is no slavery, there is therefore no serving one another in the resurrection; whereas the gospel teaches that there is more serving one another there than in the world. The constitutional distinctions and offices of the sexes belong to their original paradisaical state; and there is no proof in the Bible or in reason, that they are ever to be abolished, but abundance of proof to the contrary (1 Cor. 11:3–11). The saying of Paul that in Christ "there is neither Jew nor Greek, neither male nor female," etc., simply means that the unity of life which all the members of Christ have in him, overrides all individual distinctions. In the same sense as that in which the apostle excludes distinctions of sexes, he also virtually excludes distinction of persons; for he adds, "Ye are all one in Christ Jesus." Yet the several members of Christ, in perfect consistency with their spiritual unity, remain distinct persons; and so the sexes, though one in their innermost life, as members of Christ, yet retain their constitutional distinctions.

Proposition 6. In the kingdom of heaven, the intimate union of life and interests, which in the world is limited to pairs, extends through the whole body of believers; i.e. *complex* marriage takes the place of simple (John 17:21). Christ prayed that *all* believers might be one, *even as* he and the Father are one. His unity with the Father is defined in the words, *"All mine are thine, and all thine are mine"* (v. 10). This perfect community of interests, then will be the condition of *all*, when his prayer is answered. The universal unity of the members of Christ, is described in the same terms that are used to describe marriage-unity. Compare 1 Cor. 12:12–27 with Gen. 2:24. See also I Cor. 6:15–17, and Eph. 5:30–32. . . .

Proposition 9. The abolishment of sexual exclusiveness is involved in the love-relation required between all believers by the express injunction of Christ and the apostles, and by the whole tenor of the New Testament. "The new commandment is, that we love one another," and that, not by pairs, as in the world, but *en masse.* We are required to love one another *fervently* (1 Pet. 1:22), or, as the original might be rendered, *burningly.* The fashion of the world forbids a man and woman who are otherwise appropriated, to love one another burningly—to flow into each other's hearts. But if they obey Christ they must do this; and whoever would allow them to do this, and yet would forbid them (on any other ground than that of present expediency) to express their unity of hearts by bodily unity, would "strain at a gnat and swallow a camel;" for unity of hearts is as much more important than the bodily expression of it, as a camel is bigger than a gnat. . . .

Proposition 10. The abolishment of worldly restrictions on sexual intercourse, is involved in the anti-legality of the gospel. It is incompatible with the state of perfected freedom towards which Paul's gospel of 'grace without law' leads, that man should be allowed and required to *love* in all directions, and yet be forbidden to express love in its most natural and beautiful form, except in one direction. In fact, Paul says with direct reference to sexual intercourse—"All things are *lawful* for me, but all things are not expedient;" "all things are lawful for me, but I will not be brought under the power of any" (1 Cor. 6:12); thus placing the restrictions which were necessary in the transition period on the basis, not of law, but of expediency and the demands of spiritual freedom, and leaving it fairly to be inferred that in the final state, when hostile surroundings and powers of bondage cease, all restrictions also will cease. . . .

In a perfect state of things, where corrupting attractions have no place, and all susceptibilities are duly subordinated and trained, the denying exercise of the will ceases, and attraction reigns without limitation. In such a state, what is the difference between the love of man towards man, and that of man towards woman? Attraction being the essence of love in both cases, the difference lies in this, that man and woman are so adapted to each other by the differences of their natures, that attraction can attain a more perfect union between them than between man and man, or between woman and woman. . . . Love between man and man can only advance to something like plain contact; while love between man and woman can advance to interlocked contact. In other words, love between the different sexes, is peculiar, not in its essential nature, but because they are so constructed with reference to each other, both spiritually and physically, (for the body is an index of the life,) that more intimate unity, and of course more intense happiness in love, is possible between them than between persons of the same sex. . . .

Proposition 16. The restoration of true relations between the sexes, is a matter second in importance only to the reconciliation of man to God. The distinction of male and female is that which makes man the image of God, i.e. the image of the Father and the Son (Gen. 1:27). The relation of male and female was the first social relation (Gen. 2:22). It is therefore the root of all other social relations. The derangement of this relation was the first result of the original breach with God (Gen. 3:7; cf. 2:25). Adam and Eve were, at the beginning, in open, fearless, spiritual fellowship, first with God, and secondly, with each other. Their transgression produced two corresponding alienations, viz., first, an alienation from God, indicated by their fear of meeting him, and their hiding themselves among the trees of the garden; and, secondly, an alienation from each other, indicated by their shame at their nakedness, and their hiding themselves from each other by clothing. These

were the two great manifestations of original sin—the only manifestations presented to notice in the inspired record of the apostasy.
The first thing then to be done, in an attempt to redeem man
and reorganize society, is to bring about reconciliation with God;
and the second thing is to bring about a true union of the sexes.
In other words, religion is the first subject of interest, and sexual
morality the second, in the great enterprise of establishing the
kingdom of God on earth. . . .

Proposition 17. Dividing the sexual relation into two branches,
the amative and propagative, the amative or love-relation is first
in importance, as it is in the order of nature. God made woman
because "he saw it was not good for man to be alone" (Gen. 2:18);
i.e. for social, not primarily for propagative purposes. Eve was
called Adam's "help-meet." In the whole of the specific account
of the creation of woman, she is regarded as his companion, and
her maternal office is not brought into view (Gen. 2:18–25).
Amativeness was necessarily the first social affection developed in
the garden of Eden. The second commandment of the eternal
law of love—"thou shalt love thy neighbor as thyself"—had
amativeness for its first channel; for Eve was at first Adam's only
neighbor. Propagation, and the affections connected with it, did
not commence their operation during the period of innocence.
After the fall, God said to the woman, "I will greatly multiply thy
sorrow and thy conception" from which it is to be inferred that
in the original state, conception would have been comparatively
infrequent. . . .

Proposition 19. The propagative part of the sexual relation is in
its nature the expensive department. (1) While amativeness keeps
the capital stock of life circulating between two, propagation intro-
duces a third partner. (2) The propagative act, i.e. the emission
of the seed, is a drain on the life of man, and when habitual,
produces disease. (3) The infirmities and vital expenses of woman
during the long period of pregnancy, waste her constitution.
(4) The awful agonies of child-birth heavily tax the life of
woman. (5) The cares of the nursing period bear heavily on
woman. (6) The cares of both parents, through the period of the
childhood of their offspring, are many and burdensome. (7) The

labor of man is greatly increased by the necessity of providing for children. A portion of these expenses would undoubtedly have been curtailed, if human nature had remained in its original integrity, and will be, when it is restored. But it is still self-evident, that the birth of children, viewed either as a vital or a mechanical operation, is in its nature expensive; and the fact that multiplied conception was imposed as a curse, indicates that it was so regarded by the Creator. . . .

Note: The grand problem which must be solved before redemption can be carried forward to immortality, is this:—*How can the benefits of amativeness be secured and increased, and the expenses of propagation be reduced to such limits as life can afford?* The human mind has labored much on this problem. Shakerism is an attempt to solve it. Ann Lee's attention, however, was confined to the latter half of it—the reduction of expenses; (of which her own sufferings in child-birth gave her a strong sense;) and for the sake of stopping propagation she prohibited the union of the sexes— thus shutting off the profitable as well as the expensive part of the sexual relation. This is cutting the knot—not untying it. Robert Dale Owen's *Moral Physiology* is another attempted solution of the grand problem. He insists that sexual intercourse is of some value by itself, and not merely as a bait to propagation. He proposes therefore to limit propagation, and retain the privilege of sexual intercourse, by the practice of withdrawing previous to the emission of the seed, after Onan's fashion (Gen. 38:9). This method, it will be observed, is unnatural, and even more wasteful of life, so far as the man is concerned, than ordinary practice; since it gives more freedom to desire, by shutting off the propagative consequences. The same may be said of various French methods. The system of producing abortions, is a still more unnatural and destructive method of limiting propagation, without stopping sexual intercourse. A satisfactory solution of the grand problem, must propose a method that can be shown to be natural, healthy for both sexes, favorable to amativeness, and effectual in its control of propagation. Such a solution will be found in what follows.

Chapter 4

SHOWING HOW THE SEXUAL FUNTION IS TO BE REDEEMED, AND TRUE
RELATIONS BETWEEN THE SEXES RESTORED

Proposition 20. The amative and propagative functions of the sexual organs are distinct from each other, and may be separated practically. They are confounded in the world, both in the theories of physiologists and in universal practice. The amative function is regarded merely as a bait to the propagative, and is merged in it. The sexual organs are called "organs of reproduction," or "organs of generation," but not organs of love or organs of union. But if amativeness is, as we have seen, the first and noblest of the social affections, and if the propagative part of the sexual relation was originally secondary, and became paramount by the subversion of order in the fall, we are bound to raise the amative office of the sexual organs into a distinct and paramount function. It is held in the world, that the sexual organs have two distinct functions, viz., the urinary and the propagative. We affirm that they have three—the urinary, the propagative, and the amative. i.e., they are conductors, first of the urine, secondly of the semen, and thirdly of the social magnetism. And the amative is as distinct from the propagative, as the propagative is from the urinary. In fact, strictly speaking, the organs of propagation are *physiologically* distinct from the organs of union in both sexes. The testicles are the organs of reproduction in the male, and the uterus in the female. These are distinct from the organs of union. The sexual conjunction of male and female, no more necessarily involves the discharge of the semen than of the urine. The discharge of the semen, instead of being the main act of sexual intercourse, properly so called, is really the sequel and termination of it. Sexual intercourse, pure and simple, is the conjunction of the organs of union, and the interchange of magnetic influences, or conversation of spirits, through the medium of that conjunction. The communication from the seminal vessels to the uterus, which constitutes the propagative act, is distinct from, subsequent to, and not necessarily connected with, this intercourse. (On the one hand, the seminal discharge can be voluntarily withheld in sexual connection; and on the other, it can be produced without sexual connection, as it is in masturbation. This latter fact demonstrates that the discharge of the semen and the pleasure connected with it, is not essentially social, since it can be produced in solitude; it is a personal and not a dual affair. This, indeed, is evident from a physiological analysis of it. The pleasure of the act is not produced by contact and interchange of life with the female, but by the action of the seminal fluid on certain internal nerves of the male organ. The appetite and that which satisfies it, are both within the man, and of course the pleasure is personal, and may be obtained without sexual intercourse.) We insist then that the amative function—that which consists in a simple union of persons, making "of twain one flesh," and giving a medium of magnetic and spiritual interchange—is a distinct and independent function, as superior to the reproductive as we have shown amativeness to be to propagation....

Note 3: Here is a method of controlling propagation, that is natural, healthy, favorable to amativeness, and effectual. First, It is natural. The useless expenditure of seed certainly is not natural. God cannot have designed that men should sow seed by the way-side, where they do not expect it to grow, or in the same field where seed has already been sown, and is growing; and yet such is the practice of men in ordinary sexual intercourse. They sow seed habitually where they do not wish it to grow. This is wasteful of life, and cannot be natural. So far the Shakers and Grahamites are right. Yet it is equally manifest that the natural instinct of our nature demands frequent congress of the sexes, not for propagative, but for social and spiritual purposes. It results from these opposite indications, that simple congress of the sexes, without the propagative crisis, is the order of nature for the gratification of ordinary amative instincts; and that the act of propagation should be reserved for its legitimate occasions, when conception is intended. The idea that sexual intercourse, pure and simple, is impossible or difficult, and therefore not natural, is contradicted by the experience of many. Abstinence from masturbation is impossible or difficult, where habit has made it a second nature; and yet no one will say that habitual masturbation is natural. So abstinence from the propagative part of sexual intercourse may seem impracticable to depraved natures, and yet be perfectly natural and easy to persons properly trained to chastity. Our method simply proposes the subordination of the flesh to the spirit, teaching men to seek principally the elevated spiritual pleasures of sexual intercourse, and to be content with them in their general intercourse with women, restricting the more sensual part to its proper occasions. This is certainly natural and easy to spiritual men, however difficult it may be to the sensual.

Secondly, this method is *healthy*. In the first place, it secures woman from the curses of involuntary and undesirable procreation; and secondly, it stops the drain of life on the part of man. This cannot be said of Owen's system, or any other method that merely prevents the *propagative effects* of the emission of the seed, and not the emission itself.

Thirdly, this method is *favorable* to amativeness. Owen can only say of his method that it does not *much diminish* the pleasure of sexual intercourse; but we can say of ours, that it *vastly increases* that pleasure. Ordinary sexual intercourse (in which the amative and propagative functions are confounded) is a momentary affair, terminating in exhaustion and disgust. If it begins in the spirit, it soon ends in the flesh; i.e., the amative, which is spiritual, is drowned in the propagative, which is sensual. The exhaustion which follows, naturally breeds self-reproach and shame, and this leads to dislike and concealment of the sexual organs, which contract disagreeable associations from the fact that they are the instruments of pernicious excess. This undoubtedly is the philosophy of the origin of shame after the fall. Adam and Eve first sunk the spiritual in the sensual, in eating the forbidden fruit; and then, having lost the true balance of their natures, they sunk the spiritual in the sensual in their intercourse with each other, by pushing prematurely beyond the amative to the propagative, and so became ashamed, and began to look with an evil eye on the instruments of their folly. On the same principle we may account for the process of "cooling off" which takes place between lovers after marriage, and often ends in indifference and disgust. Exhaustion and self-reproach make the eye evil not only toward the instruments of excess, but toward the person who tempts to it. In contrast with all this, lovers who use their sexual organs simply as the servants of their spiritual natures, abstaining from the propagative act, except when procreation is intended, may enjoy the highest bliss of sexual fellowship for any length of time, and from day to day, without satiety or exhaustion; and thus marriage life may become permanently sweeter than courtship, or even the honeymoon.

Fourthly, this method of controlling propagation is *effectual*. The habit of making sexual intercourse a quiet affair, like conversation, restricting the action of the organs to such limits as are necessary to the avoidance of the sensual crisis, can easily be established, and then there is no risk of conception without intention.

Note 4: Ordinary sexual intercourse, i.e., the performance of the propagative act, without the intention of procreation, is properly to be classed with masturbation. The habit in the former case is less liable to become besotted and ruinous, than in the latter, simply because a woman is less convenient than the ordinary means of masturbation. It must be admitted, also, that the amative affection favorably modifies the sensual act to a greater extent in sexual commerce than in masturbation. But this is perhaps counterbalanced by the cruelty of forcing or risking undesired conception, which attends sexual commerce, and does not attend masturbation.

Note 5: Our theory, separating the amative from the propagative, not only relieves us of involuntary and undesirable procreation, but opens the way for *scientific* propagation. We are not opposed, after the Shaker fashion, or even after Owen's fashion, to the increase of population. We believe that the order to "multiply" attached to the race in its original integrity, and that propagation, rightly conducted, and kept within such limits as life can fairly afford, is the next blessing to sexual love. But we are opposed to *involuntary* procreation. A very large proportion of all children born under the present system, are begotten contrary to the wishes of both parents, and lie nine months in their mother's womb under their mother's curse, or a feeling little better than a curse. Such children cannot be well organized. We are opposed to excessive, and of course oppressive procreation, which is almost universal. We are opposed to *random* procreation, which is unavoidable in the marriage system. But we are in favor of *intelligent, well-ordered* procreation. The physiologists say that the race cannot be raised from ruin till propagation is made a matter of science; but they point out no way of making it so. True, propagation is controlled and reduced to a science in the case of valuable domestic brutes; but marriage and fashion forbid any such system among human beings. We believe the time will come when involuntary and random propagation will cease, and when scientific combination will be applied to human generation as freely and successfully as it is to that of other animals. The way will be open for this, when amativeness can have its proper gratification without drawing after it procreation, as a necessary sequence. And at all events, we believe that good sense and benevolence will very soon sanction and enforce the rule, that women shall bear children only when they choose. They have the principal burdens of breeding to bear, and they, rather than men, should have their choice of time and circumstances, at least till science takes charge of the business.

Note 6: The political economist will perhaps find in our discovery some help for the solution of the famous "population question." Carey, and other American writers on political economy, seem to have exploded the old Malthusian doctrine that population necessarily outruns subsistence; but there is still a difficulty in the theoretical prospect of the world in regard to population, which they do not touch. Admitting that the best soils are yet in reserve, and that with the progress of intelligence, means of subsistence may for the present increase faster than population; it is nevertheless certain that the actual area of the earth is a limited thing, and it is therefore certain that if its population goes on doubling, as we are told, once in twenty-five years, a time must come at last when there will not be standing-room! Whether such a catastrophe is worth considering and providing for or not, we may be certain, that man, when he has grown wise enough to be

worthy of his commission as Lord of nature, will be able to determine for himself what shall be the population of the earth,
instead of leaving it to be determined by the laws that govern the
blind passions of brutes.

Note 7: The separation of the amative from the propagative,
places amative sexual intercourse on the same footing with other
ordinary forms of intercourse, such as conversation, kissing, shaking hands, embracing, etc. So long as the amative and propagative
are confounded, sexual intercourse carries with it physical consequences which necessarily take it out of the category of mere
social acts. If a man under the cover of a mere social call upon a
woman, should leave in her apartments a child for her to breed and
provide for, he would do a mean wrong. The call might be made
without previous negotiation or agreement, but the sequel of the
call—the leaving of the child—is a matter so serious that it is to be
treated as a business affair, and not be done without good reason
and agreement of the parties. But the man who under the cover
of social intercourse, commits the propagative act, leaves his child
with the woman in a meaner and more oppressive way, than if he
should leave it full born in her apartments; for he imposes upon
her not only the task of breeding and providing for it, but the
sorrows and pains of pregnancy and child-birth. It is right that law,
or at least public opinion, should frown on such proceedings even
more than it does; and it is not to be wondered at that women,
to a considerable extent, look upon ordinary sexual intercourse
with more dread than pleasure, regarding it as a stab at their life,
rather than a joyful act of fellowship. But separate the amative
from the propagative—let the act of fellowship stand by itself—and
sexual intercourse becomes a purely social affair, the same in kind
with other modes of kindly interchange, differing only by its superior intensity and beauty. Thus the most popular, if not the most
serious objection to free love and sexual intercourse, is removed.
The difficulty so often urged, of knowing to whom children belong
in complex-marriage, will have no place in a community trained
to keep the amative distinct from the propagative. Thus also the
only plausible objection to amative intercourse between near relatives, founded on the supposed law of nature that "breeding in and

in" deteriorates offspring (which law however was not recognized in Adam's family) is removed; since science may dictate in this case as in all others, in regard to propagation, and yet amativeness may be free.

Note 7: In society trained in these principles, as propagation will become a science, so amative intercourse will have place among the "fine arts." Indeed it will take rank above music, painting, sculpture, &c.; for it combines the charms and benefits of them all. There is as much room for cultivation of taste and skill in this department as in any.

Note 8: The practice which we propose will advance civilization and refinement at railroad speed. The self-control, retention of life, and ascent out of sensualism, which must result from making freedom of love a bounty on the chastening of physical indulgence, will at once raise the race to new vigor and beauty, moral and physical. And the refining effects of sexual love (which are recognized more or less in the world) will be increased a thousand-fold, when sexual intercourse becomes a method of ordinary conversation, and each is married to all.

16. Sarah Grimké: From Abolition to Suffrage

Sarah Grimké's *Letters on the Equality of the Sexes and the Condition of Women* (1837–1838) grew out of her experiences as a public speaker on the question of abolition. She was a member of the Quaker opposition to slavery which organized an educational campaign against it in the early nineteenth century. Sarah Grimké's *Letters* were written ten years before the event usually cited as the beginning of the formal organization of the nineteenth-century women's movement (the Seneca Falls Convention of 1848) and hence are an early expression of feminism in America. The letters were addressed to Mary Parker, President of the Boston Female Anti-Slavery Society, who had suggested to Sarah that she set down her thoughts on the topic of women in a form suitable for publication.[1]

The route by which Sarah Grimké entered the movement for women's rights was an indirect one. She and her younger sister Angelina, daughters of a South Carolina slaveholder, early in life developed an aversion to slavery as an institution. So strongly repelled were they by the southern acceptance of slavery that, upon reaching adulthood, they moved to Philadelphia and joined the Quaker sect. The Quakers at that time were devoted to the cause of abolition, and the Grimké sisters enthusiastically participated in the antislavery campaign.

The Quaker movement was an exceptional one in yet another way: women exercised leadership and performed ministerial functions within the sect because they no less than men were thought to be led directly by the Spirit. The sisters received valuable training within the Quaker fold as public speakers. This ability they put to use at first by making speeches to women's circles in private homes on the issue of slavery, but their popularity soon necessitated their moving to larger quarters. Men were then drawn to the churches and halls to hear the remarkable pair with the result that the audiences became "mixed." During the sisters' tour of New England in 1837, the region's Council of Congregationalist Ministers, who represented traditional Protestantism, became alarmed at the spectacle of women publicly addressing audiences which included men and championing controversial causes. It drew up a "pastoral letter" outlining the deleterious effects of women's assuming the place of public reformers and moral leaders, roles which had usually been reserved for male clergy, which leaned heavily on arguments derived from the Bible. In Sarah Grimké's Letter 3, parts of which are printed below, she refers to passages from the Congregationalist ministers' rebuke and delivers an appropriately feminist response.[2]

It was not, however, merely the traditional clergymen who opposed the sisters' activities. Even the men who had dedicated their lives to the abolition movement expressed anxiety over Sarah's and Angelina's writing and lecturing, though for reasons quite different from those proffered by the spokesmen for Massachusetts's Congregationalism. Some men did not oppose the sisters' public lecturing per se, but their lecturing on the condition of women. Both John Greenleaf Whittier and Theodore Weld (who later took Angelina to wife despite his earlier vow not to marry until the slaves were freed) were concerned that if the sisters became embroiled in feminist causes, the campaign against slavery might suffer. As Whittier wrote them in 1837, "Is it not forgetting the great and dreadful wrongs of the slave in a selfish crusade against some paltry grievance of [your] own?"[3] Weld took a "humanist" line: if the public could be convinced of the importance of human rights in general and be sufficiently aroused to the horrors of slavery to rectify that injustice, then it would be "an easy matter to take millions of females from their knees and set them on their feet, or in other words, transform them from babies into women."[4] A practical compromise was reached: the sisters would no longer devote their lectures to women's rights, but Sarah would complete and publish the articles she was writing, the *Letters on the Equality of the Sexes*.[5] After doing so, she apparently gave up her public advocacy of women's issues and devoted herself to the Weld household. Much later she reappears, walking about the countryside at the age of seventy-nine, selling copies of John Stuart Mill's feminist tract, *The Subjection of Women*.[6]

Sarah Grimké, as a Quaker Christian, clearly wished to uphold the Bible as an ethical guide. Passages which did not bend easily to her feminist interpretation she sometimes labeled "mistranslations," or, at the very least, she would point out that men had "misinterpreted" the meaning of the particular verse in question. She thought that if Scripture were understood in its true intention it would be seen to support the equality of women for the most part. Her attempt to read the Bible in a spiritual and reformist manner was a brave one, not only because of the novelty of her feminist stance, but also because she was writing at a time when Americans as yet knew little or nothing about the "higher criticism" of the Bible.[7]

Despite her lack of formal theological education, Sarah Grimké was sensitive to the nuances of Scripture. Her defense of the equality of men and women as based on the opening chapters of Genesis is a strong one. She demonstrated her theological perceptivity in noting that women's "worship" of men, from a Christian standpoint, was idolatrous. Phrases from her work have found their way into the rhetoric of American feminism, especially her famous words, "I ask no favors for my sex. I surrender not our claim to equality. All I ask of our brethern is, that they will take their feet from off our necks, and permit us to stand upright on that ground which God designed us to occupy."

Grimké's generally positive evaluation of the Bible contrasts sharply with the more critical views of Elizabeth Cady Stanton in the next selection.

From Sarah Grimké, Letter 3 of *Letters on the Equality of the Sexes and the Condition of Woman* (1838; New York: Burt Franklin, 1970).

The Pastoral Letter of the General Association of Congregational Ministers of Massachusetts.

Haverhill, 7th Mo. 1837.

Dear friend,

When I last addressed thee, I had not seen the Pastoral Letter of the General Association. It has since fallen into my hands, and I must digress from my intention of exhibiting the condition of women in different parts of the world, in order to make some remarks on this extraordinary document. I am persuaded that when the minds of men and women become emancipated from the thraldom of superstition and "traditions of men," the sentiments contained in the Pastoral Letter will be recurred to with as much astonishment as the opinions of Cotton Mather and other distinguished men of his day, on the subject of witchcraft; nor will it be deemed less wonderful, that a body of divines should gravely assemble and endeavor to prove that woman has no right to "open her mouth for the dumb," than it now is that judges should have sat on the trials of witches, and solemnly condemned nineteen persons and one dog to death for witchcraft.

But to the letter. It says, "We invite your attention to the dangers which at present seem to threaten the FEMALE CHARACTER with wide-spread and permanent injury." I rejoice that they have called the attention of my sex to this subject, because I believe if woman investigates it, she will soon discover that danger is impending, though from a totally different source from that which the Association apprehends—danger from those who, having long held the reins of usurped authority, are unwilling to permit us to fill that sphere which God created us to move in, and who have entered into league to crush the immortal mind of woman. I rejoice, because I am persuaded that the rights of woman, like the rights of slaves, need only be examined to be understood and asserted, even by some of those, who are now endeavoring to smother the irrepressible desire for mental and spiritual freedom which glows in the breast of many, who hardly dare to speak their sentiments.

"The appropriate duties and influence of women are clearly stated in the New Testament. Those duties are unobtrusive and private, but the sources of *mighty power*. When the mild, *dependent*, softening influence of woman upon the sternness of man's opinions is fully exercised, society feels the effects of it in a thousand ways." No one can desire more earnestly than I do, that woman may move exactly in the sphere which her Creator has assigned her; and I believe her having been displaced from that sphere has introduced confusion into the world. It is, therefore, of vast importance to herself and to all the rational creation, that she should ascertain what are her duties and her privileges as a responsible and immortal being. The New Testament has been referred to, and I am willing to abide by its decisions, but must enter my protest against the false translation of some passages by the MEN who did that work, and against the perverted interpretation by MEN who undertook to write commentaries thereon. I am inclined to think, when we are admitted to the honor of studying Greek and Hebrew, we shall produce some various readings of the Bible a little different from those we now have.

The Lord Jesus defines the duties of his followers in his Sermon on the Mount. He lays down grand principles by which they should be governed, without any reference to sex or condition: "Ye are the light of the world. A city that is set on a hill cannot be hid. Neither do men light a candle and put it under a bushel, but on a candlestick, and it giveth light unto all that are in the house. Let your light so shine before men, that they may see your good works, and glorify your Father which is in Heaven." I follow him through all his precepts, and find him giving the same directions to women as to men, never even referring to the distinction now so strenuously insisted upon between masculine and feminine virtues: this is one of the anti-christian "traditions of men" which are taught instead of the "commandments of God." Men and women were CREATED EQUAL; they are both moral and accountable beings, and whatever is *right* for man to do, is *right* for woman.

But the influence of woman, says the Association, is to be private and unobtrusive; her light is not to shine before man like that of her brethren; but she is passively to let the lords of the creation, as they call themselves, put the bushel over it, lest peradventure it might appear that the world has been benefitted by the rays of her candle. So that her quenched light, according to their judgment, will be of more use than if it were set on the candlestick. "Her influence is the source of mighty power." This has ever been the flattering language of man since he laid aside the whip as a means to keep woman in subjection. He spares her body; but the war he has waged against her mind, her heart, and her soul, has been no less destructive to her as a moral being. How monstrous, how anti-christian, is the doctrine that woman is to be dependent on man! Where, in all the sacred Scriptures, is this taught? Alas! she has too well learned the lesson, which MAN has labored to teach her. She has surrendered her dearest RIGHTS, and been satisfied with the privileges which man has assumed to grant her; she has been amused with the show of power, whilst man has absorbed all the reality into himself. He has adorned the creature whom God gave him as a companion, with baubles and gew-gaws, turned her attention to personal attractions, offered incense to her vanity, and made her the instrument of his selfish gratification, a plaything to please his eye and amuse his hours of leisure. "Rule by obedience and by submission sway," or in other words, study to be a hypocrite, pretend to submit, but gain your point, has been the code of household morality which woman has been taught. The poet has sung, in sickly strains, the loveliness of woman's dependence upon man, and now we find it re-echoed by those who profess to teach the religion of the Bible. God says, "Cease ye from man whose breath is in his nostrils, for wherein is he to be accounted of?" Man says, depend upon me. God says, "HE will teach us of his ways." Man says, believe it not, I am to be your teacher. This doctrine of dependence upon man is utterly at variance with the doctrine of the Bible. In that book I find nothing like the softness of woman, nor the sternness of man: both are equally commanded to bring forth the fruits of the Spirit, love meekness, gentleness, &c.

But we are told, "the power of woman is in her dependence, flowing from a consciousness of that weakness which God has given her for her protection." If physical weakness is alluded to, I cheerfully concede the superiority; if brute force is what my brethren are claiming, I am willing to let them have all the honor they desire; but if they mean to intimate, that mental or moral weakness belongs to woman, more than to man, I utterly disclaim the charge. Our powers of mind have been crushed, as far as man could do it, our sense of morality has been impaired by his interpretation of our duties; but no where does God say that he made any distinction between us, as moral and intelligent beings.

"We appreciate," say the Association, "the unostentatious prayers and efforts of woman in advancing the cause of religion at home and abroad, in leading religious inquiries TO THE PASTOR for instruction." Several points here demand attention. If public prayers and public efforts are necessarily ostentatious, then "Anna the prophetess (or preacher) who departed not from the temple, but served God with fastings and prayers night and day," "and spake of Christ to all them that looked for redemption in Israel," was ostentatious in her efforts. Then, the apostle Paul encourages women to be ostentatious in their efforts to spread the gospel, when he gives them directions how they should appear, when engaged in praying, or preaching in the public assemblies. Then, the whole association of Congregational ministers are ostentatious, in the efforts they are making in preaching and praying to convert souls.

But women may be permitted to lead religious inquirers to the PASTORS for instruction. Now this is assuming that all pastors are better qualified to give instruction than woman. This I utterly deny. I have suffered too keenly from the teaching of man, to lead any one to him for instruction. The Lord Jesus says, "Come unto me and learn of me." He points his followers to no man; and when woman is made the favored instrument of rousing a sinner to his lost and helpless condition, she has no right to substitute any teacher for Christ; all she has to do is, to turn the contrite inquirer to the "Lamb of God which taketh away the sins of the world." More souls have probably been lost by going down to Egypt for help, and by trusting in man in the early stages of religious experience, than by any other error. Instead of the petition being offered to God—"Lead me in thy truth, and TEACH me, for thou art the God of my salvation"—instead of relying on the precious promises, "What man is he that feareth the Lord? Him shall HE TEACH in the way that he shall choose; "I will instruct thee and TEACH thee in the way which thou shalt go; I will guide thee with mine eye," the young convert is directed to go to man, as if he were in the place of God, and his instructions essential to an advancement in the path of righteousness. That woman can have but a poor conception of the privilege of being taught of God, what he alone can teach, who would turn the "religious inquirer aside" from the fountain of living waters, where he might slake his thirst for spiritual instruction, to those broken cisterns which can hold no water, and therefore cannot satisfy the panting spirit. The business of men and women, who are ORDAINED of GOD to preach the unsearchable riches of Christ to a lost and perishing world, is to lead souls to Christ, and not to Pastors for instruction.

The General Association say, that "when woman assumes the place and tone of man as a public reformer, our care and protection of her seem unnecessary; we put ourselves in self-defence against her, and her character becomes unnatural." Here again the unscriptural notion is held up, that there is a distinction between the duties of men and women as moral beings; that what is virtue in man, is vice in woman; and women who dare to obey the command of Jehovah, "Cry aloud, spare not, lift up thy voice like a trumpet, and show my people their transgression," are threatened with having the protection of the brethren withdrawn. If this is all they do, we shall not even know the time when our chastisement is inflicted; our trust is in the Lord Jehovah, and in him is everlasting strength. The motto of woman, when she is engaged in the great work of public reformation should be, "the Lord is my light and my salvation; of whom shall I be afraid?" She must feel, if she feels rightly, that she is fulfilling one of the important duties laid upon her as an accountable being, and that her character, instead of being "unnatural," is in exact accordance with the will of Him to whom, and to no other, she is responsible for the talents and the gifts confided to her. As to the pretty simile, introduced into the "Pastoral Letter," "If the vine whose strength and beauty is to lean upon the trellis work, and half conceal its clusters, thinks to assume the independence and the overshadowing nature of the elm," etc., I shall only remark that it might well suit the poet's fancy, who sings of sparkling eyes and coral lips, and knights in armor clad; but it seems to me utterly inconsistent with the dignity of a Christian body, to endeavor to draw such an anti-scriptural distinction between men and women. Ah! how many of my sex feel in the dominion, thus unrighteously exercised over them, under the gentle appellation of *protection*, that what they have leaned upon has proved a broken at best and oft a spear.

Thine in the bonds of womanhood.

Sarah M. Grimké.

17. Elizabeth Cady Stanton and
The Woman's Bible

The Woman's Bible is one of the most remarkable products of nineteenth-century feminism. Inspired and directed by Elizabeth Cady Stanton, prime theoretician of women's suffrage, the book is a commentary on passages from the Old and New Testaments dealing with women.

Not all of the women who collaborated with Stanton in the 1890s to produce this commentary shared her radical views on religion. Although she was not an atheist (she believed in a "Supreme Intelligence" which governed the world by natural law), she had no use for the doctrines and ethical teachings of the Christian churches of her time. In fact, she thought that organized religion had been far more of a barrier to the freedom of women than had disfranchisement.[1]

The seeds of Elizabeth Cady Stanton's nonconformity and irreverent attitudes had apparently been sown in her youth. She tells us in her autobiography that she had been a rebellious child who had received a boy's education and had been bitterly disappointed when she was not allowed, because of her sex, to attend Union College along with her male friends.[2] Shortly after her marriage to the abolitionist Henry B. Stanton, she attended the World's Anti-Slavery Convention in London. The women in the American delegation were not permitted to sit with the men on the floor of the conference. The ministers present were among the most vociferous defenders of male privilege on that occasion. "The clergymen seemed to have God and his angels especially in their care and keeping, and were in agony lest the women should do or say something to shock the heavenly hosts."[3] Her attitudes toward the church did not mellow with the years. She gave not one iota of thanks to the ecclesiastical establishment for the movement towards women's freedom; women, she said, could rather thank religion for emphasizing their "inferiority and subjection."[4] In retrospect, her viewpoint appears to have been exaggerated, for many ministers did lend their support—and the support of the Christian religion—to the suffrage cause.[5]

In the latter part of the century, the women's movement had split on the issue of the scope of its platform. Some thought that feminists should stick only to the matter of winning the vote; others wished to expand the debate to include a whole spectrum of concerns relating to women. It has been argued that those who wanted to work only for suffrage really "sold out" the potential of the feminist movement; they overemphasized the changes which the vote would bring and neglected to explore the psychological, social, and economic bonds which imprisoned women.[6] Stanton was always on the side of those who stressed the wider issues: women's domestic situation, marriage and divorce laws, the conditions of working women. Freedom for women meant more than obtaining the vote; women must be able to exercise their God-given right to determine their own "spheres of activity,"[7] especially if these were different from the traditional ones to which they had been assigned. But for women to regulate their own lives, they first had to be freed from the false consciousness and psychological oppression which kept them enslaved.

It was to help women free themselves from this psychological bondage that Stanton sought, toward the end of her long and active career in the suffrage movement, to organize a group of her colleagues who could write a commentary on biblical passages relating to women. Stanton believed that the Bible, which had given to Western civilization its values and worldview, not only had contributed to the suppression of women in society, but also had shaped the low self-image of women. Her first attempt to enlist friends and associates to work on the project failed, in 1886, from lack of cooperation.[8] But in the 1890s she did succeed in gaining support for her proposal and two volumes of *The Woman's Bible* were forthcoming.

The reception of Stanton's book was very cool. In the closing years of the nineteenth century the National American Woman Suffrage Association voted to disclaim any official connection with *The Woman's Bible*. This decision reflects the fact that feminism had become "respectable"; women of more conventional values than Stanton now made up the core of the movement and they were not happy to be associated with her biting criticism of Judaism and Christianity. Stanton, however, adopted a long-range perspective on that rejection; she noted, in her autobiography, that many of her past activities had been criticized at first but praised later on—and so it would be with *The Woman's Bible*.

Elizabeth Cady Stanton, from whose pen all of the following passages come, argued her case in a variety of ways. When it fit her purposes, she praised the biblical authors, such as the author of Genesis 1, for writing in a manner which suggested the equality of the sexes. At other times, she took a far more critical approach toward the Bible. Nor did she shrink from interpreting the biblical stories so that they demonstrated a feminist moral. Thus Jephthah's nameless daughter, if the women's movement could have reached her, might have said to her father, "Self-development is a higher duty than self-sacrifice." And the editor of Matthew would no doubt have been amazed to learn that the parable of the wise and foolish virgins was in actuality a lesson in "the cultivation of courage and self-reliance" for females. In these passages we see an image of a new kind of woman being forged which was in direct confrontation with the older views. The modern women's movement builds on Stanton's belief that woman's oppression cannot be overcome without her liberation from a false consciousness of her own potentialities and place in life. That today we see *The Woman's Bible* as a pioneering attack on the psychological and spiritual oppression of women is a vindication of Stanton's own faith.

From Elizabeth Cady Stanton, *The Woman's Bible*, Parts 1, 2, and Appendix (1895–98; reprinted—New York: Arno Press, 1972).

The Woman's Bible

THE OLD TESTAMENT

Genesis 1: 26, 27, 28:

. . . Here is the sacred historian's first account of the advent of woman; a simultaneous creation of both sexes, in the image of God. It is evident from the language that there was consultation in the Godhead, and that the masculine and feminine elements were equally represented. Scott in his commentaries says, "this consultation of the Gods is the origin of the doctrine of the trinity." But instead of three male personages, as generally represented, a Heavenly Father, Mother, and Son would seem more rational.

The first step in the elevation of woman to her true position, as an equal factor in human progress, is the cultivation of the religious sentiment in regard to her dignity and equality, the recognition by the rising generation of an ideal Heavenly Mother, to whom their prayers should be addressed, as well as to a Father.

If language has any meaning, we have in these texts a plain declaration of the existence of the feminine element in the Godhead, equal in power and glory with the masculine. The Heavenly Mother and Father! "God created man in his own image, male and female." Thus Scripture, as well as science and philosophy, declares the eternity and equality of sex. . . .

The above texts plainly show the simultaneous creation of man and woman, and their equal importance in the development of the race. All those theories based on the assumption that man was prior in the creation have no foundation in Scripture.

As to woman's subjection, on which both the canon and the civil law delight to dwell, it is important to note that equal dominion is given to woman over every living thing, but not one word is said giving man dominion over woman.

Here is the first title deed to this green earth giving alike to the sons and daughters of God. No lesson of woman's subjection can be fairly drawn from the first chapter of the Old Testament. . . .

Judges 11: 30–37:

A woman's vow, as we have already seen, could be disallowed at the pleasure of any male relative; but a man's was considered sacred even though it involved the violation of the sixth commandment, the violation of the individual rights of another human being. These loving fathers in the Old Testament, like Jephthah and Abraham, thought to make themselves specially pleasing to the Lord by sacrificing their children to Him as burnt offerings. If the ethics of their moral code had permitted suicide, they might with some show of justice have offered themselves, if they thought that the first-born kid would not do; but what right had they to offer up their sons and daughters in return for supposed favors from the Lord?

The submission of Isaac and Jephthah's daughter to this violation of their most sacred rights is truly pathetic. But, like all oppressed classes, they were ignorant of the fact that they had any natural, inalienable rights. We have such a type of womanhood even in our day. If any man had asked Jephthah's daughter if she would not like to have the Jewish law on vows so amended that she might disallow her father's vow, and thus secure to herself the right of life, she would no doubt have said, "No; I have all the rights I want," just as a class of New York women said in 1895, when it was proposed to amend the constitution of the State in their favor.

The only favor which Jephthah's daughter asks, is that she may have two months of solitude on the mountain tops to bewail the fact that she will die childless. Motherhood among the Jewish women was considered the highest honor and glory ever vouchsafed to mortals. So she was permitted for a brief period to enjoy her freedom, accompanied by young Jewish maidens who had hoped to dance at her wedding.

Commentators differ as to the probable fate of Jephthah's daughter. Some think that she was merely sequestered in some religious retreat, others that the Lord spoke to Jephthah as He did to Abraham forbidding the sacrifice. We might attribute this helpless condition of woman to the benighted state of those times if we did not see the trail of the serpent through our civil laws and church discipline.

This Jewish maiden is known in history only as Jephthah's daughter—she belongs to the no-name series. The father owns her absolutely, having her life even at his disposal. We often hear people laud the beautiful submission and the self-sacrifice of this nameless maiden. To me it is pitiful and painful. I would that this page of history were gilded with a dignified whole-souled rebellion. I would have had the daughter receive the father's confession with a stern rebuke, saying: "I will not consent to such a sacrifice. Your vow must be disallowed. You may sacrifice your own life as you please, but you have no right over mine. I am on the threshold of life, the joys of youth and of middle age are all before me. You are in the sunset; you have had your blessings and your triumphs; but mine are yet to come. Life is to me full of hope and of happiness. Better that you die than I, if the God whom you worship is pleased with the sacrifice of human life. I consider that God has made me the arbiter of my own fate and all my possibilities. My first duty is to develop all the powers given to me and to make the most of myself and my own life. Self-development is a higher duty than self-sacrifice. I demand the immediate abolition of the Jewish law on vows. Not with my consent can you fulfill yours." This would have been a position worthy of a brave woman. . . .

THE NEW TESTAMENT

"Great is Truth, and mighty above all things." 1 Esdras 4:41.

Does the New Testament bring promises of new dignity and of larger liberties for woman? When thinking women make any criticisms on their degraded position in the Bible, Christians point to her exaltation in the New Testament, as if, under their religion, woman really does occupy a higher position than under the Jewish dispensation. While there are grand types of women presented under both religions, there is no difference in the general estimate of the sex. In fact, her inferior position is more clearly and emphatically set forth by the Apostles than by the Prophets and the Patriarchs. There are no such specific directions for woman's subordination in the Pentateuch as in the Epistles.

We are told that the whole sex was highly honored in Mary being the mother of Jesus. Surely a wise and virtuous son is more indebted to his mother than she is to him, and is honored only by reflecting her superior characteristics. Why the founders of the Christian religion did not improvise an earthly Father as well as an earthly Mother does not clearly appear. The questionable position of Joseph is unsatisfactory. As Mary belonged to the Jewish aristocracy, she should have had a husband of the same rank. If a Heavenly Father was necessary, why not a Heavenly Mother? If an earthly Mother was admirable, why not an earthly Father? The Jewish idea that Jesus was born according to natural law is more rational than is the Christian record of the immaculate conception by the Holy Ghost, the third person of the Trinity. These Biblical mysteries and inconsistencies are a great strain on the credulity of the ordinary mind.

Matthew 25:1–12:

In this chapter we have the duty of self-development impressively and repeatedly urged in the form of parables, addressed alike to man and to woman. The sin of neglecting and of burying one's talents, capacities, and powers, and the penalties which such a course involve, are here strikingly portrayed.

. . . .It [this parable] fairly describes the two classes which help to make up society in general. The one who, like the foolish virgins, have never learned the first important duty of cultivating their own individual powers, using the talents given to them, and keeping their own lamps trimmed and burning. The idea of being a helpmeet to somebody else has been so sedulously drilled into most women that an individual life, aim, purpose and ambition are never taken into consideration. They oftimes do so much in other directions that they neglect the most vital duties to themselves.

We may find in this simple parable a lesson for the cultivation of courage and of self-reliance. These virgins are summoned to the discharge of an important duty at midnight, alone, in darkness, and in solitude. No chivalrous gentleman is there to run for oil and to trim their lamps. They must depend on themselves, unsupported, and pay the penalty of their own improvidence and unwisdom. Perhaps in that bridal procession might have been seen fathers, brothers, friends, for whose service and amusement the foolish virgins had wasted many precious hours, when they should have been trimming their own lamps and keeping oil in their vessels.

And now, with music, banners, lanterns, torches, guns, and rockets fired at intervals, come the bride and the groom, with their attendants and friends numbering thousands, brilliant in jewels, gold and silver, magnificently mounted on richly caparisoned horses—for nothing can be more brilliant than were those nuptial solemnities of Eastern nations. As this spectacle, grand beyond description, sweeps by, imagine the foolish virgins pushed aside, in the shadow of some tall edifice, with dark, empty lamps in their hands, unnoticed and unknown. And while the castle walls resound with music and merriment, and the lights from every window stream out far into the darkness, no kind friends gather round them to sympathize in their humiliation, nor to cheer their loneliness. It matters little that women may be ignorant, dependent, unprepared for trial and for temptation. Alone they must meet the terrible emergencies of life, to be sustained and protected amid danger and death by their own courage, skill, and self-reliance, or perish.

Woman's devotion to the comfort, the education, the success of men in general, and to their plans and projects, is in a great measure due to her self-abnegation and self-sacrifice having been so long and so sweetly lauded by poets, philosophers and priests as the acme of human goodness and glory.

Now, to my mind, there is nothing commendable in the action of young women who go about begging funds to educate young men for the ministry, while they and the majority of their sex are too poor to educate themselves, and if able, are still denied admittance into some of the leading institutions of learning throughout our land. It is not commendable for women to get up fairs and donation parties for churches in which the gifted of their sex may neither pray, preach, share in the offices and honors, nor have a voice in the business affairs, creeds and discipline, and from whose altars come for Biblical interpretations in favor of woman's subjection.

It is not commendable for the women of this Republic to expend much enthusiasm on political parties as now organized, nor in national celebrations, for they have as yet no lot or part in the great experiment of self-government.

In their ignorance, women sacrifice themselves to educate the men of their households, and to make of themselves ladders by which their husbands, brothers and sons climb up into the kingdom of knowledge, while they themselves are shut out from all intellectual companionship, even with those they love best; such are indeed like the foolish virgins. They have not kept their own lamps trimmed and burning; they have no oil in their vessels, no resources in themselves; they bring no light to their households nor to the circle in which they move; and when the bridegroom cometh, when the philosopher, the scientist, the saint, the scholar, the great and the learned, all come together to celebrate the marriage feast of science and religion, the foolish virgins, though present, are practically shut out; for what know they of the grand themes which inspire each tongue and kindle every thought? Even the brothers and the sons whom they have educated, now rise to heights which they cannot reach, span distances which they cannot comprehend.

The solitude of ignorance, oh, who can measure its misery!

The wise virgins are they who keep their lamps trimmed, who burn oil in their vessels for their own use, who have improved every advantage for their education, secured a healthy, happy, complete development, and entered all the profitable avenues of labor, for self-support, so that when the opportunities and the responsibilities of life come, they may be fitted fully to enjoy the one and ably to discharge the other.

These are the women who to-day are close upon the heels of man in the whole realm of thought, in art, in science, in literature, and in government. With telescopic vision they explore the starry firmament, and bring back the history of the planetary world. With chart and compass they pilot ships across the mighty deep, and with skilful fingers send electric messages around the world. In galleries of art, the grandeur of nature and the greatness of humanity are immortalized by them on canvas, and by their inspired touch, dull blocks of marble are transformed into angels of light. In music they speak again the language of Mendelssohn, of Beethoven, of Chopin, of Schumann, and are worthy interpreters of their great souls. The poetry and the novels of the century are theirs; they, too, have touched the keynote of reform in religion, in politics and in social life. They fill the editors' and the professors' chairs, plead at the bar of justice, walk the wards of the hospital, and speak from the pulpit and the platform.

Such is the widespread preparation for the marriage feast of science and religion; such is the type of womanhood which the bridegroom of an enlightened public sentiment welcomes to-day; and such is the triumph of the wise virgins over the folly, the ignorance and the degradation of the past as in grand procession they enter the temple of knowledge, and the door is no longer shut. . . .

APPENDIX

. . . The real difficulty in woman's case is that the whole foundation of the Christian religion rests on her temptation and man's fall, hence the necessity of a Redeemer and a plan of salvation. As the chief cause of this dire calamity, woman's degradation and subordination were made a necessity. If however, we accept the Darwinian theory, that the race has been a gradual growth from the lower to a higher form of life, and that the story of the fall is a myth, we can exonerate the snake, emancipate the woman, and reconstruct a more rational religion for the nineteenth century, and thus escape all the perplexities of the Jewish mythology as of no more importance than those of the Greek, Persian, and Egyptian.

18. Women and Marriage, Vatican Style: *The Casti Connubii*

The pronouncements of the papacy within the last century concerning women and sexuality were made in response to a variety of factors. The Vatican since the time of Leo XIII (1878–1903) had attempted to bring the Catholic church more into dialogue with the society of its time than Leo's predecessors had seen fit. Many social changes had taken place by the late nineteenth century concerning woman and her role. In some countries, such as England and America, the suffrage movement had made great strides. Thousands of females had joined the work force outside the home; they were spending part of their lives in a "man's world," with all the attendant privileges and responsibilities, not the least of which was earning their own money. In addition, various developments in contraception had taken place which gave to women (and men) greater control over their reproductive faculties than had been possible earlier.[1] And as the 1920s dawned, the movement toward sexual freedom for women, accompanied by a revolution in female dress, brought a new consciousness and style of life to young women.

For traditional Catholicism, these developments were unsettling. From Leo XIII to Pius XI, popes repudiated the Marxist critique of traditional marriage as a bourgeois institution. They expressed uneasiness at women's entrance into the world of professions and politics with the accompanying desertion of the home as the center of her existence, and appeared scandalized by the lack of modesty in female dress.[2] But the decisive shock to Catholic thinking came in the summer of 1930 when Anglican bishops meeting at Lambeth Palace issued a statement sanctioning the use of birth control for members of the Church of England. Their pronouncement was a blow to Catholics who felt that the Anglican communion, of all the Protestant denominations, was the one closest to their own. In response, Pius XI thought the time was at hand for a clarification of Catholic views on marriage.

The *Casti Connubii*, Pius's famous encyclical[3] on the subject, is structured around Augustine's analysis of the threefold "goods" of marriage. Under the first purpose of marriage as described by Augustine, offspring, Pius discussed the issues of birth control (forbidden as "against nature" and "intrinsically vicious"), abortion ("the direct murder of the innocent"), and sterilization. The second of Augustine's "goods," conjugal fidelity, was taken by Pius to exclude any kind of extramarital sexual experimentation. And the "sacramental bond" was interpreted by the pope, as it was by Augustine, to mean the prohibition of divorce except in very rare cases. Thus the church of the 1930s portrayed itself as retaining the same ideals of sexual morality upheld by the bishop of Hippo over 1500 years before.

A clearly formulated notion of the position of women is also present in the encyclical. Although Pius was aware that women in contemporary society were permitted more civil and legal rights than they had formerly enjoyed, he wished women to use these in such a way that the traditional idea of the female role, especially the function of wife and mother, was not overturned. Women are reminded that, despite the rights now granted to them, they are to be in "ready subjection" to the chief of the family, the husband. Husbands and children are to be the center of their existence. Activities in the larger world outside the home are sanctioned only insofar as they do not interfere with the calling of motherhood and do not injure the modesty and fragility of the "female temperament." Pius saw the feminist movement as offering women a false freedom and he condemned it. The liberty offered women under the feminist banner is considered to be "debasing" to the female character. Catholics are also warned against enthusiastically espousing the relaxation of the divorce laws; greater freedom of divorce is seen as not only damaging the family structure, but also as lowering the position of women, leaving them helpless and undefended in a ruthless male world. And in a section not included in the following passages from the encyclical, the state is called upon to aid the church by forbidding abortion and sterilization, and by helping to ensure youthful modesty.

The views of the *Casti Connubii* set the tone for Catholic attitudes in the years following. Various Vatican pronouncements clarified and developed the themes of the encyclical. Starting in the middle 1940s, Pius XII delivered a number of speeches on women's roles in which he stressed the spiritual equality of men and women and acknowledged the new social role of women, but upheld, in addition, the more traditional attitudes toward family life.[4] Perhaps the most important of these statements was "The Apostolate of the Midwife," issued in 1951, which, although it championed the church's stand against abortion and contraception in general, did permit the use of the "rhythm" method of birth control in some circumstances.[5]

In light of the rapid development and improvement of methods of contraception, many lay Catholics were hopeful when Pope Paul VI, in response to discussions concerning marriage and sexuality which took place at the Second Vatican Council,[6] set up a special commission to study the problem of contraception. Catholics throughout the world thought that perhaps there would be a change in viewpoint on the issue of contraception. Although the Majority Report of the Pope's commission recommended a relaxation of the church's strict attitude in view of newer understandings of "human nature," the personal values present in the marriage relationship, and the changed place of women in society, it did not meet with the Vatican's approval.[7] In response, Pope Paul VI issued the encyclical *Humanae Vitae* in 1968, which once again strongly condemned all forms of contraception except for the "rhythm" method and announced that even "rhythm" should be employed only in distressed circumstances.[8] The restrictiveness of this encyclical prompted a sharp response from Catholic laity and the more liberally minded clergy alike, and precipitated a crisis of confidence in the church with which Catholics are still dealing.[9]

On Christian Marriage

Encyclical Letter Casti Connubii, December 31, 1930

(10) Now when We come to explain, Venerable Brethren, what are the blessings that God has attached to true matrimony, and how great they are, there occur to Us the words of that illustrious Doctor of the Church whom We commemorated recently in Our encyclical Ad Salutem on the occasion of the fifteenth centenary of his death: "These," says St. Augustine, "are all the blessings of matrimony on account of which matrimony itself is a blessing: offspring, conjugal faith and the sacrament." And how under these three heads is contained a splendid summary of the whole doctrine of Christian marriage, the holy Doctor himself expressly declares when he said: "By conjugal faith it is provided that there should be no carnal intercourse outside the marriage bond with another man or woman; with regard to offspring, that children should be begotten of love, tenderly cared for and educated in a religious atmosphere; finally, in its sacramental aspect that the marriage bond should not be broken and that a husband or wife, if separated, should not be joined to another even for the sake of offspring. This we regard as the law of marriage by which the fruitfulness of nature is adorned and the evil of incontinence is restrained."

(11) Thus amongst the blessing of marriage, the child holds the first place. And indeed the Creator of the human race Himself, Who in His goodness wished to use men as His helpers in the propagation of life, taught this when, instituting marriage in Paradise, He said to our first parents, and through them to all future spouses: "Increase and multiply, and fill the earth." As St. Augustine admirably deduces from the words of the holy Apostle

From Pius XI, Casti Connubii ("On Christian Marriage") in The Church and the Reconstruction of the Modern World: The Social Encyclicals of Pius XI, ed. T. P. McLaughlin, Garden City: Doubleday & Co., Image Books, 1957).

St. Paul to Timothy when he says: "The Apostle himself is therefore a witness that marriage is for the sake of generation: 'I wish,' he says, 'young girls to marry.' And, as if someone said to him, 'Why?' he immediately adds: 'To bear children, to be mothers of families.'"...

(13) But Christian parents must also understand that they are destined not only to propagate and preserve the human race on earth, indeed not only to educate any kind of worshipers of the true God, but children who are to become members of the Church of Christ, to raise up fellow citizens of the saints, and members of God's household, that the worshipers of God and Our Saviour may daily increase.

(14) For although Christian spouses, even if sanctified themselves, cannot transmit sanctification to their progeny, nay, although the very natural process of generating life has become the way of death by which original sin is passed on to posterity, nevertheless, they share to some extent in the blessings of that primeval marriage of Paradise, since it is theirs to offer their offspring to the Church in order that by this most fruitful Mother of the children of God they may be regenerated through the laver of Baptism unto supernatural justice and finally be made living members of Christ, partakers of immortal life, and heirs of that eternal glory to which we all aspire from our inmost heart. . . .

(16) The blessing of offspring, however, is not completed by the mere begetting of them, but something else must be added, namely the proper education of the offspring. For the most wise God would have failed to make sufficient provision for children that had been born, and so for the whole human race, if he had not given to those to whom he had entrusted the power and right to beget them, the power also and the right to educate them. For no one can fail to see that children are incapable of providing wholly for themselves, even in matters pertaining to their natural life, and much less in those pertaining to the supernatural, but require for many years to be helped, instructed and educated by others. Now it is certain that both by the law of nature and of God this right and duty of educating their offspring belongs in the first place to those who began the work of nature by giving them birth, and they

are indeed forbidden to leave unfinished this work and so expose it to certain ruin. But in matrimony provision has been made in the best possible way for this education of children that is so necessary, for, since the parents are bound together by an indissoluble bond, the care and mutual help of each is always at hand.

(17) Since, however, we have spoken fully elsewhere on the Christian education of youth, let Us sum it all up by quoting once more the words of St. Augustine: "As regards the offspring, it is provided that they should be begotten lovingly and educated religiously,"—and this is also expressed succinctly in the Code of Canon Law—"The primary end of marriage is the procreation and the education of children." . . .

(26) Domestic society being confirmed, therefore, by this bond of love, there should flourish in it that "order of love," as St. Augustine calls it. This order includes both the primacy of the husband with regard to the wife and children, the ready subjection of the wife and her willing obedience, which the Apostle commends in these words: "Let women be subject to their husbands as to the Lord, because the husband is the head of the wife, as Christ is the head of the church."

(27) This subjection, however, does not deny or take away the liberty which fully belongs to the woman both in view of her dignity as a human person, and in view of her most noble office as wife and mother and companion; nor does it bid her obey her husband's every request if not in harmony with right reason or with the dignity due to a wife; nor, in fine, does it imply that the wife should be put on a level with those persons who in law are called minors, to whom it is not customary to allow free exercise of their rights on account of their lack of mature judgment, or of their ignorance of human affairs. But it forbids that exaggerated liberty which cares not for the good of the family; it forbids that in this body which is the family, the heart be separated from the head to the great detriment of the whole body and the proximate danger of ruin. For if the man is the head, the woman is the heart, and as he occupies the chief place in ruling, so she may and ought to claim for herself the chief place in love.

(28) Again, this subjection of wife to husband in its degree and

manner may vary according to the different conditions of persons, place and time. In fact, if the husband neglect his duty, it falls to the wife to take his place in directing the family. But the structure of the family and its fundamental law, established and confirmed by God, must always and everywhere be maintained intact. . . .

(53) And now, Venerable Brethren, We shall explain in detail the evils opposed to each of the benefits of matrimony. First consideration is due to the offspring, which many have the boldness to call the disagreeable burden of matrimony and which they say is to be carefully avoided by married people, not through virtuous continence (which Christian law permits in matrimony when both parties consent), but by frustrating the marriage act. Some justify this criminal abuse on the ground that they are weary of children and wish to gratify their desires without their consequent burden. Others say that they cannot on the one hand remain continent nor on the other can they have children because of the difficulties, whether personal or on the part of the mother or on the part of family circumstances.

(54) But no reason, however grave, may be put forward by which anything intrinsically against nature may become conformable to nature and morally good. Since, therefore, the conjugal act is destined primarily by nature for the begetting of children, those who in exercising it deliberately frustrate its natural power and purpose sin against nature and commit a deed which is shameful and intrinsically vicious.

(55) Small wonder, therefore, if Holy Writ bears witness that the Divine Majesty regards with greatest detestation this horrible crime and at times has punished it with death. As St. Augustine notes: "Intercourse even with one's legitimate wife is unlawful and wicked where the conception of the offspring is prevented. Onan, the son of Juda, did this and the Lord killed him for it."

(56) Since, therefore, openly departing from the uninterrupted Christian tradition, some recently have judged it possible solemnly to declare another doctrine regarding this question, the Catholic Church, to whom God has entrusted the teaching and defense of the integrity and purity of morals, standing erect in the midst of the moral ruin which surrounds her, in order that she may

preserve the chastity of the nuptial union from being defiled by this foul stain, raises her voice in token of her divine ambassadorship and through Our mouth proclaims anew: any use whatsoever of matrimony exercised in such a way that the act is deliberately frustrated in its natural power to generate life is an offense against the law of God and of nature, and those who indulge in such are branded with the guilt of a grave sin. . . .

(58) As regards the evil use of matrimony, to pass over the arguments which are shameful, not infrequently others that are false and exaggerated are put forward. Holy Mother Church very well understands and clearly appreciates all that is said regarding the health of the mother and the danger to her life. And who would not grieve to think of these things? Who is not filled with the greatest admiration when he sees a mother risking her life with heroic fortitude, that she may preserve the life of the offspring which she has conceived? God alone, all bountiful and all merciful as He is, can reward her for the fulfillment of the office allotted to her by nature, and will assuredly repay her in a measure full to overflowing.

(59) Holy Church knows well that not infrequently one of the parties is sinned against rather than sinning, when for a grave cause he or she reluctantly allows the perversion of the right order. In such a case there is no sin, provided that, mindful of the law of charity, he or she does not neglect to seek to dissuade and to deter the partner from sin. Nor are those considered as acting against nature who in the married state use their right in the proper manner, although on account of natural reasons either of time or of certain defects new life cannot be brought forth. For in matrimony as well as in the use of the matrimonial rights there are also secondary ends, such as mutual aid, the cultivating of mutual love, and the quieting of concupiscence which husband and wife are not forbidden to consider so long as they are subordinated to the primary end and so long as the intrinsic nature of the act is preserved.

(60) We are deeply moved by the sufferings of those parents who, in extreme want, experience great difficulty in rearing their children.

(61) However, they should take care lest the calamitous state of their external affairs should be the occasion for a more calamitous error. No difficulty can arise that justifies the putting aside of the law of God which forbids all acts intrinsically evil. There are no possible circumstances in which husband and wife cannot, strengthened by the grace of God, fulfill faithfully their duties and preserve in wedlock their chastity unspotted. . . .

(63) But another very grave crime is to be noted, Venerable Brethren, which regards the taking of the life of the offspring hidden in the mother's womb. Some wish it to be allowed and left to the will of the father or the mother; others say it is unlawful unless there are weighty reasons which they call by the name of medical, social, or eugenic "indication." Because this matter falls under the penal laws of the State by which the destruction of the offspring begotten but unborn is forbidden, these people demand that the "indication," which in one form or another they defend, be recognized as such by the public law and in no way penalized. There are those, moreover, who ask that the public authorities provide aid for these death-dealing operations, a thing which, sad to say, everyone knows is of very frequent occurrence in some places.

(64) As to the medical and therapeutic "indication" to which, using their own words, We have made reference, Venerable Brethren, however much We may pity the mother whose health and even life is gravely imperiled in the performance of the duty allotted to her by nature, nevertheless what could ever be a sufficient reason for excusing in any way the direct murder of the innocent? This is precisely what we are dealing with here. Whether inflicted upon the mother or upon the child, it is against the precept of God and the law of nature: "Thou shalt not kill." The life of each is equally sacred, and no one has the power, not even the public authority, to destroy it. It is of no use to appeal to the right of taking away life, for here it is a question of the innocent, whereas that right has regard only to the guilty; nor is there here question of defense by bloodshed against an unjust aggressor (for who would call an innocent child an unjust aggressor?); again there is no question here of what is called the "law of extreme

necessity" which could never extend to the direct killing of the innocent. . . .

(65) All of which agrees with the stern words of the Bishop of Hippo in denouncing those wicked parents who seek to remain childless, and, failing in this, are not ashamed to put their offspring to death: "Sometimes this lustful cruelty or cruel lust goes so far as to seek to procure sterilizing poisons, and if this fails, the foetus conceived in the womb is in one way or another smothered or evacuated, in the desire to destroy the offspring before it has life, or if it already lives in the womb, to kill it before it is born. If both man and woman are party to such practices they are not spouses at all; and if from the first they have carried on thus they have come together not for honest wedlock, but for impure gratification; if both are not party to these deeds, I make bold to say that either the one makes herself a mistress of the husband, or the other simply the paramour of his wife." . . .

(74) The same false teachers who try to dim the luster of conjugal faith and purity do not scruple to do away with the honorable and trusting obedience which the woman owes to the man. Many of them even go further and assert that such a subjection of one party to the other is unworthy of human dignity, that the rights of husband and wife are equal; wherefore, they boldly proclaim, the emancipation of women has been or ought to be effected. This emancipation, in their opinion, must be threefold, in the ruling of the domestic society, in the administration of family affairs and in the rearing of the children. It must be social, economic, physiological: physiological, that is to say, the woman is to be freed at her own good pleasure from the burdensome duties properly belonging to a wife as companion and mother (We have already said that this is not an emancipation but a crime); social, inasmuch as the wife being freed from the care of children and family, should, to the neglect of these, be able to follow her own bent and devote herself to business and even public affairs; finally economic, whereby the woman even without the knowledge and against the will of her husband may be at liberty to conduct and administer her own affairs, giving her attention chiefly to these rather than to children, husband and family.

(75) This, however, is not the true emancipation of woman, nor that rational and exalted liberty which belongs to the noble office of a Christian woman and wife; it is rather the debasing of the womanly character and the dignity of motherhood, and indeed of the whole family, as a result of which the husband suffers the loss of his wife, the children of their mother and the home and the whole family of an ever watchful guardian. More than this, this false liberty and unnatural equality with the husband is to the detriment of the woman herself, for if the woman descends from her truly regal throne to which she has been raised within the walls of the home by means of the Gospel, she will soon be reduced to the old state of slavery (if not in appearance, certainly in reality) and become, as amongst the pagans, the mere instrument of man.

(76) This equality of rights, which is so much exaggerated and distorted, must indeed be recognized in those rights which belong to the dignity of the human soul and which are proper to the marriage contract and inseparably bound up with wedlock. In such things undoubtedly both parties enjoy the same rights and are bound by the same obligations; in other things there must be a certain inequality and due accommodation, which is demanded by the good of the family and the right ordering and unity and stability of home life.

(77) As, however, the social and economic conditions of the married woman must in some way be altered on account of the changes in social intercourse, it is part of the office of the public authority to adapt the civil rights of the wife to modern needs and requirements, keeping in view what the natural disposition and temperament of the female sex, good morality, and the welfare of the family demand, and provided always that the essential order of the domestic society remain intact, founded as it is on something higher than human authority and wisdom, namely on the authority and wisdom of God, and so not changeable by laws or at the pleasure of private individuals. . . .

(85) The advocates of the neopaganism of today have learned nothing from the sad state of affairs, but instead, day by day, more and more vehemently, they continue by legislation to attack the

indissolubility of the marriage bond, proclaiming that the lawfulness of divorce must be recognized, and that the antiquated laws
should give place to a new and more humane legislation. Many
and varied are the grounds put forward for divorce, some arising
from the wickedness and the guilt of the persons concerned, others
arising from the circumstances of the case; the former they describe
as subjective, the latter as objective, in a word, whatever might
make married life hard or unpleasant. They strive to prove their
contentions regarding these grounds for the divorce legislation they
would bring about, by various arguments. Thus, in the first place,
they maintain that it is for the good of both parties that the one
who is innocent should have the right to separate from the guilty,
or that the guilty should be withdrawn from a union which is un-
pleasing to him and against his will. In the second place, they argue,
the good of the child demands this, for either it will be deprived
of a proper education or the natural fruits of it, and will too
easily be affected by the discords and shortcomings of the parents,
and drawn from the path of virtue. And thirdly, the common good
of society requires that these marriages should be completely dissolved which are now incapable of producing their natural results,
and that legal reparations should be allowed when crimes are to
be feared as the result of the common habitation and intercourse
of the parties. This last, they say, must be admitted to avoid the
crimes being committed purposely with a view to obtaining the
desired sentence of divorce for which the judge can legally loose
the marriage bond, as also to prevent people from coming before
the courts when it is obvious from the state of the case that they
are lying and perjuring themselves—all of which brings the court
and the lawful authority into contempt. Hence the civil laws, in
their opinion, have to be reformed to meet these new requirements,
to suit the changes of the times and the changes in men's opinions,
civil institutions and customs. Each of these reasons is considered
by them as conclusive, so that all taken together offer a clear proof
of the necessity of granting divorce in certain cases.

(86) Others, taking a step further, simply state that marriage,
being a private contract, is like other private contracts, to be left
to the consent and good pleasure of both parties, and so can be
dissolved for any reason whatsoever.

(87) Opposed to all these reckless opinions, Venerable Brethren, stands the unalterable law of God, fully confirmed by Christ, a law that can never be deprived of its force by the decrees of men, the ideas of a people, or the will of any legislator: "What God hath joined together, let no man put asunder." And if any man, acting contrary to this law, shall have put asunder, his action is null and void, and the consequence remains, as Christ Himself has explicitly confirmed: "Every one that putteth away his wife and marrieth another committeth adultery: and he that marrieth her that is put away from her husband committeth adultery." Moreover, these words refer to every kind of marriage, even that which is natural and legitimate only; for, as has already been observed, that indissolubility by which the loosening of the bond is once and for all removed from the whim of the parties and from every secular power is a property of every true marriage. . . .

(89) If, therefore, the Church has not erred and does not err in teaching this, and consequently it is certain that the bond of marriage cannot be loosed even on account of the sin of adultery, it is evident that all the other weaker excuses that can be and usually brought forward are of no value whatsoever. . . .

(90) To revert again to the expressions of Our predecessor, it is hardly necessary to point out what an amount of good is involved in the absolute indissolubility of wedlock and what a train of evils follows upon divorce. Whenever the marriage bond remains intact, then we find marriage contracted with a sense of safety and security, while, when separations are considered and the dangers of divorce are present, the marriage contract itself becomes insecure, or at least gives ground for anxiety and surprises. On the one hand we see a wonderful strengthening of good will and cooperation in the daily life of husband and wife, while, on the other, both of these are miserably weakened by the presence of a facility for divorce. Here we have at a very opportune moment a source of help by which both parties are enabled to preserve their purity and loyalty; there we find harmful inducements to unfaithfulness. On this side we find the birth of children and their tuition and upbringing effectively promoted, many avenues of discord closed amongst families and relations, and the beginnings of rivalry and jealousy easily suppressed; on that, very great obstacles to the

birth and rearing of children and their education, and many occasions of quarrels, and seeds of jealousy sown everywhere. Finally,
but especially, the dignity and position of women in civil and
domestic society are integrally restored by the former; while by
the latter they are shamefully lowered and the danger is incurred
"of their being considered outcasts, slaves of the lust of men." . . .

19. The Triumph of Patriarchalism in the Theology of Karl Barth

Karl Barth, the originator of what is often labeled "Neo-orthodox" theology, is considered by many to have been the most important Protestant thinker since Schleiermacher. Born in Basel, Switzerland in 1886, he received his theological education from such distinguished representatives of nineteenth-century German Liberalism as Adolph Harnack and Wilhelm Hermann. Protestant Liberalism of that era stressed the essential goodness of man's nature and his ability to assist God in bringing the Kingdom of brotherly love and peace to earth; in doing so, it underplayed the classical Christian understanding of God's mysterious Otherness and man's radical sinfulness.

Barth spent the years of the First World War preaching in the Swiss village of Safenwil. As he viewed the misery and anxiety of his war-weary flock, he came to see the impotence of Liberalism. He and his lifelong friend Edward Thurneysen turned for comfort and inspiration to the Bible, like "shipwrecked people whose everything had gone overboard."[1] In those years, Barth was beginning to understand the very point which "liberal theology had tended to obscure, namely, the fundamental discontinuity between God and man."[2] This dramatic shift in his thinking resulted in several editions of a theological exposition on Paul's epistle to the Romans. Barth's work on Romans, which is often cited as signaling the change from Liberalism to Neo-orthodoxy, emphasized the absolute disjunction between the Wholly Other God and man, upon whose sin God delivers a resounding "No!" The book made a sensation throughout Europe; Barth registered his own amazement at the response he had evoked by comparing his position to that of a man on "the dark staircase of a church tower" who reaches for the bannister but pulls the bell rope instead.[3]

But this was only the first of the shifts in Barth's theological viewpoint; another came during the 1930s, as he became increasingly concerned to voice the "Yes" of God's loving and reconciling acceptance of man as his "covenant-partner" in Jesus Christ, in whom "the humanity of God" is revealed. In retrospect, Barth wrote that his declamation of judgment on man's sin was appropriate at the time the Römerbrief appeared (he congratulates himself: "Well-roared, lion"),[4] but he sensed that another word was needed for the decades following. This new attitude governed the writing of the multivolumed Church Dogmatics, from which our selections are taken. In this theological masterpiece, Barth shows that he was constantly revising and rethinking his position. For someone who wrote thirteen volumes of dogmatics, he retained a remarkably "undogmatic" approach to his own work. As is often observed, Barth was no Barthian.

It is of course impossible to summarize the ideas of those thirteen volumes in these few pages, but some of the theological themes which touch upon his views of the male-female relationship can be noted. First of all, Barth's description of God gives us some clues to a proper understanding of human associations, for God is a Being who is in relationship. In the Old Testament, he pledges himself to be in covenant with Israel. The creation stories tell us of a God who wanted a counterpart, man. Even the doctrine of the Trinity testifies to the notion that God is not a solitary being, but even within his transcendent majesty is in relationship with himself.[5] When the Bible proclaims that man was made in God's image, we are to understand that he was fashioned as a social being. This "analogy of relation" between God and man has been called "the most pervasive and most formative" of all the principles in Barth's theology.[6]

Likewise, the biblical description of Christ informs us of what humans are to be like; Christ is "the secret truth about the essential nature of man."[7] One of Jesus' prime characteristics was that he gave himself willingly and freely *for* others, thus setting the pattern for our being *with* others.[8] Of course, we cannot be *for* others in the nonreciprocal way that Jesus was;[9] nonetheless, he exemplified the truly human life of relationship which sets the pattern for our associations with others.

There is a second reason why the biblical portrayal of Jesus is important for our lives: in the picture of Jesus' voluntary subordiation of himself to the Father, mankind is shown the radical obedience God demands (or, as Barth would say, "permits")[10] of us. Out of our Christological understanding, we move into the realm of ethics.[11] Out of God's doing comes the possibility of man's doing. "Faith" becomes "obedience."

Both in his divinity and his humanity, God has shown us that we were meant to be with and for others, to live in "cohumanity" (*Mitmenschlichkeit*). Man's humanity, for Barth, "consists in the determination of his being as a being with the other."[12] We are to look each other in the eye, says Barth, engage in mutual speech and hearing, and render each other help and assistance.[13] When we perform these actions, we are exhibiting our humanity as the *Mitmenschlichkeit* of which the male-female relation is the primary example.

Barth also wishes us to understand a second point about cohumanity: in all human relations, no matter how close the friendship or deep the intimacy, there is always an I and a Thou which do not merge but remain distinct from one another. There is no interchangeability of persons; the I does not swallow up the Thou, nor does the I grovel in self-abasement and slavery before the Other.[14] Neither of these two types of behavior represents *Mitmenschlichkeit*. Barth's stress on the preservation of this duality governs his insistence upon the affirmation and preservation of sexual discreteness.

For Barth is convinced that Gensis 1 and 2 relate a truth which is valid today as it was thousands of years ago: God created humans in two kinds, wanting us to understand that sexual differentiation is the most basic of all human distinctions.[15] Sexual difference represents a basic minimum duality to which we must stick. It is part of our "vocation," Barth affirms, to preserve the differences of masculinity and femininity.[16] He criticizes sharply all attempts to overcome or relax the borders between maleness and femaleness; in fact, he sees in such efforts blasphemous attempts to aspire to divinity. Thus Barth has no sympathy with the androgynous vision of feminists like Simone de Beauvoir[17] and is both puzzled by and wary of Schleiermacher's interest in exploring his own femaleness.[18] Likewise, he protests against all women who act as if they "want to be men."[19] To be a woman means that a female must respect the characteristics which define the male but not envy them nor wish to possess them herself; she must remember that "his strength and precedence are the reality without which she could not be woman."[20] Thus in discussing the creation story of Genesis 2, Barth writes that the text means that the woman "in her being and existence" belongs to the man. "She is ordained to be his helpmeet";[21] "she would not be woman if she had even a single possibility apart from being man's helpmeet."[22]

Accepting one's maleness or femaleness is only the first step in maintaining a correct sexual ethic. Even within the relation which God has ordained and from which neither male nor female must flee, a further command is given: man is to be superordinate, woman subordinate, man is A and woman is B, man is the initiator, woman the follower. This pattern, Barth thinks, has the sanction of the New Testament. He quotes Ephesians 5 with evident satisfaction: just as Christ is the "head" of the Christian community, the "bridegroom" for the "bride," so the man is the "head" of the sexual relationship.[23] To be fair to Barth, we must note his own emphasis: the woman is not subordinating herself to the man so much as she is to the order God has established, an order to which man *also* subordinates himself.[24] Yet a feminist would be quick to see that the "order" to which the man submits himself is one which emphasizes the characteristics men have displayed throughout history: assertiveness, initiative, and so forth, whereas the woman's subjection to the "order" leaves her in the position of oppression which has been her lot until recent times. Barth denies that women are inferior to men, nor does he sanction a male tyrannical role which encourages the woman to be a "pliable kitten."[25] Nonetheless, he asserts that God has commanded human relations to conform to a certain "order";[26] being "one in Jesus Christ" does not imply that sexual differentiation is negated,[27] as groups so diverse as some early Christian sects and the Shakers believed. Barth appears to be hampered in his attempt to think about male-female relations by his inability to imagine them in anything but sequential—one might almost say hierarchical—terms.[28]

Feminists, as one would expect, find Barth's views either infuriating or laughable. The traditional line of "secondary but not inferior status" status for women no longer will receive support from many educated females of the present era. Barth probably wished to affirm sexual differentiation and female subordination *without* implying female inferiority, but this, as the conservative theologian Paul Jewett has pointed out, was not a realized goal.[29] For all his cultural sophistication, Barth seems oblivious to the large variation in sexual roles and behavior as uncovered by psychosexual research. He speaks as if people were somehow basically determined in their functions and personality characteristics by their sex. The notion that there is a special "vocation" attached to one's sex is an idea which is particularly irksome to feminists. It is interesting that Barth, who was such a courageous defender of human rights in the face of Nazi oppression, cannot shake himself free from his conservatism on the subject of women. In the case of the Nazis, he was willing to defy the New Testament's injunctions on rebellion against governing authorities; feminists find it significant that he does *not* take a similar stance against the New Testament passages oppressive of women.

It has been suggested that part of Barth's difficulty with feminism stems from his views on the composition and correct interpretation of the Bible. Although he certainly was familiar with the results of biblical criticism, "he will not take seriously the historical conditioning which the subordination texts presuppose and promote. . . ."[30] Thus in the *Church Dogmatics*, he selects some of the more antifeminist passages—such as 1 Corinthians 11 and Ephesians 5—to undergird his views. n his discussion of these texts, he can even compare the superordination of men to Christ in his divinity, and the subordination of women to Christ in his humanity: lord and servant. Christ in his glorious divinity is like the male, in his humble servitude is like the female. "His is the place of man, and His the place of woman."[31] Presumably Barth wants us to think that Christ then represents *both* sexes, but his language rather conveys to contemporary women the message of female oppression. (And his position is not radically improved, in the eyes of feminists, by his notion that men must be subordinate to the divine order as well.)[32] He tells us—with remarkable lack of embarrassment—about some encounters he had in 1948 at the World Council of Churches meeting in Amsterdam. When the Commission on Women appropriated Paul's text on "no male and female" as its watchword, Barth felt compelled to remind it that Paul had said many other things about women which should be taken into consideration.[33] We could interpret Barth's remarks merely as an attempt to be "dialectical," but we think it was more than a commitment to the dialectical principle that led Barth to uphold the biblical verses which reinforce traditional attitudes toward women.

Would Barth have changed his mind had he lived longer and been more fully exposed to the ideas of the modern woman's movement? He remarked in *How I Have Changed My Mind* that if he were a young American theologian, he would write a theology of liberation. And he asked, "Will such a specific American theology one day arise? I hope so."[34] Barth's notion of "liberation" is so different from feminism's that it is dubious whether he would have accepted a work such as Mary Daly's *Beyond God the Father* as a contribution to liberation theology. But Barth was an open person and throughout his life maintained an unusual personal relationship with his collaborator Charlotte von Kirschbaum, who lived in the Barth household for many years. If one thinks that personal experience goes far to shape a person's ideology, it is conceivable to imagine that "grace" might have triumphed over Barth's patriarchalism.

(From Karl Barth, "The Doctrine of Creation," *Church Dogmatics*, vol. 3, sec. 4, ed. G. W. Bromiley and T. F. Torrance (Edinburgh: T. and T. Clark, 1961).

The Doctrine of Creation

. . . The command of God comes to man and woman in the relationship and order in which God created them to be together as His image, as the likeness of His covenant of grace, in the male or female existence which they gain in His eyes within the framework of their character as likeness and image. Thus it is the command of God itself which tells them what here and now is their male or female nature, and what they have to guard faithfully as such. As the divine command is itself free from the systematisation by which man and woman seek to order and clarify their thoughts about their differentiation, so, in requiring fidelity, it frees man and woman from the self-imposed compulsion of such systematisation. To what male or female nature must they both be true? Precisely to that to which they are summoned and engaged by the divine command—to that which it imposes upon them as it confronts them with its here-and-now requirement. As this encounters them, their particular sexual nature will not be hidden from them. And in this way the divine command permits man and woman continually and particularly to discover their specific sexual nature, and to be faithful to it in this form which is true before God, without being enslaved to any preconceived opinions.

The temptation which arises in face of this first and fundamental demand for fidelity has two forms. The first is that the sexes might wish to exchange their special vocations, what is required of the one or the other as such. This must not happen. . . . Of course, it is not a question of keeping any special masculine or feminine standard. We have just seen that the systematisations to which we might be tempted in this connexion do not yield any practicable imperatives. Different ages, peoples and cultures have had very different ideas of what is concretely appropriate, salutary and necessary in man and woman as such. But this does not mean that the distinction between masculine and non-masculine or feminine and unfeminine being, attitude and action is illusory. Just because the command of God is not bound to any standard it makes this distinction all the more sharply and clearly. This distinction insists upon being observed. It must not be blurred on either side. The command of God will always point man to his position and woman to hers. In every situation, in face of every task and in every conversation, their functions and possibilities, when they are obedient to the command, will be distinctive and diverse, and will never be interchangeable. . . .

But the temptation which we have to see and avoid in this connexion may take a very different form. The desire to violate fidelity to one's own sex does not now think in terms of an exchange with the nature and characteristics of the opposite sex. It aspires beyond its own and the opposite sex to a third and supposedly higher mode of being, possible to both sexes and indifferent to both. What is sought is a purely human being which is male or female only externally, incidentally and on a lower plane, in respect of psychological and biological conditioning. . . . It is a movement in which man and woman aspire to overcome their sexual and separated mode of existence and to transcend it by a humanity which is neither distinctively male nor female but both at once, or neither. . . .

. . . But the fact remains that if the divine command is valid and relevant in this sphere we must object no less earnestly to this view and the resultant conduct than to everything which necessarily entails effeminacy in the male or mannishness in the female. We can certainly accept the humanisation of this sphere, but not in such a way as would neutralise the sexes, for this would finally mean dehumanisation. Outside their common relationship to God, there is no point in the encounter and fellowship of man and woman at which even as man and woman they can also transcend their sexuality. . . . God is the One for them, and this very fact saves them from having to become one amongst themselves and prevents them from trying to do so. That God created man as male and female, and therefore as His image and the likeness of the covenant of grace, of the relationship between Himself and His people, between Christ and His community, is something which can never lead to a neutral It, nor found a purely external, incidental and transient sexuality, but rather an inward, essential and lasting order of being as He and She, valid for all time and also for eternity. . . .

We should include in the category of "flight from one's own sex" the conception and teaching which Simone de Beauvoir derived from the existentialism of J. P. Sartre and expounded in the two volumes of her *Le Deuxième Sexe* (1949), a book which is worth noting for all that is very pagan in spirit. The myth of the androgyne is not used in this case. But sexuality is definitely interpreted as a mere *condition* which is not necessary and proper to the human being and individual as such. It characterises merely the situation under the presupposition and by means of which, and in conflict with which, the human individual both male and female has again and again to affirm itself, to win and keep its freedom. Sexuality is not an absolute requirement like the physical basis of existence, nor like mortality an unshakeably fixed boundary of human life which cannot be thought away. *On ne naît pas femme, on le devient.* Woman becomes this under that presupposition and in the process of that conflict: by the mastery of her femininity in virtue of the human freedom in which she is born. Not even the necessity of continuing the race can make sexuality an essential condition of human life, for the phenomenon of parthogenesis and the existence of hermaphroditism in other spheres of nature proves that race-continuance is conceivable and possible in the human sphere as well by other than sexual means. Sexuality and its differentiation is only that of the situation which must be lived out in responsibility by the individual and transcended in freedom. This is more difficult of accomplishment for woman, since for man there is no conflict between his freedom and subjectivity on the one hand and his masculinity on the other, but unhindered by the imposed conditioning he can and does act as *homo faber*, as the creator of values, as a huntsman and warrior, conquering the world, and especially in so doing making woman (who is more hindered by her role as child bearer) his object, his other, whom he then no less artfully glorifies in all kinds of myths. Woman is still faced with the task of bringing her destiny as an autonomous human individual into accord with her special human conditioning, of getting to grips with her situation and mastering it, of abolishing that very myth of femininity which man has devised only for the purpose of maintaining his own control, of fulfilling her existence as *être humain*, feminine only pro-

visionally and not essentially. It is not a question of her happiness
but of her freedom. She must cut right across and transcend
the given conditions, which are of course only those of her
situation. To remain involved in feminine immanence, i.e., in
these given conditions, and in the setting of the masculine
myth of woman, or to lapse into this immanence, is for her the
absolute evil, no matter whether she elects to do so spontaneously
or whether she allows herself to be coerced into so doing by man,
i.e., under the pressure of the circumstances which he fashions.
It is unfortunately the case not only that man has made woman
his object but that she has to a large extent allowed him to do so
and thus willed it. But to-day she is in revolt in the interests of
an equal and fruitful encounter between herself and man in which
she will master her feminine situation just as man has always
mastered his in virtue of the easier conditions imposed upon him.
As there are negroes and Jews, so there are women. But as there is
no specifically negro soul or Jewish character, so there is no "eternal
feminine." In the last analysis we can only say of sexual differentiation that it is perhaps superfluous and will one day disappear, and
that even though it is for the time being strikingly evident it is
only a secondary reality in comparison with man's act of freedom.
In the words of Sartre, it is only "essence," not existence; and
"l'existence précède l'essence."

What are we to say to this? The book of Simone de Beauvoir
has its merits. Whatever reservations we may have in detail, the
description of the way in which man has made and still makes himself master of woman, the presentation of the myth with which
he invests her in this process and for this purpose, and the unmask-
ing of this myth, are all worthy of attention especially on the part
of men and not least of Christian theologians. Far too much has
been said about man and woman which, in view of the suggestions
of this book or the light which it casts, are better not said at all,
or only with caution and reserve. But this does not mean that we
can and may countenance the thesis of this book. For if Simone de
Beauvoir unmasks the myth of the woman and makes no use of
the idealistic myth of the androgyne, it is plain that she proclaims
another new myth so much the more powerfully and unreservedly

—that of the human individual who in the achievement of freedom overcomes his masculinity or her femininity, mastering it
from a superior plane, so that sexuality is only a condition by
which he is not finally conditioned, with which he can dispense
and whose operation he can in any case control. Even in the
masculine form presupposed by Simone de Beauvoir, is not this
individual a product of wishful thinking rather than a reality? Is
he not more a man-God or God-man than a real human figure?
Man no doubt dreams of that radiant victorious freedom from his
conditioning—and sometimes woman too, as *figura* shows. But
he does not live in it. Can it be well, therefore, to commend this
ideal to woman as one in the realisation of which she will achieve
her own emancipation and humanity? Why is it that the whole
emancipation programme of this woman, who in her way fights so
valiantly and skilfully, is still orientated on man, and particularly
on this highly unreal man? Can she really expect to call women
to repentance and conversion, let alone men, by proclaiming this
picture of man which is only a product of wishful thinking? Yet
in the last analysis we cannot criticise even this myth, for it lives
by other powers than its own inner necessity and consistency. We
can only recognise that it is a myth, and one which, although not
identical with that of the androgyne, is very closely related to it.
Indeed, it has the same basic *logos*—the freeing of man in the
form of his emancipation—and especially in this case the emancipation of woman—from sex. But in its execution, not to speak of its
relationship to the divine command, this liberation can only end
in the negation of real man, and therefore it cannot be a true
logos. . . .

We proceed to a second principle, which again extends to the
whole sphere. Looking now in the opposite direction, we maintain
that in obedience to the divine command there is no such thing
as a self-contained and self-sufficient male life or female life. In
obedience to the divine command, the life of man is ordered,
related and directed to that of the woman, and that of the woman
to that of the man. . . .

. . . It is always in relationship to their opposite that man and
woman are what they are in themselves. We must be clear that

relationship does not mean transition and dissolution. It does not
.mean a denial of one's own sex or an open or secret exchange with
its opposite. On the contrary, it means a firm adherence to this
polarity and therefore to one's own sex, but only in so far as such
adherence is not self-centred but expansive, not closed but open,
not concentric but eccentric. Relationship to woman in this sense
makes the man a man, and her relationship to man in this sense
makes the woman a woman. To become sexually awake, ripe and
active, to be true to one's own sex, means for both man and woman
to be awake to this polar relationship, ripe for it and active in it,
to remain true to it. To this extent our second principle corresponds
with the first, and the first can be properly grasped only in the
light of the second. It is the equivalence of the being of both sexes
with this relationship which legitimately replaces the many typo-
logies which have been attempted, and makes them completely
superfluous. . . .

As against this, everything which points in the direction of male
or female seclusion, or of religions or secular orders or communities,
or of male or female segregation—if it is undertaken in principle
and not consciously and temporarily as an emergency measure—is
obviously disobedience. All due respect to the comradeship of a
company of soldiers! But neither men nor women can seriously
wish to be alone, as in clubs and ladies' circles. Who commands
or permits them to run away from each other? That such an
attitude is all wrong is shown symptomatically in the fact that
every artificially induced and maintained isolation of the sexes
tends as such—usually very quickly and certainly morosely and
blindly—to become philistinish in the case of men and precious
in that of women, and in both cases more or less inhuman. It is
well to pay heed even to the first steps in this direction.

These first steps may well be symptoms of the malady called
homosexuality. This is the physical, psychological and social sickness, the phenomenon of perversion, decadence and decay, which
can emerge when man refuses to admit the validity of the divine
command in the sense in which we are now considering it. In
Romans 1, Paul connected it with idolatry, with changing the
truth of God into a lie, with the adoration of the creature instead

of the Creator (v. 25). "For this cause God gave them up into vile affections: for even their women did change the natural use into that which is against nature: and likewise also the man, leaving the natural use of the woman, burned in their lust one toward another; men with men working that which is unseemly, and receiving in themselves the recompence of their error which was meet" (vv. 26–27). From the refusal to recognise God there follows the failure to appreciate man, and thus humanity without the fellow–man (C.D., vol. 3, sec. 2, p. 229ff.). And since humanity as fellow–humanity is to be understood in its root as the togetherness of man and woman, as the root of this inhumanity there follows the ideal of a masculinity free from woman and a femininity free from man. And because nature or the Creator of nature will not be trifled with, because the despised fellow–man is still there, because the natural orientation on him is still in force, there follows the corrupt emotional and finally physical desire in which—in a sexual union which is not and cannot be genuine—man thinks that he must seek and can find in man, and woman in woman, a substitute for the despised partner. But there is no sense in reminding man of the command of God only when he is face to face with this ultimate consequence, or pointing to the fact of human disobedience only when this malady breaks out openly in these unnatural courses. Naturally the command of God is opposed to these courses. This is almost too obvious to need stating. It is to be hoped that, in awareness of God's command as also of His forgiving grace, the doctor, the pastor trained in psychotherapy, and the legislator and judge—for the protection of threatened youth—will put forth their best efforts. But the decisive word of Christian ethics must consist in a warning against entering upon the whole way of life which can only end in the tragedy of concrete homosexuality. We know that in its early stages it may have an appearance of particular beauty and spirituality, and even be redolent of sanctity. Often it has not been the worst people who have discovered and to some extent practised it as a sort of wonderful esoteric of personal life. Nor does this malady always manifest itself openly, or, when it does so, in obvious or indictable forms. Fear of ultimate consequences can give as little protection in this case, and condemnation may be as feeble a deterrent, as the thought of painful consequences in the case of fornication. What is needed is that the recognition of the divine command should cut sharply across the attractive beginnings. The real perversion takes place, the original decadence and disintegration begins, where man will not see his partner of the opposite sex and therefore the primal form of fellow-man, refusing to hear his question and to make a responsible answer, but trying to be human in himself as sovereign man or woman, rejoicing in himself in self-satisfaction and self-sufficiency. The command of God is opposed to the wonderful esoteric of this *beata solitudo*. For in this supposed discovery of the genuinely human man and woman give themselves up to the worship of a false god. It is here, therefore, that for himself and then in relation to others each must be brought to fear, recollection and understanding. This is the place for protest, warning and conversion. The command of God shows him irrefutably—in clear contradiction to his own theories—that as a man he can only be genuinely human with woman, or as a woman with man. In proportion as he accepts this insight, homosexuality can have no place in his life, whether in its more refined or cruder forms. . . .

We shall now take a third step, again with reference to the whole sphere of the relationship of man and woman. It brings us to the most delicate of the general questions which call for consideration at this point. The disjunction and the conjunction of man and woman, of their sexual independence and sexual inter-relationship, is controlled by a definite order. As the attitude and function of the man and those of the woman must not be confused and interchanged but faithfully maintained, and as on the other hand they must not be divorced and played off against each other but grasped and realised in their mutual relatedness, so they are not to be equated, nor their relationship reversed. They stand in a sequence. It is in this that man has his allotted place and woman hers. It is in this that they are orientated on each other. It is in this that they are individually and together the human creature as created by God. Man and woman are not an A and a second A whose being and relationship can be described like the two halves of an hour glass, which are obviously two, but absolutely equal and therefore interchangeable. Man and woman are an A and a B, and cannot, therefore, be equated. In inner dignity and right, and therefore in human dignity and right, A has not the slightest advantage over B, nor does it suffer the slightest disadvantage. What is more, when we say A we must with equal emphasis say B also, and when we say B we must with equal emphasis have said A. We have considered this equality of man and woman as carefully as possible in our first two propositions, and not one iota of it must be forgotten or abrogated as we now turn in the third to the order in which their being no less than their being in fellowship is real, and therefore to the requirement of the divine command in so far as it includes the observance of this order. Man and woman are fully equal before God and therefore as men and therefore in respect of the meaning and determination, the imperilling, but also the promise, of their human existence. They are also equal in regard to the necessity of their mutual relationship and orientation. They stand or fall together. They become and are free or unfree together. They are claimed and sanctified by the command of God together, at the same time, with equal seriousness, by the same free grace, to the same obedience and the reception of the same benefits. Yet the fact remains—and in this respect there is no simple equality—that they are claimed and sanctified as man and woman, each for himself, each in relation to the other in his own particular place, and therefore in such a way that A is not B but A, and B is not another A but B. It is here that we see the order outside which man cannot be man nor woman be woman, either in themselves or in their mutual orientation and relationship.

Every word is dangerous and liable to be misunderstood when we try to characterise this order. But it exists. And everything else is null and void if its existence is ignored, if we refuse to recognise it as an element in the divine command, if it is left to chance. If order does not prevail in the being and fellowship of man and woman—we refer to man and woman as such and in general, to the rule which is valid both in and outside love and marriage—the only alternative is disorder. All the misuse and misunderstanding to which the conception of order is liable must not prevent us from considering and asserting the aspect of reality to which it points.

A precedes B, and B follows A. Order means succession. It means preceeding and following. It means super- and sub-ordination. But when we say this we utter the very dangerous words which are unavoidable if we are to describe what is at issue in the being and fellowship of man and woman. Let us proceed at once to the very necessary explanation. When it is a question of the true order which God the Creator has established, succession, and therefore precedence and following, super- and sub-ordination, does not mean any inner inequality between those who stand in this succession and are subject to this order. It does indeed reveal their inequality. But it does not do so without immediately confirming their equality. In so far as it demands subjection and obedience, it affects equally all whom it concerns. It does not confer any privilege or do any injustice. It lays a duty on all, but it also gives to all their right. It does not deny honour to any, but gives to each his own honour.

Thus man does not enjoy any privilege or advantage over woman, nor is he entitled to any kind of self-glorification, simply because in respect of order he is man, and therefore A, and thus precedes and is superior in relation to woman. This order simply points him to the position which, if he is obedient, he can occupy only in humility, or materially only as he is ordered, related and directed to woman in preceding her, taking the lead as the inspirer, leader and initiator in their common being and action. He cannot occupy it, then, for himself, let alone against her, or in self-exaltation, let alone in exaltation over her and therefore to her degradation, but as he humbles himself in obedience to the command which concerns them both, as he first frees himself from sexual self-sufficiency and takes seriously his orientation on woman, as he first enters into fellowship with her, as he first bows before the common law of humanity as fellow-humanity. Only as he accepts her as fellow-man, only together with her, can he be the first in his relationship to her—the first in a sequence which would have no meaning if she did not follow and occupy her own place in it. If it is understood in any other way, and not as a primacy of service, the preeminence of man is not the divine order but a particular form of human disorder. The exploitation of this order by man, in consequence of which he exalts himself over woman, making himself her lord and master and humiliating and offending her so that she inevitably finds herself oppressed and injured, has nothing whatever to do with divine order. It is understandable that woman should protest and rebel against this exploitation, although she ought to realise at once that here as elsewhere protesting and rebelling are one thing and the way from disorder to order quite another. It cannot be a question of woman attaining her rights as opposed to man and his, but of man's understanding the order and sequence and therefore the obligation in which he is the first, of his primarily submitting and rendering obedience to the common law instead of standing upon his own rights, of his not neglecting in his own favour—or his own disfavour—the required initiative of service in the common cause of humanity, but of assuming and discharging it. By simply protesting and rebelling, woman, even though she were a thousand times in the right, does not affirm and respect the order under which she also stands and by which alone she can vindicate her rights. Indeed, it may well be that her protesting and rebelling spring from the same source of contempt for order with which man offends her so deeply. The real service which she ought to render in this matter—indirectly in her own favour—is certainly not yet performed by the mere fact of her opposing man when he turns order into disorder.

For woman does not come short of man in any way, nor renounce her right, dignity and honour, nor make any surrender, when theoretically and practically she recognises that in order she is woman, and therefore B, and therefore behind and subordinate to man. This order gives her her proper place, and in pride that it is hers, she may and should assume it as freely as man assumes his. She, too, has to realise that she is ordered, related and directed to man and has thus to follow the initiative which he must take. Nor is this a trifling matter. Properly speaking, the business of woman, her task and function, is to actualise the fellowship in which man can only precede her, stimulating, leading and inspiring. How could she do this alone, without the precedence of man? How could she do it for herself and against him? How could she reject or envy his precedence, his task and function, as the one who stimulates, leads and inspires? To wish to replace him in this, or to do it with him, would be to wish not to be a woman. She does not admit any false superiority on his part when she not merely grants him this primacy of service, for it can be nothing more, but is glad that man has and exercises this function in the common service of the common cause of humanity, he himself being also subject to order in his own place. Why should not woman be the second in sequence, but only in sequence? What other choice has she, seeing she can be nothing at all apart from this sequence and her place within it? And why should she desire anything else, seeing this function and her share in the common service has its own special honour and greatness, an honour and greatness which man in his place and within the limits of his function cannot have? It is then settled—if such things can be settled—that the honour and greatness peculiar to her position, the honour and greatness possible to her in her subordinate role, cannot possibly exceed his? At least there can be no doubt that the subordination about which woman is entitled to complain is certainly not that which is envisaged in the divine order in which she has second place as woman. On the other hand the establishment of an equality with man might well lead to a state of affairs in which her position is genuinely and irreparably deplorable because both it and that of man are as it were left hanging in the void. If she occupies and retains her proper place, she will not merely complain even when man for his part does not keep to his place and thus encroaches upon her rights. The goodness and justice of the divine order are not transformed into evil and injustice even for those who have to suffer from its misunderstanding and abuse by others. Even then it is better that she on her side should not infringe but observe it. If there is a way of bringing man to repentance, it is the way of the woman who refuses to let herself be corrupted and made disobedient by his disobedience, but who in spite of his disobedience maintains her place in the order all the more firmly. . . .

But let us now return to our discussion of obedience to the divine command and therefore observance of the order. We referred to the mature woman. This woman will never let herself be pushed into the role of the compliant wife, whether she has to do with

the strong or the tyrannical man. She will endorse the strength of
the strong man which is the strength of his sense of responsibility
and service, and successfully or otherwise she will negate the
tyranny of the tyrant. She will do both because she is an independent element in the order which binds both man and woman.
The mature woman is as such the woman who knows and takes
her proper place, not in relation to man but in relation to the order.
She realises that as between man and woman there can be no
question of claim and counter-claim or the brutal struggle for
power, but of rivalry only in regard to the right following of the
path common to both but specifically allotted to each. Therefore,
while she compares herself to the man, she will not compare her
place and right to his. If she is challenged by him, it is not whether
his attitude and function might not equally well be hers, but
whether she is truly fulfilling the position and function assigned her.
If she is orientated on him, it is not with the intention of imitating
him, but with that of doing her part in fellowship with him. In
this self-knowledge there is no resignation on the part of woman.
By it she asserts rather her independence, showing her mastery,
her true equality with man. There can be in it no shadow of sad-
ness and resignation and therefore no spark of rebellion even in
relation to the tyrannical and weak man. In face of an erring man
the mature woman will not only be sure of herself in her quiet
self-restriction, but she will also know her duty and witness towards
him. Successfully or otherwise—and we now turn over another
leaf—she is in her whole existence an appeal to the kindness of
man. In human relationships kindness is not the same thing as
condescension. It means the free impulse in which a man interests
himself in his neighbour because he understands him and is aware
of his obligation towards him. The self-restricting woman appeals
to the kindness of man. She puts him under an obligation to be
kind. The opposite is also true, but in this respect the advantage is
perhaps with woman. She may win the respect of man. If he is
capable of this at all, it is in face of the mature and therefore self-
restricting woman. He understands such a woman, not condescend-
ingly, or superciliously, or complacently in respect of her pliability,
but with a sincere and non-patronising respect for the inde-

pendence, mastery and equality which she thus evinces. Such a woman puts man under an obligation. He can and must take such a one seriously. If anything can disturb his male tyranny and there fore his male weakness, if anything can challenge him to goodness and therefore to the acceptance of woman, it is encounter with the self-restricting woman. Why? Because her maturity is displayed in her self-restriction. She need not wait for the kind man to know and limit herself, as he need not wait for the modest woman to be kind. For kindness belongs originally to his particular responsibility as a man. But we come to the point where woman may in fact be the educator of man, so long, be it noted, as she does not evade her proper subordination. And now the circle may be closed. For the kind man, who is instructed in kindness by the self-knowledge and self-restriction of the woman, is identical with the strong man with whom we commenced this discussion. What is manly strength if not the power with which man in his relationships with woman may in obedience to the order of things seize responsibility and take the initiative? As a strong man he confirms the order, the order in which woman in her place is not simply subordinate to him, but stands at his side.

20. Radical Feminism, Radical Religion: Mary Daly

Although the nineteenth-century suffrage movement resulted in the ratification in 1920 of a constitutional amendment giving woman the right to vote, it accomplished less than what some of its partisans had hoped. Elizabeth Cady Stanton, for example, had envisioned the movement as ushering into American life far-reaching social changes; the realization of that vision was hampered by the course of events in the early twentieth century.

Probably several factors contributed to the failure of those dreams. Many women who joined the suffrage campaign in its closing stages concentrated their efforts solely on winning the vote; so important was that issue to them that they neglected to address themselves to the social, economic, and psychological changes which would be required before a genuine equality of the sexes was reached.[1] And although the 1920s saw the abandonment of double standard sexual morality, the norm of domestic life—marriage and family—remained basically the same for the flappers as it had been for their mothers and grandmothers.

The Depression of the next decade resulted in a scarcity of jobs; women were encouraged to retreat from the labor market so that male "breadwinners" could find positions. The period of the Second World War did see thousands of American women going to work outside the home, some of them taking jobs traditionally reserved for men, but upon the signing of the armistice, they relinquished their positions and returned to domesticity. The postwar period has been described as the nadir of feminism in America. Women flocked to the suburbs, immersed themselves in the home, children, and volunteer activities, and adopted the gospel of popular Freudianism regarding their appropriate sexual roles.

With the birth of radical politics in the 1960s, American women sprang to life again. Many young females became involved in student, civil rights, and antiwar movements. But as that decade wore on, veteran female activists came to realize that these movements were not the liberating forces they had hoped. Women's services as coffee-makers and envelope-lickers were gratefully received by their male colleagues, but policy was being made elsewhere. In particular, many women came to feel that the men in these movements were sexually exploitative.[2] By 1967, some radical women were gathering for discussion and analysis of their own situation: what it meant to be female at that time and place in American history.

And to the political analyses of these women were added the questions of others. A grass-roots feminist movement was taking shape all over the country. Housewives who, a decade before had gladly traded their independence for the joys of suburban motherhood suddenly started asking themselves and each other, "What is wrong? I have everything I dreamed of, yet I feel empty and unfulfilled." Betty Friedan's *The Feminine Mystique* was the classical expression of this "housewife's syndrome," which she called "the problem that has no name."[3]

Lastly, the federal government in the 1960s was becoming alert to the discrimination against women which American law up to that point had tolerated. Beginning with Title VII of the 1964 Civil Rights Act (which forbade discrimination in federally regulated employment on various grounds, including that of sex, "unless sex is a bona fide occupational qualification"), the executive, legislative, and judicial branches of government all took steps to assure to women equal opportunity under the law in various pursuits of life.[4]

Out of these three streams was born the modern feminist movement, which soon incorporated itself in a wide range of organizations, from the reformist National Organization for Women to the Radical Feminists and the Redstockings. Many spheres of American life were analyzed and criticized by women who saw themselves as carrying forward the unfinished aims of nineteenth-century feminism. Not only did they ask that laws be changed to eliminate discrimination against females, they investigated other aspects of social life. They sought greater freedom of choice for individuals in their domestic arrangements, more and better child-care facilities, and the elimination of sex-role stereotyping in children's literature and in the public schools. They asked for the right to control their own reproductive functions and determine their own sexuality. They criticized the image of woman presented through the mass media and encouraged young females to resist the pressures exerted upon them to devote themselves to the cultivation of physical beauty rather than to self-development and personal accomplishment.

Growing awareness of all these issues contributed to the undertaking of a feminist analysis and criticism of religion. The argument for extending the feminist critique to Christianity has been put cogently by Elizabeth Farians:

> The basic argument for women's rights is justice. The hardness of the line is most evident in relation to the church. The church itself, i.e,. its doctrine, practice and law, cannot be excepted. Justice does not admit of exception. If something is due, it is due. If women have rights, they have rights in the church the same as anywhere else.[5]

Acting on this understanding, women undertook two campaigns in regard to Christianity. On the one hand, they began to rebel against the practices of the church which had forced them into subordinate roles—the cookie-bakers and Sunday School teachers—and had excluded them from the centers of power and the opportunity to shape polity and doctrine. It was painfully obvious that some denominations did not ordain women to the ministry at all; others which did rarely gave them positions of importance in the more prestigious churches. The movement for women's ordination—and steps to ensure full equality with male ministers once ordination is attained—is one of the present goals of feminists in religious life.[6]

But feminists have also undertaken an analysis of the beliefs

and ideals of Christianity, past and present. Here again they found
the church to be lacking. Despite the claims of Christianity that
God is "above sex," it has characteristically depicted and referred
to God as "He," and the sacred writings have been interpreted to
show how "He" commands the subordination of women. Even
the ethical arguments of theologians have rarely taken into account
women's experience with and attitudes on the issues which concern
them the most, such as contraception and abortion. These are
but two of the topics which have been singled out by women
freshly appraising Christianity's message.

One of the most articulate of the feminist critics of Christianity
is Mary Daly, a theology professor at Boston College, who caught
public attention in 1968 with her book, The Church and the
Second Sex. In that work, she denounced the sexist attitudes and
practices of Christianity, particularly Roman Catholicism, but
remained optimistic that the church would endeavor to correct its
past injustice toward women. Her position shifted rather rapidly
in the years thereafter to a more negative estimate of traditional
Christianity and its willingness to undergo self-correction. In the
following article, and especially in her most important work to
date, Beyond God the Father: Toward a Philosophy of Women's
Liberation,[7] she presents us with a far-reaching feminist analysis
of the Christian religion.

Although many might imagine that Daly in this book was con-
structing an "antitheology," the book in fact follows with rigorous
precision the classical Christian outline of a systematic theology;
she discusses, in order, God, creation, Fall, Christ and Redemption,
ethics, the church, and eschatology. But the content of these
doctrines emerges in startling contrast to the meanings given them
by orthodox Christian theologians. Far from extolling God the
Father, Daly proclaims that his death is necessary for the liberation of women; the Supreme Phallus, as she puts it, must be cut
away.[8] Her point is not just the one made by earlier thinkers who
affirmed the nonsexual nature of God; rather, she is proceeding
from the intuition that as long as God is perceived as male, then
"the male is God."[9] Theology, in other words, serves as a justification for human values; hence, the "maleness" of God tends to

uphold the patriarchal order. Daly does not object to God-talk, but insists that the Deity can be better described as ultimate reality and meaning, the power of being, as a process, not a person[10]— phrases reminiscent of Tillich and Whitehead, to whom she is theologically indebted. Insofar as Daly understands the women's movement to be a spiritual phenomenon,[11] such language, she thinks, is appropriate.

Likewise, her interpretation of creation and Fall is a radical one. Classical Christian teaching posited that mankind had been created as free but had abused that freedom in its Fall into sin, which took place as early as the days of Adam and Eve in Eden. For Daly, sin, Fall, and freedom are set in a new configuration. As far back as history takes us, we find the "original sin of sexism" present in the world, wreaking its destructive effects upon women.[12] What is needed at present, in fact, is a "Fall"—a "Fall" into freedom,[13] in which we exorcise the evil associated traditionally with womankind and cease affirming the values which males have projected onto us. Only then will Eve learn to name herself, to become all she can be. We are to define ourselves not by some mythic character who was blamed for the primordial sin, but by the ideal of womanhood which still looks to the future for its realization.

From this "original sin of sexism" we cannot find liberation through a male symbol, the God-Man.[14] We must rather redeem ourselves by repudiating the "myth of feminine evil," and by refusing to give our energies and support to the "structures and ideologies of patriarchy."[15] Only then will we understand that God was not incarnate just in one particular male, Jesus of Nazareth; the Power of Being, rather, is present in all persons.[16] Daly views this healing process as a "movement toward androgynous being," in which both men and women will strive for the "completeness of human being."[17]

The male orientation of classical Christianity also resulted in an ethics which overlooked women's experience.[18] The "unholy Trinity" of rape, genocide, and warfare,[19] which were condoned in various ways by traditional theologies, needs to be replaced by a new Trinity of "love, power, and justice"[20]—a scheme Daly borrows from Tillich but corrects with the rueful note that women have been all too given to self-abasing "love"; they need now to affirm power and justice more ardently. The kinds of ethical issues with which women grapple (for instance, abortion),[21] are ones of which men have no direct experience, yet they are the persons who have dictated the rules under which females have suffered.

For the traditional notion of the church, Daly substitutes the community of sisterhood, struggling against "the social extension of the male Incarnation myth, as this has been objectified in the structures of political power."[22] The following article presents us with a vision of what such a community means for Daly. And lastly, far from looking to the return of Jesus as the signal of the eschaton's arrival, Daly anticipates the coming of "female presence,"[23] women breaking through to a new consciousness, a new life which will include a "covenant" with the whole cosmos (ecological issues pertain to this topic).[24] Radical feminism, she concludes, is the "final cause"—the Aristotelian term for the purpose, goal, and explanation—of human existence, because it alone can demonstrate that sexism is the basic model and source for all oppression, and it alone can open up to our consciousness the striving for a nonhierarchical, nonoppressive society.[25] This, then, is Daly's hope for the world "beyond God the Father."

As one might expect, *Beyond God the Father* was received with varying degrees of enthusiasm. One feminist called it "brilliant and profoundly provocative;"[26] a male writer, on the other hand, dubbed it a "misbegotten and silly book" which reveals the "fascism of the dyspeptic feminist intellectual who wants a world created in her own image and likeness."[27]

From the article, "The Women's Movement: An Exodus Community," we have excerpted a sermon Daly gave at Harvard Memorial Church in 1971. As she pointed out, it was the first time a woman had ever preached at a Sunday service in that church for its entire history of 336 years! At the conclusion of the service, an "exodus" was staged in which those committed to the search for a new community favorable to women exited from "the land of the fathers." That the experience was one of great significance for the participants is revealed in the letters some of them wrote afterwards, in which they spoke of their feeling that they had arrived as

"whole persons for the first time,"[28] that they left the church to go
to their faith.[29] The theme of the sermon—the women's movement
as an "exodus"—demonstrates how ancient religious events and
concepts can be interpreted in the context of twentieth-century
feminism.

The Women's Movement:
An Exodus Community

Sisters and other esteemed members of the congregation:

There are many ways of refusing to see a problem—such as
the problem of the oppression of women by society in general and
religion in particular. One way is to make it appear trivial. For
example, one hears: "Are you on that subject of women again
when there are so many *important* problems—like war, racism,
pollution of the environment." One would think, to hear this,
that there is no connection between sexism and the rape of the
Third World, the rape of the Blacks, or the rape of land and water.
Another way of refusing to see the problem of the oppression of
women is to particularize it. For instance, one hears: "Oh, that's
a Catholic problem. The Catholic church is so medieval." One
would imagine, to listen to this, that there is no patriarchy around
here. Another method of refusing to see is to spiritualize, that is, to
refuse to look at concrete oppressive facts. There is a significant
precedent for this in Christian history: Paul wrote that "in Christ
there is neither male nor female," but was not exactly concerned
about social equality for women. The repetition of that famous
line from Paul by would-be pacifiers of women invites the response
that even if "in Christ there is neither male nor female," everywhere
else there damn well is. Finally, some people, especially academics,
attempt to make the problem disappear by universalizing it. One
frequently hears: "But isn't the *real* problem *human* liberation?"
The difficulty with this is that the words spoken may be "true,"

From Mary Daly, "The Women's Movement: An Exodus Community,"*Religious Education* 67, (September/October 1972): 327–
333.

but when used to avoid the issue of sexism they are radically untruthful.

There *is* a problem. It is this: There exists a world-wide phenomenon of sexual caste, which is to be found not only in Saudi Arabia but also in Sweden. This planetary sexual caste system involves birth-ascribed, hierarchically ordered groups whose members have unequal access to goods, services, prestige, and physical and mental well-being. This exploitative system is masked by sex role segregation. Thus it is possible for a woman with a Ph.D. to fail to recognize any inequity in church regulations which forbid her to serve Mass while permitting a seven year old retarded boy to do so. Sexual caste is masked also by women's duality of status, for women have a derivative status stemming from relationships with men, which serves to hide our infrahuman condition as women. Finally, it is masked by ideologies and institutions that alienate women from our true selves, deluding us with false identifications, sapping our energies, deflecting our anger and our hope.

It is easy, then, to fail to see the problem of sexual caste. Moreover, patriarchal religion has made it more difficult to see through the injustices of the system by legitimating and reinforcing it. The long history of legitimation of sexism by religion is too well known to require detailed repetition here. I need not recite those infamous Pauline passages on women. I need not allude to the misogynism of the church Fathers—for example, Tertullian, who informed women in general: "You are the devil's gateway," or Augustine, who opined that women are not made to the image of God. I can omit reference to Thomas Aquinas and his numerous commentators and disciples who defined women as misbegotten males. I can overlook Martin Luther's remark that God created Adam lord over all living creatures but Eve spoiled it all. I can pass over the fact that John Knox composed a "First Blast of the Trumpet against the Monstrous Regiment of Women." All of this, after all, is past history.

Perhaps, however, we should take just a cursory glance at more recent history. Pope Pius XII more or less summarized official ecclesiastical views on women when he wrote that "the mother who complains because a new child presses against her bosom seeking nourishment at her breast is foolish, ignorant of herself, and unhappy." In another address he remarked that "she loves it the more, the more pain it has cost her." It may be objected, however, that in the year 1970 the official Catholic position leaped into the twentieth century, for in that year chaste lay women (c-h-a-s-t-e) willing to take vows of chastity were offered special consecration in what was called the answer to the modern world's obsession with sex. . . . The question unasked was: Just whose obsession is this?

Meanwhile on the Protestant front things have not really been that different. Theologian Karl Barth proclaimed that woman is ontologically subordinate to man as her "head." Dietrich Bonhoeffer in his famous *Letters and Papers from Prison*, in which he had proclaimed the attack of Christianity upon the adulthood of the world to be pointless, ignoble, and unchristian—in this very same volume—insists that women should be subject to their husbands.

Theology which is overtly and explicitly oppressive to women is by no means a thing of the past. Exclusively masculine symbolism for God, for the notion of divine "incarnation" in human nature, and for the human relationship to God reinforces sexual hierarchy. Tremendous damage is done, particularly in ethics, when theologians construct one-dimensional arguments that fail to take women's experience into account. This is evident in biased ethical arguments concerning abortion—for example, those of some well-known professors at this university. To summarize briefly the situation: The entire conceptual apparatus of theology, developed under the conditions of patriarchy, has been the product of males and serves the interests of sexist society.

To a large extent in recent times the role of the church in supporting the sexual caste system has been assumed by psychoanalysis. Feminists have pointed out that it is by no accident that Freudian theory emerged as the first wave of feminism was cresting. This was part of the counterrevolution, the male backlash. Psychoanalysis has its own creeds, priesthood, spiritual counseling, its rules, anathemas, and jargon. Its power of psychological intimidation is enormous. Millions who might smile at being labeled "heretic" or "sinful" for refusing to conform to the norms of sexist society can be cowed and kept in line by the labels "sick," "neurotic," or "unfeminine." This Mother Church of contemporary secular patriarchal religions has sent its missionaries everywhere, not excluding the traditional churches themselves.

It isn't "prudent" for women to see all of this. Seeing means that everything changes: the old identifications and the old securities are gone. Therefore the ethic that is emerging in the women's movement is not an ethic of prudence but one whose dominant theme is existential courage. This is the courage to see and to be in the face of the nameless anxieties that surface when a woman begins to see through the masks of sexist society and to confront the horrifying fact of her own alienation from her authentic self.

The courage to be and to see that is emerging in the women's revolution expresses itself in sisterhood—an event which is new under the sun. The so-called "sisterhoods" of patriarchy were and are in fact mini-brotherhoods, serving male interests and ideals. The ladies' auxiliaries of political parties, college sororities, religious orders of nuns—all have served the purposes of sexist society. In contrast to these, the new sisterhood is the bonding of women for liberation from sex role socialization. The very word itself says liberation and revolution.

There is no reason to think that sisterhood is easy. Women suffer from a duality of consciousness, as do the members of all oppressed groups. That is, we have internalized the image that males have created of "the woman," and this is in constant conflict with our authentically striving selves. One of the side effects of this duality is a kind of paralysis of the will. This is sometimes experienced as fear of ridicule, or of being considered abnormal, or—more basically—simply of being rejected, unwanted, unloved. Other effects of this dual consciousness are self-depreciation and emotional dependence. All of this is expressed in feminine antifeminism—the direction by women of our self-hatred toward each other. Each of us has internalized the "male chauvinist pig." It exists inside our heads and it is a devil that must be exorcised and exterminated.

How can we do this? For women, the first salvific moment comes when we realize the fact of our exploitation and oppression. But—and this is an important "but"—unless the insight gives birth to externalized action it will die. This externalized action, or *praxis*, authenticates insight and creates situations out of which new knowledge can grow. It must relate to the building of a new community, to the bonding of women in sisterhood.

Sisterhood is both revolutionary and revelatory. By refusing—together—to be objects, we can break down the credibility of sex stereotyping and bring about a genuine psychic revolution. By the same token, sisterhood is revelation. The plausibility of patriarchal religion is weakening. Nietzsche, the prophet, asked: "What are these churches now if they are not the tombs and sepulchres of God?" Nietzsche's misogynism did not permit him to see that the God who had to die was the patriarchal tyrant. Women who are "getting it together" are beginning to see that as long as God is imaged exclusively as male, then the male can feel justified in playing God. The breakdown of the idols of patriarchal religion, then, is consequent upon women's new consciousness. Out of our courage to be in the face of the absence of these idols—in the face of the experience of non-being—can emerge a new sense of transcendence, that is, a new and more genuine religious consciousness. This means that a transvaluation of values can take place. Faith, instead of being blind acceptance of doctrines handed down by authority, can be a state of ultimate concern that goes beyond bigotry. Hope, instead of being reduced to passive expectation of a reward for following rules allegedly set down by the Father and his surrogates, can be a communal creation of the future. Love, instead of being abject acceptance of exploitation, can become clean and free, secure in the knowledge that the most loving thing we can do in an oppressive situation is to work against the structures that destroy both the exploited and the exploiter. The transvaluation of values that is implied in the revolution of sisterhood touches the very meaning of human life itself. It may be the key to turning our species away from its course of destroying life on this planet.

Sisterhood, then, is in a very real sense an anti-church. In creating a counter-world to the society endorsed by patriarchal religion women are at war with sexist religion *as sexist*. This is true whether we concern ourselves directly with religion or not. Women whose consciousness has been raised are spiritual exiles whose sense of transcendence is seeking alternative expressions to those available in institutional religion.

Sisterhood is also functioning as church, proclaiming dimensions of truth which organized religion fails to proclaim. It is a space set apart, in which we can be ourselves, free of the mendacious contortions of mind, will, and feeling demanded of us "out there." It is a charismatic community, in which we experience prophecy and healing. It is a community with a mission to challenge the distortions in sexually unbalanced society, to be a counter-force to the prevailing sense of reality by building up a new sense of reality. Finally, sisterhood is an *exodus community* that goes away from the land of our fathers—leaving that behind because of the promise in women that is still unfulfilled. It is an exodus community that, perhaps for the first time in history, is putting our own cause—the liberation of women—*first*. It is a positive refusal to be co-opted any more—a positive refusal based on the prophetic insight that the sisterhood of women opens out to universal horizons, pointing outward to the sisterhood of man.

Sisters:

The sisterhood of man cannot happen without a real exodus. We have to go out from the land of our fathers into an unknown place. We can this morning demonstrate our exodus from sexist religion —a break which for many of us has already taken place spiritually. We can give physical expression to our exodus community, to the fact that we must go away.

We cannot really belong to institutional religion as it exists. It isn't good enough to be token preachers. It isn't good enough to have our energies drained and co-opted. Singing sexist hymns, praying to a male god breaks our spirit, makes us less than human. The crushing weight of this tradition, of this power structure, tells us that we *do not even exist*.

The women's movement is an exodus community. Its basis is not merely in the promise given to our fathers thousands of years ago. Rather its source is in the unfulfilled promise of our mothers' lives, whose history was never recorded. Its source is in the promise of our sisters whose voices have been robbed from them, and in our own promise, our latent creativity. We can affirm now our promise and our exodus as we walk into a future that will be our own future.

Sisters—and brothers, if there are any here: Our time has come. We will take our own place in the sun. We will leave behind the centuries of silence and darkness. Let us affirm our faith in ourselves and our will to transcendence by rising and walking out together.

Notes

1. Introduction

1. Karl Barth, *Church Dogmatics* vol. 3, sec. 4, ed. and trans. G. W. Bromiley and T. F. Torrance (Edinburgh: T. & T. Clark, 1961), p. 171.

2. Bachofen's famous theory was set forth in *Myth, Religion and Mother Right* (1861; reprint ed. Princeton: Princeton University Press, 1967).

3. Among Morgan's works are *Ancient Society* (1877), *Houses and Houselife of the American Aborigines* (1881), and *The Indian Journals, 1859–62* (1959).

4. See, for example, Joan Bamberger, "The Myth of Matriarchy," in M. Z. Rosaldo and L. Lamphere, eds., *Woman, Culture and Society* (Stanford: Stanford University Press, 1974). Some twentieth-century women (e.g., Elizabeth Gould Davis, *The First Sex* [New York: G. P. Putnam's Sons, 1971]) have sought to establish the historical credibility of matriarchy, but their theories have not received confirmation from the scholarly community. Such books have nonetheless served as imaginative inspiration to some feminists who see in them the message that patriarchy is not a future inevitability.

5. The "economic" interpretation of sexual relations received its classic expression in Friedrich Engels, *The Origin of the Family, Private Property and the State* (1884; reprint ed., New York: International Press, 1942). Engels wrote, "The modern individual family is founded on the open or concealed domestic slavery of the wife. . . ." (p. 65). His formula for the overcoming of patriarchy was putting females into the public labor market, which he understood would involve "the abolition of the monogamous family as the economic unit of society" (p. 66).

6. See M. Kay Martin and Barbara Voorhies, *Female of the Species* (New York: Columbia University Press, 1975).

7. For an attempt to "periodize" the development of sexual relationships, see Herbert W. Richardson, *Nun, Witch, Playmate: The Americanization of Sex* (New York: Harper and Row, 1971).

8. See, for example, Aristotle's discussion of friendship in Books 8 and 9 of the *Nicomachean Ethics*. The highest kind of friendship, one based on

"virtue," is that in which the persons are similar to each other (1156b). Since most husbands and wives are not equals, the wife cannot be a true friend (an "other self" [1166a]) to her spouse. Aristotle admits that there are exceptional cases in which the relation might be based on "virtue" rather than on "utility" or "pleasure" (1162a).

9. There has been considerable scholarly debate on the position of women in fifth-century Athens: to what extent *did* they lead secluded lives? See footnotes 6 and 7, p. 277 below for a list of some relevant materials.

10. Aeschylus, *Choephori*, 11. 594–638. The "myth of feminine evil" is explored by H. R. Hays in *The Dangerous Sex: The Myth of Feminine Evil* (New York: G. P. Putnam's Sons, 1964).

11. Judges 16.

12. For various scholarly views on the origins of the Olympian goddesses and their original connections—or lack of connections—with fertility, see Martin Nilsson, *A History of Greek Religion* (Oxford: Clarendon Press, 1952); Martin Nilsson, *The Minoan-Mycenean Religion and its Survival in Greek Religion* (2nd rev. ed. New York: Biblo and Tanner, 1971); and Abel W. Persson, *The Religion of Greece in Pre-Historic Times* (Berkeley: University of California Press, 1942).

13. Sarah Pomeroy, *Goddesses, Whores, Wives and Slaves: Women in Classical Antiquity* (New York: Schocken Books, 1975), pp. 4–9. As Pomeroy points out (p. 8), none of the female Olympians gives us a picture of a "fully realized female." The distribution of desirable characteristics among a number of females rather than their concentration in one being is appropriate to a patriarchal society. The dictum of Demosthenes (59, 118–122) indicates how female functions might be distributed on the human level: "We have *hetairai* for our enjoyment, concubines to serve our person, and wives to bear legitimate children."

14. Although, as pointed out by Joseph Blenkinsopp, *Sexuality and the Christian Tradition* (Dayton: Pflaum Press, 1969), the celibacy of the Hebrew God meant that the understanding of human sexuality "is no longer derived from mythical archetypes but from reflection on experience" (p. 25).

15. Judges 19.

16. Aeschylus, *Eumenides*, 11. 657–661.

17. Genesis 16, 18, 21, 29 and 1 Samuel 1.

18. "Regressions" we will take to mean a return to patriarchal or traditional values at a time when more liberal views of the status of women had already been expressed.

19. The "enthusiasts" would do well to note the words of D. S. Bailey, "Christianity displayed from the first a marked inclination towards conservatism" on matters relating to women and marriage (*Sexual Relation in Christian Thought* [New York: Harper & Bros., 1959], p. 6), and those of Rosemary R. Ruether, "Misogynism and Virginal Feminism in the Fathers of the Church," in *Religion and Sexism: Images of Woman in the Jewish and Christian Traditions*, ed. R. R. Ruether (New York: Simon and Schuster, 1974): the position

of the married woman in Christianity fell below that of women in late antiquity. "Thus the frequent claim that Christianity elevated the position of woman must be denied. It actually lowered the position of woman compared to more enlightened legislation in later Roman society as far as the married woman was concerned, and elevated woman only in her new 'unnatural' and antifemale role as 'virgin' " (p. 165).

20. For views of the developing freedom of Roman women, see J. P. V. D. Balsdon, Roman Women: Their History and Habits (London: The Bodley Head, 1962), and Sarah Pomeroy, Goddesses, Whores.

21. See in particular Leonard Swidler, "Jesus Was a Feminist," Catholic World 212 (January 1971): 177–183.

22. For example, Luke 8:1–3; Acts 9:36–43; Acts 18:18–28; Philippians 4:3.

23. Sarah Pomeroy, Goddesses, Whores, pp. 79–81, and Louis Epstein, Sex Laws and Customs in Judaism, 2nd ed. (New York: Ktav, 1967), chap. 4.

24. Ecclesiastical legislation directed against "spiritual marriage" appears as early as the third century.

25. Jean Daniélou, The Ministry of Women in the Early Christian Church (London: Faith Press, 1961), pp. 16–23; D. S. Bailey, Sexual Relation in Christian Thought, pp. 66–69; George Tavard, Woman in Christian Tradition (Notre Dame: University of Notre Dame Press, 1973), pp. 94–95.

26. See Elaine Pagels, "What Became of God the Mother? Conflicting Images of God in Early Christianity," forthcoming, Signs.

27. Clement of Alexandria, "Who Is the Rich Man That Shall Be Saved?, 37" Ante-Nicene Fathers, vol. 2, ed. A. Roberts and J. Donaldson (Grand Rapids: William B. Eerdmans Publishing Company, 1967), p. 601.

28. See the selections from Jerome and Augustine below.

29. Church literature from the early second century on denounces these practices in explicit terms. See John Noonan, Contraception: A History of its Treatment by the Catholic Theologians and Canonists (New York: New American Library, 1967), chap. 3.

30. See Elizabeth Clark, "Sexual Politics in the Writings of John Chrysostom," forthcoming in The Anglican Theological Review.

31. See below, pp. 61–62.

32. See the discussion of this point in Rosemary Ruether, "Misogynism and Virginal Feminism," pp. 160–161.

33. Sarah Pomeroy, Goddesses, Whores. . . , pp. 84–86, 169.

34. Joan Morris, The Lady Was a Bishop; The Hidden History of Women with Clerical Ordination and the Jurisdiction of Bishops (New York: The Macmillan Company, 1973).

35. For a variety of viewpoints on the rise of romantic love, see C. S. Lewis, The Allegory of Love (Oxford: Oxford University Press, 1936); Robert Flacelière, Love in Ancient Greece (New York: Crown Press, 1962); Maurice Valency, In Praise of Love (New York: The Macmillan Company, 1958); and John C. Moore, Love in Twelfth Century France (Philadelphia: University of Pennsylvania Press, 1972).

36. Robert Flacelière, *Love in Ancient Greece,* chap. 3, and Maurice Valency, *In Praise of Love,* pp. 5–6, 15.

37. For a criticism of the view that the exaltation of Mary contributed to a rise in the status of real women, see Mary Daly, *The Church and the Second Sex* (New York: Harper & Row, 1968), pp. 46ff.

38. "The most important instance of the church identified with a woman is, of course, that of the bride in the Canticles. It is in this love affair between God and His church that we find the strongest antidote to the anti-femininism of theologians, since it forces the male writer and his audience to identify with the female role." Joan M. Ferrante, *Woman As Image in Medieval Literature from the Twelfth Century to Dante* (New York: Columbia University Press, 1975), p. 26.

39. See below, p. 86.

40. See pp. 134 ff.

41. See Walter M. Abbott, S. J., ed., *The Documents of Vatican II* (New York: Guild Press, 1966), pp. 249–258, for the relevant portions of "The Church in the Modern World" (*Gaudium et Spes*).

42. Spiritualistic movements throughout Christian history have tended to give a fuller role to women; Montanism is a prime example from the early centuries of Christianity.

43. For Barth's views on Schleiermacher, see p. 242.

44. See John Noonan, *Contraception,* pp. 469 and 485.

45. See below, pp. 165 ff.

46. See below, pp. 221–224.

2. Aeschylus: Queens, Goddesses, Furies

1. See the fascinating interpretation of Orestes, "the epitome of the fifth century Athenian," who rejects his mother and devotes himself to his father, in Philip E. Slater's *The Glory of Hera: Greek Mythology and the Greek Family* (Boston: Beacon Press, 1968), p. 192. Slater uses the Greek myths to show that the principal strains in "the Greek family system were in cross-sex parent-child dyads, as both cause and consequence of the sex antagonism prevailing in the culture as a whole" (p. 399). For a critique of Slater's thesis by a classical scholar, see Sarah B. Pomeroy, *Goddesses, Whores, Wives, and Slaves: Women in Classical Antiquity* (New York: Schocken Books, 1975), pp. 95–96.

2. George D. Thomson, *Aeschylus and Athens: A Study in the Social Origins of Drama* (New York: Haskell House, 1967), p. 286.

3. See the article on "Erinyes" in *The Oxford Classical Dictionary,* ed. N. G. L. Hammond and H. H. Scullard, 2nd ed. (Oxford: Clarendon Press, 1970), pp. 406–407.

4. George Thomson, *Aeschylus and Athens,* sees in the subordination and denunciation of women an important principle in Aeschylus's notion of a society based on private property. Inheritance is through the male line and

women are viewed as so many chattels for ensuring the correct application of the inheritance law. Thomson notes that Plato and Aristophanes, attacking the problem from a different viewpoint, "perceived that the abolition of private property would involve the emancipation of woman" (p. 288).

5. Athena's case presents an interesting parallel with one we find in early Christianity: females who devote themselves to Christian virginity are said to be "manly" or even to have "become males." Such women were thought of as spiritual equals to men, unlike other women, who, by their involvement with sexual and reproductive functions, could never attain the status of the male.

6. For example, Arnold W. Gomme, "The Position of Women in Athens in the 5th and 4th C.B.C.," *Essays in Greek History and Literature* (Oxford: B. Blackwell, 1937). His position has been upheld more recently by Donald C. Richter, "The Position of Women in Classical Athens," *Classical Journal* 67 (1971), pp. 1–8. See also Marilyn B. Arthur, "Early Greece: The Origins of the Western Attitude toward Women," *Arethusa* 6 (1973): 7–58.

7. See Sarah Pomeroy, *Goddesses*; also Robert Flacelière, *Daily Life in Greece at the Time of Pericles* (New York: Macmillan Company, 1965) and *Love in Ancient Greece* (New York: Crown, 1962); and Hans Licht (pseud.), *Sexual Life in Ancient Greece* (New York: Barnes and Noble, 1953).

8. Pomeroy, *Goddesses*, p. x, and chap. 8. J. P. V. D. Balsdon, *Roman Women: Their History and Habits* (London: The Bodley Head, Ltd., 1962), pp. 14–15, gives a somewhat rosier picture of the freedom of Roman women.

3. The Old Testament

1. Phyllis Bird, "Images of Women in the Old Testament," *Religion and Sexism: Images of Woman in the Jewish and Christian Traditions*, ed. Rosemary R. Ruether (New York: Simon and Schuster, 1974), p. 41.

2. Phyllis Trible, "Good Tidings of Great Joy: Biblical Faith Without Sexism," *Christianity and Crisis* 34, no. 1 (February 4, 1974): 12.

3. See the selection given below, pp. 265–271.

4. Some scholars think that women had more freedom in the earlier days of Hebrew society but that it became progressively curtailed in the postexilic period. Louis Epstein, *Sex Laws and Customs in Judaism*, 2nd ed. (New York: Ktav, 1967), pp. 5, 13.

5. Elizabeth Mary MacDonald, *The Position of Women as Reflected in Semitic Codes of Law* (Toronto: University of Toronto Press, 1931).

6. H. R. Hays, *The Dangerous Sex: The Myth of Feminine Evil* (New York: G. P. Putnam's Sons, 1964).

7. See Herbert Richardson, *Nun, Witch, Playmate: The Americanization of Sex* (New York: Harper and Row, 1974), pp. 21–22.

8. See Elizabeth Cady Stanton's assessment of that story below, pp. 219–220.

9. See M. Kay Martin and Barbara Voorhies, *Female of the Species* (New York: Columbia University Press, 1975).

10. Of course, the image can be read the other way around. Thus Samuel Terrien can point out, "Toward a Biblical Theology of Womanhood," *Religion in Life* (Autumn 1973), p. 327 that the covenant between Yahweh and Israel could never have been described as a "marriage" unless womanhood was viewed as not degrading.

11. David M. Feldman, *Birth Control in Jewish Law* (New York: New York University Press, 1968), p. 104.

12. See, for example, Tertullian, *On the Apparel of Women* 1.

13. Phyllis Trible, "Depatriarchalizing in Biblical Interpretation," *Journal of the American Academy of Religion* 41 (1973): 35–42.

14. Phyllis Trible, "Good Tidings," p. 16.

4. The New Testament

1. Leonard Swidler, "Jesus Was a Feminist," *Catholic World* 212 (January 1971): 177–183.

2. Tom F. Driver, "Sexuality and Jesus," *New Theology, no. 3,* ed. M. Marty and D. Peerman (New York: The Macmillan Company, 1966), pp. 118–132; William Phipps, *Was Jesus Married? The Distortion of Sexuality in the Christian Tradition* (New York: Harper & Row, 1970) and, by the same author, *The Sexuality of Jesus: Theological and Literary Perspectives* (New York: Harper & Row, 1973).

3. The Greek text of this verse says (in translation) "neither Jew nor Greek, neither slave nor free, no male and female." The change of wording in the last phrase indicates that Paul was calling to mind the words of Genesis 1:27, that God had created mankind as "male and female." English translations of the verse do not usually bring out this distinction.

4. Biblical translators usually render this word as "deaconess," although there is no reason, based on the Greek text, why she should not rather be called a "deacon."

5. For a discussion of leadership roles for women in the early church, see André Dumas, "Biblical Anthropology and the Participation of Women in the Ministry of the Church," *World Council of Churches' Statement Concerning the Ordination of Women* (Geneva: The World Council of Churches, 1964), pp. 12–40; Jean Daniélou, S. J., *The Ministry of Women in the Early church* (London: Faith Press, 1961); and Haye van der Meer, S. J., *Women Priests in the Catholic Church? A Theological-Historical Investigation* (Philadelphia: Temple University Press, 1973).

6. Elaine H. Pagels, "Paul and Women: A Response to Recent Discussion," *Journal of the American Academy of Religion* 42 (1974): 542.

7. For example, Robin Scroggs, "Paul and the Eschatological Woman," *Journal of the American Academy of Religion* 41 (1972): 283–303; also a more popular version of the same argument, "Paul: Chauvinist or Liberationist?" *The Christian Century* 89 (March 15, 1972): 307–309. A recent article simply concludes that 1 Corinthians 11:2–16 in its entirety is an interpolation.

See William O. Walker, Jr., "I Corinthians 11:2–16 and Paul's Views Regarding Women," *Journal of Biblical Literature* 94 (1975): 94–110. The most recent production on this theme is Derwood C. Smith, "Paul and the Non-Eschatological Woman," *Ohio Journal of Religious Studies* 4, no. 1 (1976): 11–18.

8. Scroggs, "Paul and the Eschatological Woman," p. 284.

9. The above-mentioned articles by Scroggs and Pagels have been the chief items in the debate so far. Scroggs, attempting to claim Paul for women's liberation, argues that Paul thought that the old order had passed away and the new world had arrived with the coming of Christ; Christians were living an eschatological existence in which male dominance had been brought to an end. He relies heavily on Paul's break with traditional Jewish understandings of marriage in 1 Corinthians 7 as indicating Paul's eagerness for women's emancipation. Even the headcoverings of 1 Corinthians 11 are viewed by Scroggs not as a sign of women's inferiority, but as signaling woman's entrance to the eschatological order of freedom. His argument has been answered by Elaine Pagels, a feminist scholar noted especially for her work in Gnosticism. She questions whether there can be such a term as *eschatological woman*: surely the eschaton, for Paul, meant that sexual differences would become irrelevant. Moreover, she claims, Paul's view of marriage in 1 Corinthians 7 is not one which stresses the "liberty" involved, ·as Scroggs suggests, but the "bondage" which prohibits the partners from devoting their full energies to the Lord. And 1 Corinthians 11, she points out, contains too many allusions to female subordination for it to be used as a text affirming the equality of women; if anything, it represents Paul reverting to traditional notions of women's place in the social order. Whatever theoretical ideas Paul may have had about women's equality, he did nothing, as far as we know, to change the social structures which have contributed to their subordination. She concludes that feminists had better look to themselves (and even to Professor Scroggs!) rather than to Paul for inspiration on how to handle the difficulties of women in our own era (p. 547).

10. Such as castration. See Elaine Pagels, "Paul and Women," p. 541.

11. Joan Morris, *The Lady Was a Bishop; The Hidden History of Women with Clerical Ordination and the Jurisdiction of Bishops* (New York: The Macmillan Company, 1973).

12. Constance F. Parvey, "The Theology and Leadership of Women in the New Testament," *Religion and Sexism: Images of Woman in the Jewish and Christian Traditions*, ed. Rosemary R. Ruether (New York: Simon and Schuster, 1974), p. 146.

13. "The Protevangelium of James," Edgar Hennecke, *New Testament Apocrypha*, vol. 1, ed. W. Schneemelcher (Philadelphia: The Westminster Press, 1963), p. 385.

14. The "immaculate conception" does not mean that Mary's mother was also a virgin; rather, the conception took place in the usual manner, but God intervened so that original sin would not be passed to the child.

15. For a feminist discussion of Mary's role and function in Christianity, see Mary Daly, *Beyond God the Father: Toward a Philosophy of Women's Liberation* (Boston: Beacon Press, 1973), pp. 81–92.

16. See the selections below from the writings of the early church fathers, especially Jerome, pp. 56–68.

5. Clement of Alexandria and the Gnostics:
Women, Sexuality and Marriage in Orthodoxy and Heterodoxy

1. Quotation marks are put around this word advisedly. What the church later considered "orthodox" teaching was, in the second century, still a matter of opinion.

2. "On Marriage" is part of a larger work by Clement, the *Stromateis*, usually translated as *Miscellanies*, which suggests the rather rambling, unsystematic character of Clement's musings on various aspects of Christian life and thought. Clement worked in the closing years of the second century and the opening ones of the third, largely in Alexandria, where church tradition tells us he was associated with a Christian catechetical school. Part of Clement's enduring interest lies in his attempt to link the best of classical learning and culture with the Christian tradition, to demonstrate that Christianity could appeal to the more cultivated and educated classes within Greco-Roman society rather than only to the rabble, as some of his contemporaries affirmed.

3. Hans Jonas, *The Gnostic Religion*, 2nd ed. (Boston: Beacon Press, 1963), p. 32. Jonas's book provides a number of the most important primary source documents from the Gnostic sects as well as lucid commentary by one of the foremost scholars of Gnosticism.

4. W. E. G. Floyd in *Clement of Alexandria's Treatment of the Problem of Evil* (Oxford: Oxford University Press, 1971), p. 91, notes that "Clement of Alexandria's speculation on the problem of evil is in large measure dictated by his anti-gnostic polemic."

5. See Jonas, *The Gnostic Religion*, chap. 11.

6. Floyd, *Clement*, p. 28.

7. See below, p. 45. A similar argument about Jesus being married was developed by William Phipps, *Was Jesus Married? The Distortion of Sexuality in the Christian Tradition* (New York: Harper & Row, 1970).

8. For a discussion of this "middle way" of passion, *metriopatheia*, see Salvatore R. C. Lilla, *Clement of Alexandria: A Study in Christian Platonism and Gnosticism* (Oxford: Oxford University Press, 1971), pp. 103–104.

9. John Ferguson, in *Clement of Alexandria* (New York: Twayne Publishers, Inc., 1974), p. 131, disagrees with commentators who argue that Clement would have liked people to desist from sexual relations altogether: "Clement's ideal is not to feel sexual desire, and let sexual union be determined wholly by will."

10. Irenaeus, *Against Heretics* 1. 1.

11. Ibid., 1. 1–7.

12. In Robert M. Grant, *Gnosticism: A Sourcebook of Heretical Writings from the Early Christian Period* (New York: Harper & Bros., 1961), p. 70.

13. Tertullian, *On the Prescription of Heretics*, 41.

14. As explained by Henri-Charles Puech, the gospel is probably a compilation of two originally separate parts. E. Hennecke and W. Schneemelcher, *New Testament Apocrypha*, vol. 1 (Philadelphia: Westminster Press, 1963), p. 344.

15. As Elaine Pagels points out in "What Became of God the Mother? Conflicting Images of God in Early Christianity," forthcoming in *Signs*, Peter is often depicted as warring against women in Gnostic literature; perhaps he is representative of attitudes among the orthodox? In view of her suggestion, it is of interest to recall that in Paul's version of the people witnessing the resurrected Jesus (1 Corinthians 15), Peter has usurped the place given to Mary Magdalene and the other women in the Gospels.

6. Jerome: The Exaltation of Christian Virginity

1. For the most recent account of Jerome's life and work, see J. N. D. Kelly, *Jerome: His Life, Writings and Controversies*, (New York: Harper & Row, 1976). A slightly older work is Jean Steinmann, *Saint Jerome and His Times*, trans. Ronald Matthews (Notre Dame: Fides Publishers, 1959). For a shorter account, see pp. 333–386 of Pierre de Labriolle's *History and Literature of Christianity from Tertullian to Boethius*, trans. Herbert Wilson (New York, Barnes and Noble, 1968).

2. Kelly, *Jerome*, p. 48, discusses the difficulty of pinpointing the period which Jerome spent in the desert.

3. Letter 48, 20.

4. See the selections below, p. 56.

5. For Jerome's borrowing from the classical antifeminist tradition, see David Wiesen, *St. Jerome as a Satirist: A Study in Christian Latin Thought and Letters* (Ithaca: Cornell University Press, 1964), chap. 4 and Harold Hagendahl, *Latin Fathers and the Classics: A Study in the Apologists, Jerome and Other Christian Writers* (Göteborg: Universitetet Press, 1958), pp. 147–161. Kelly, *Jerome*, p. 12, doubts that Jerome really was familiar with Juvenal.

6. Wiesen, *St. Jerome*, p. 119.

7. Ibid., p. 160, n. 160.

8. For a discussion of these women, see chapter 10 of Kelly, *Jerome*. Jerome was so close to his female friends that his behavior aroused the suspicions of the Roman clergy, who asked him to leave their city in the summer of 385.

9. Jerome was one of the few early Christian fathers who learned Hebrew. His motives for doing so appear to have been mixed: not only did he have a scholarly desire to master the language of the Old Testament, he also believed that the study of Hebrew would help calm his sex drive (Letter 125, 12).

10. Kelly, *Jerome*, p. 91, offers this explanation: "Strongly sexed but also,

because of his convictions, strongly repressed as well, his nature craved for female society, and found deep satisfactions in it when it could be had without doing violence to his principles."

11. Here Jerome was referring to the *agapetae* or *subintroductae*. They were women who had devoted themselves to celibacy but nonetheless lived with monks. Although the couples claimed that they remained chaste, the church was scandalized by the practice. Jerome was one of the church fathers who refused to believe that the relationships were innocent. He wrote Letter 117 to a mother and daughter who each had been living under such arrangements, urging them to to seek other roommates.

12. Letter 48.

13. Ibid., 3.

14. For an attempt to defend Jerome against charges of misogyny in the *Against Jovinian*, see Gerard Campbell, "St. Jerome's Attitude Toward Marriage and Women," *The American Ecclesiastical Review* 143 (1960): 310–320, 384–394.

15. *Against Helvidius*, 16 and 17.

16. Ibid., 21.

17. Hans von Campenhausen, *The Virgin Birth in the Theology of the Ancient Church* (Napierville, Ill.: Alec R. Allenson, 1964).

18. For further material on Mary, see below, pp. 103–104, 286 n. 8.

7. Augustine: Sinfulness and Sexuality

1. *Confessions* 4. 2. Augustine was born in North Africa in 354 and received his early education there before journeying to Rome and Milan. In the latter city, under the influence of Ambrose's powerful preaching, he resolved to take the step of baptism. After this initiatory rite, he returned to North Africa and became associated with the church at Hippo where eventually he was raised to the bishopric. He remained in Hippo until his death in 430.

2. *Confessions* 8. 8 and 11. See Kenneth Burke, *The Rhetoric of Religion; Studies in Logology* (Boston: Beacon Press, 1961), pp. 86 and 114f., for an interesting discussion of how Augustine changed his "loves." Augustine's ambivalence about his sexual life is revealed in his famous prayer, "Grant me chastity and continence—but not yet" (*Confessions* 8. 7).

3. *Confessions* 6. 15.

4. *Confessions* 9. 9.

5. Ibid.

6. For a discussion of Manicheanism, see see Geo. Widengren, *Mani and Manichaeism* (London: Weidenfeld and Nicolson, 1965).

7. John T. Noonan, Jr., *Contraception: A History of its Treatment by the Catholic Theologians and Canonists* (New York: The New American Library, 1967), p. 151. Augustine's views on Manichean sexual practices can be found in *On the Morals of the Manicheans* 18. 65 and *Against Faustus* 22. 30.

8. Michael F. Valente, *Sex: The Radical View of a Catholic Theologian* (New York: Bruce Publishing Company, 1970), p. 46.

9. *Confessions* 6. 14.

10. For a discussion of Pelagius and his views, see John Ferguson, *Pelagius: A Historical and Theological Study* (Cambridge, England: W. Heffer, 1956) or Robert Evans, *Pelagius: Inquiries and Reappraisals* (London: A. & C. Black, 1968). Pelagius, a British visitor to Rome at the end of the fourth century, was shocked by the moral laxity of the Christians he observed in the imperial city. In 412 he arrived in North Africa where he took up a fierce literary debate with Augustine on the topics of God's grace and man's free will. Councils in the following years made a variety of pronouncements regarding the "correct" opinion; in 529 the Council of Orange accepted in essence the Augustinian position regarding the ravages of original sin but stressed the sacrament of baptism as the means for alleviating its dire results.

11. Selections from Pelagius's writings can be found in Henry Bettenson, ed., *Documents of the Christian Church*, 2nd ed. (Oxford: Oxford University Press, 1967), pp. 52–54.

12. *The City of God* 22. 30.

13. Noonan, *Contraception*, p. 167.

14. *Retractions* 2. 22.

15. As revealed, for example, in his *Treatise on the Sermon on the Mount* 1. 15, 41: the good Christian is to love woman insofar as she is a human being, a creature of God, but he is to hate what in her belongs to being a female, which Augustine associates with sexual intercourse. Thus the Christian is enjoined to love his wife as he would an enemy, for the human potential in her, not for what is distinctive to her sexual nature.

16. Earlier in his career, Augustine had considered other options regarding the sex life of Adam and Eve in Eden. See *On the Good of Marriage* 2.

17. Rosemary R. Ruether, "Misogynism and Virginal Feminism in the Fathers of the Church," in *Religion and Sexism: Images of Woman in the Jewish and Christian Tradition*, ed. Rosemary R. Ruether (New York: Simon and Schuster, 1974), p. 162.

18. Noonan, *Contraception*, pp. 170–175.

8. Thomas Aquinas: The Man Who Should Have Known Better

1. Feminists raise the same issue in regard to modern theologians. Mary Daly, for example, notes that Paul Tillich laid the basis for a nonsexist theology in his notion of God as " the Ground of Being." *Beyond God the Father: Toward a Philosophy of Women's Liberation* (Boston: Beacon Press, 1973), chap. 1.

2. *ST* 1. 92. 4 ad 2. The patristic speculation that Eve was created through the mediation of angels rather than directly by God was one means of according her a lower status than Adam. Citations from the *Summa Theologica* will be abbreviated as *ST* throughout. The above reference, for example, indicates that the material can be found in part 1, question 92, article 4, reply to ob-

jection 2. Where no concluding number is given, the citation is from the "I answer that" section of the article.

3. Aristotle, for Thomas, was "the Philosopher." Thomas wished to make known to Latin Christendom Aristotle's physical and metaphysical writings which had not been available to Christian thinkers of the early Middle Ages. Thomas did not follow Aristotle blindly, nor did he necessarily try to "make a Christian" of him. As F. C. Copleston has written, "He was not concerned with patching together Aristotle as Aristotle with Christian theology. If he adopted and adapted a number of Aristotelian theories, this was not because he thought them 'useful,' but because he believed them to be true." *Aquinas* (Baltimore: Penguin Books, 1955), p. 63.

4. Eleanor Commo McLaughlin, "Equality of Soul, Inequality of Sexes: Women in Medieval Theology," in *Religion and Sexism: Images of Woman in the Jewish and Christian Traditions*, ed. Rosemary R. Ruether (New York: Simon and Schuster, 1974), p. 256.

5. *On the Generation of Animals* 2. 3 and 4. 2.

6. Aristotle's theory of female defectiveness, feminists point out, finds its modern counterpart in the Freudian theory that girls see themselves as "castrated."

7. *ST* 1. 92. 1 ad 1.

8. *ST* 1. 99. 2 ad 2 and ad 3. The attempt to decide the sex of the child may soon be a possibility through developments in biogenetic engineering. Feminists might worry, however, that our society would choose to produce more males than females, contrary to Thomas's expectations.

9. *ST* 1. 92. 1 ad 1.

10. *ST* 1. 99. 2.

11. Copleston, *Aquinas*, p. 89.

12. *On the Generation of Animals* 1. 20. See John Noonan, *Contraception: A History of its Treatment by the Catholic Theologians and Canonists* (New York: The New American Library, 1967), p. 116.

13. *On the Generation of Animals* 2. 3.

14. *ST* 2-2. 26. 10 ad 1.

15. Ibid.

16. *ST* 1. 85. 7.

17. *ST* 2-2. 156. 1 ad 1.

18. *ST* 1. 92. 1.

19. *ST* 3 Supplement, 64. 5. The idea is also found in Aristotle, *On the Generation of Animals* 1. 20.

20. *ST* 2-2. 165. 2 ad 1; *ST* 2-2. 163. 4.

21. *ST* 1. 92. 1 ad 2.

22. Note below, p. 97, how Thomas downplays the clerical status of women in early Christianity.

23. *ST* 3 Supplement, 39. 1.

24. *ST* 3 Supplement, 39. 1 ad 1.

25. *ST* 1. 92. 2.

26. *ST* 1. 92. 3.

27. *ST* 1. 92. 2.

28. *ST* 1. 98. 1 and 2.

29. *ST* 1. 98. 2 ad 4.

30. *ST* 1. 98. 2.

31. *ST* 1. 98. 2 ad 3.

32. *ST* 3 Supplement. 49. 6.

33. *ST* 3 Supplement. 49. 6 ad 4.

34. See below, pp. 191–205.

35. *ST* 1-2 91. 2.

36. See Copleston, *Aquinas,* p. 214, for a discussion of this point regarding natural law. For a longer exploration of Thomas's idea of the natural law, see Walter Farrell, O.P., *The Natural Moral Law According to St. Thomas and Suarez* (Ditchling: St. Dominic's Press, 1930).

37. *ST* 1-2. 94. 2.

38. The Catholic Church's condoning of the "rhythm" method of contraception is predicated on a person's ability to control his or her sexual behavior through reason and will.

39. For articles critical of the Vatican's interpretation of natural law and contraception, see Daniel Callahan, ed., *The Catholic Case for Contraception* (New York: The Macmillan Company, 1969).

40. Mary Daly, *The Church and the Second Sex* (New York: Harper & Row, 1975), p. 95.

9. Dame Julian of Norwich and Margery Kempe:
Divine Motherhood and Human Sisterhood

1. Dante recounts the change in his conception of love as the consequence of his love for Beatrice in his *La Vita Nuova.* In his later *Divine Comedy* Beatrice becomes his guide and leads him towards the vision of God.

2. See the Margery Kempe reading and compare it with the *Malleus Maleficarum.*

3. On the nominalist stress on the sovereignty of God, see Heiko Oberman, *The Harvest of Mediaeval Theology* (Cambridge: Harvard University Press, 1963). Compare with Julian of Norwich, *The Revelations of Divine Love* (Westminister, Md.: Newman Press, 1952), chap. 4, "Jesus Cryst est amor meus." Katherine Cholmeley, *Margery Kempe, Genius and Mystic* (London: Longmans, Green and Co., 1947), p. 20.

5. Two volumes that present the most recent challenges to the traditional concept are *The Meaning of Courtly Love,* ed. F. X. Newman (Albany: State University of New York Press, 1968) and *In Pursuit of Perfection,* ed. Joan Ferrante and George Economou (Port Washington: Kennikat Press, 1975). Ferrante sums up the present critical position, saying, "A distinction must be made between an established doctrine, a rigid system of rules of behavior, which did not exist, and a mode of thought, expressed in literary conventions,

which can be traced through so much mediaeval literature from the twelfth century onwards" (p. 3). According to this view, it is consistent to regard courtly love poetry as having no actual social effect, but being merely "self-mockery for the sake of preserving an ideal" (p. 101). The problem with this view is that it presupposes that ideals do not affect and change social behavior. For an alternative viewpoint, see Herbert Richardson, *Nun, Witch, Playmate* (New York: Harper & Row, 1974).

6. *New Catholic Encyclopedia*, vol. 4 (New York: McGraw Hill, 1967), p. 395.

7. Ibid.

8. The first festivals in the Western church which celebrated Mary's immaculate conception took place in the twelfth century, although the official papal proclamation of the immaculate conception took place in 1854 (*Ineffabilis Deus*). In the same way, there was already devotional and theological belief in her bodily assumption, but this was proclaimed only in 1950 (*Munificentissimus Deus*). The reason for the long time lag is that the official proclamation of a dogma by the Catholic Church takes place only after there has been popular approval and theological preparation for it. For historical reasons, therefore, it is usually more helpful to look for the earliest celebrations of festivals or the first informal papal allusion to a doctrine if we are to see when it began to have influence. The first papal allusion to the spiritual motherhood of Mary, a point of special importance for this introduction, was by Sixtus IV in 1477. This archetypal notion ("motherhood") is probably a more influential religious idea than either the dogmas of immaculate conception or bodily assumption.

9. *New Catholic Encyclopedia*, vol. 9, pp. 352, 366.

10. *The Revelations*, chap. 58–60. See below, p. 108–112.

11. Ibid., chap. 86.

12. Margery Kempe, *The Book of Margery Kempe*, ed. W. Butler-Bowen (London: Jonathan Cape, 1936), chap. 18, pp. 72–74. See below, pp. 112–113.

13. P. Franklin Chambers, *Juliana of Norwich* (New York: Harper & Row, 1955), p. 28f.

14. *The Book of Margery Kempe*, chap. 61.

15. *New Catholic Encyclopedia*, vol. 8, p. 149.

16. *The Book of Margery Kempe*, chap. 76.

17. Cholmeley, *Margery Kempe*, p. 57.

18. Ibid., p. 93.

19. Ibid.

20. "Mystical Marriage," *New Catholic Encyclopedia*, vol. 10, p. 170f. See also David Knowles, *The English Mystical Tradition* (New York: Allenson, 1961), pp. 114–150.

21. "This creature" is Margery's usual, humble way of referring to herself.

22. I.e., by means of sexual intercourse.

23. In a previous communication with Jesus, he had put Margery under strict obedience to observe a meatless fast on Fridays.

10. The *Malleus Maleficarum*: The Woman as Witch

1. Rosemary Ruether, "The Persecution of Witches," *Christianity and Crisis* 34 (December 23, 1974): 293.
2. Andrea Dworkin, "What Were Those Witches Really Brewing?" *Ms.* 2, no. 10 (April, 1974): 52.
3. Hugh Trevor-Roper, "Witches and Witchcraft (II)," *Encounter* 28, no. 6 (June, 1967): 16ff.
4. Dworkin, "What Were Those Witches," p. 52.
5. Hugh Trevor-Roper, "Witches and Witchcraft (I)," *Encounter* 28, no. 5 (May, 1967): 4.
6. Ibid. The question of night-flying is important because it is a distinctive feature of witchcraft trials of the fifteenth century, though it is not much discussed in the *Malleus Maleficarum*.
7. Ibid.
8. Margaret Murray, *The Witch-cult in Western Europe* (Oxford: The Clarendon Press, 1921). A severe critique of Murray's views is found in Norman Cohn, *Europe's Inner Demons* (New York: Basic Books, 1975), chap. 6.
9. Trevor-Roper, "Witches (I)," p. 15ff.; Cohn, *Europe's Inner Demons*, p. 254ff., lays somewhat less stress on this factor.
10. Trevor-Roper, "Witches (II)," p. 30.
11. Ibid., p. 31.
12. Ibid., p. 32
13. Trevor-Roper, "Witches (I)," p. 8.
14. See selection below, *Malleus Maleficarum*, p. 122. The devil was thought to possess some quite extraordinary sexual properties. See Trevor-Roper, "Witches (I)," p. 7; Murray, *"The Witch-cult,"* pp. 176ff.
15. *Malleus*, part 1, question 6. See below, p. 125.
16. *Malleus*, part 2, question 1. chap. 7. See below, p. 130.
17. *Malleus*, part 1, question 6.
18. Trevor-Roper, "Witches (II)," p. 33.
19. Cohn, *Europe's Inner Demons*, p. 262.
20. Ibid.
21. Herbert Richardson, *Nun, Witch, Playmate* (New York: Harper & Row, 1974), p. 65. One of the factors which Richardson sees as contributing to social upheaval is courtly love, a movement that probably was related to certain heretical practices as well as contributing to the romanicization of women, effectively raising her social status. Richardson relates witchcraft directly to courtly love, suggesting that the Witch "was nothing other than the counter face of the Lady" (p. 64). The above introduction represents both a correction and a corroboration of this theme. A selection on courtly love is not included in this volume because it is not specifically a religious movement. The new higher regard for the feminine principle in the late Middle Ages, especially the feminization of God, is here represented by the selection from Dame Julian of Norwich.

22. Trevor-Roper, "Witches (II)," pp. 26–30.

11. Luther and the Protestant Reformation: From Nun to Parson's Wife

1. Roland Bainton, Women of the Reformation in Germany and Italy (Minneapolis: Augsburg Press, 1971), p. 9.

2. "In general, without losing sight of the traditional discussions of the role of marriage to remedy incontinence and provide offspring, Protestant thought tended to increase the importance of the mutual cherishing of husband and wife, which had earlier been subservient to the purpose of procreation," wrote Jane Dempsey Douglass, "Women and the Continental Reformation," Religion and Sexism: Images of Woman in the Jewish and Christian Traditions, ed. Rosemary R. Ruether (New York: Simon and Schuster, 1974), p. 302.

3. And for rather dubious reasons: that it would please his father, spite his enemies and the devil, and convince people that he had practiced what he preached. See Letters 154, 157, and 158 in Luther's Works, vol. 49 (vol. 2 of Letters), ed. and trans. Gottfried G. Krodel (Philadelphia: Fortress Press, 1972) pp, 111, 117, and 123.

4. The puzzle is resolved by noting Luther's concept of a sacrament—and why marriage does not qualify. See The Babylonian Captivity of the Church, in Luther's Works, vol. 36, ed. and trans. A. R. Wentz (Philadelphia: Fortress Press, 1959), pp. 92–106.

5. The Catholic church undertook its own reformation in the sixteenth century, particularly through its implementation of the decrees of the Council of Trent (1545–1563).

6. See The Babylonian Captivity of the Church, pp. 80–81, 102–103.

7. Table Talk, in Luther's Works, vol. 54, ed. and trans. Theodore G. Tappert (Philadelphia: Fortress Press, 1967), pp. 160–161.

8. Luther's allowance for bigamy in difficult marital cases led to problems for the Protestant cause when one of the German Protestant princes, Philip of Hesse, undertook a bigamous marriage, contrary to imperial law, with Luther's blessing. The result was the division of the Schmalkaldic League (the Protestant military league) when sanctions were applied to Philip by the Emperor.

9. Table Talk, p. 89.

10. Table Talk, p. 191.

11. Joan Morris, The Lady Was a Bishop: The Hidden History of Women with Clerical Ordination and the Jurisdiction of Bishops (New York: The Macmillan Company, 1973).

12. John Milton: The Puritan Transformation of Marriage

1. Herbert Richardson, Nun, Witch, Playmate (New York: Harper & Row, 1974), p. 67. See also the work of William Haller on Puritan attitudes

towards love and marriage, especially William and Malleville Haller, "The Puritan Art of Love," *Huntington Library Quarterly* 5 (1942): 235–272.

2. Morton Hunt, *The Natural History of Love* (New York: Knopf, 1959), p. 252.

3. Arthur Barker, *Milton and the Puritan Dilemma, 1641–1660* (Toronto: University of Toronto, 1942).

4. For example, V. Norskov Olsen, *The New Testament Logia on Divorce* (Tübingen: J. C. B. Mohr, 1971), pp. 129ff.

5. John Halkett, *Milton and the Idea of Matrimony* (New Haven: Yale University Press, 1970), p. 3.

6. The *Tetrachordon* (1645) is a scholarly treatise seeking to harmonize Old and New Testament texts on marriage; the *Colasterion* (1645) is a reply to an anonymous attack on *The Doctrine and Discipline of Divorce.*

7. John Milton, *The Doctrine and Discipline of Divorce*, chap. 13; *The Works of John Milton*, vol. 3 (New York: Columbia University Press, 1931), p. 422.

8. Ibid., chap. 1, p. 389.

9. Ibid., chap. 11, p. 415.

10. *Paradise Lost*, 4. 299.

11. See selection on Margery Kempe in this volume.

12. *Paradise Lost*, 9. 904–907, 914–916. Mary Beacom Bowers comments, regarding this passage, "It is difficult for us here not to see Adam's act as honorable, though Milton makes it clear a little later that it is not. It is hard to see him [Adam] as 'uxorious.'" "Milton's Conception of Woman," *Ohio Journal of Religious Studies* 4, no. 1 (March, 1976): 29.

13. Ann Lee: The Messiah as Woman

1. *Testimonies of the Life, Character, Revelations and Doctrines of Mother Ann Lee* (Albany: Weed, Parsons, 1888); Calvin Green and Seth Y. Wells, *A Summary View of the Millennial Church* (Albany: van Benthuysen, 1848); Giles B. Avery, *Sketches of Shakers and Shakerism* (Albany: Weed, Parsons, and Company, 1884).

2. E. D. Andrews, *The People Called Shakers: A Search for the Perfect Society* (Oxford: University Press, 1953; New York: Dover Publications, 1963); see M. F. Melcher, *The Shaker Adventure* (Princeton: University Press, 1941; Cleveland: Western Reserve University Press, 1960).

3. E. D. Andrews, *The Gift to be Simple: Songs, Dances and Rituals of the American Shakers* (New York: Dover Publications, 1940, 1962).

4. John Whitworth says Ann Lee's "claim to inspiration and her explicit teachings . . . rested on one fundamental tenet—the idea that sexual relations were the source of all sin." (*God's Blueprints*, London and Boston: Routledge & Kegan Paul, 1975), p. 17ff. This judgment appears to overlook the complex theological imagination of the Shaker movement and its founder.

5. The Shakers "created a new, more inclusive mode of heterosociality and

they evolved a living institution that overcame the partialities of the traditional family group. The partialities of the traditional biological family are (a) that it limits the number of intimate male-female relationships to the spouses; (b) that it is based upon the distinction between the rich and the poor; and (c) that it requires women to be relegated to the status of household help. The Shakers overcame these limitations by creating a communalistic economy and family which was bound together by the ritual-sexual act of ecstatic 'shaking.' " Herbert Richardson, *Nun, Witch, Playmate* (New York: Harper & Row, 1974), p. 132.

6. Henri Desroche, *The American Shakers: From Neo-Christianity to Presocialism* (Amherst: University of Massachusetts Press, 1971).

7. See below, p. 166.

8. See below, p. 171.

14. Schleiermacher and Baader: Individuality and Androgyny

1. Friedrich Schleiermacher, a founding professor of the University of Berlin, is often called "The Father of Modern Theology." Countering both the anti-metaphysical critique of Kant and the idealistic panmetaphysics of Hegel, he grounded religion on the unity of consciousness that precedes the subject-object split, which he called the "feeling of absolute dependence" on the Whole. In this way, Schleiermacher transformed systematic theology into a "doctrine about faith" (*Glaubenslehre*) away from its traditional form as a "doctrine about God." Schleiermacher's earlier writings include the romantic *Speeches on Religion* and *Christmas Eve*. For studies on Schleiermacher, see *Schleiermacher Bibliography* (Princeton: Princeton Theological Seminary, 1966).

Franz von Baader is one of the great Catholic romantic theologians, whose contemporaries ranked him the equal of Novalis, Schelling, and Schleiermacher. He exercised specific influence over Schelling, Goethe, and Kierkegaard. From 1826 until his death he was Professor of Philosophical and Speculative Theology at the University of Munich. Baader's *Sämtliche Werke* [SW] have been edited by F. Hoffmann, J. Hamberger, and A. Lutterbeck (Leipzig, 1851–60).

2. For a characterization of the romantic influence on theology, see Paul Tillich, *Perspectives on 19th and 20th Century Protestant Theology*, ed. C. Braaten (New York: Harper & Row, 1967), pp. 76–89.

3. Schleiermacher, *Christmas Eve*, trans. T. Tice (Richmond: John Knox, 1967), p. 83.

4. Ibid., p. 85.

5. Ibid., p. 54. See below, p. 183.

6. Ibid., p. 55. See below, p. 183. Karl Barth suggests that, while writing *Christmas Eve*, Schleiermacher was preoccupied with the meaning of music and relationships with women. See *Theology and Church*, trans. Louise P. Smith (London: SCM, 1962), pp. 136–158.

7. Richard R. Niebuhr, *Schleiermacher on Christ and Religion* (New York: Charles Scribner's Sons, 1964), pp. 37–43.

8. *Lebenswelt der Romantik: Dokumente romantischen Denkens und Seins,* ed. Richard Benz (München: Nymphenburger Verlag, 1948), p. 156.

9. Ibid.

10. Ibid.

11. Ibid., pp. 156ff.

12. Martin Redeker, *Schleiermacher: Life and Thought,* trans. John Wallhausser (Philadelphia: Fortress Press, 1973). pp. 69ff.

13. *Christmas Eve.* p. 86. See below, p. 186. Says Richard Niebuhr, "The true function of Josef is not to negate or to affirm the various conceptions of the human spirit expounded, but to represent the common spirit uniting and inspiring the assembly." Niebuhr, *Schleiermacher,* p. 39.

14. The following includes a summary of Baader's position found in Richarda Huch, *Blütezeit der Romantik* (Leipzig: H. Haessel, 1920), pp. 268ff.

15. Baader's doctrine of an illuminative participation in the divine principle of knowledge is formulated against the Cartesian *cogito.* Baader asserts "*cogitor, ergo cogito, ergo sum*" (I am thought [by God], therefore I think, therefore I am).

16. Huch, *Blütezeit,* pp. 269ff.

17. *Christmas Eve,* p. 55. See below, p. 183.

18. Franz von Baader, *Vom Sinn der Gesellschaft: Schriften zur Sozialphilosophie,* ed. Hans A. Fischer-Barnicol (Köln: Verlag Jakob Hegner, 1966). Also *Sätze aus der erotischen Philosophie und andere Schriften,* ed. Gerd-Klaus Kaltenbrunner (Frankfort am Main: Insel Verlag, 1966).

19. *Sämtliche Werke,* vol. 3, 287ff.

15. Living in the Kingdom of God: John Humphrey Noyes and the Oneida Community

1. Raymond Muncy, *Sex and Marriage in Utopian Communities—19th Century America* (Bloomington, Ind.: Indiana University Press, 1973), p. 8.

2. Constance Noyes Robertson, ed., *Oneida Community: An Autobiography, 1851–1876* (Syracuse: Syracuse University Press, 1970), p. 23.

3. *Circular,* March 21, 1870, in Robertson, *Oneida Community,* p. 283.

4. Noyes does not seem to have envisioned the adoption of homosexual relationships, however. See the selection below, p. 196.

5. Richard J. DeMaria, "The Oneida Community's Concept of Christian Love," Ph.D. dissertation, University of St. Michael's College, Toronto, Ontario, 1973.

6. Muncy, *Sex and Marriage,* p. 183. Later the community went in for scientific propagation or "stirpiculture," beginning in 1869. During the first ten years of the program, fifty-eight children were born to selected couples at Oneida, nine of them fathered by Noyes himself. See Muncy, pp. 187–191, and Robertson, *Oneida Community,* pp. 335–355. Noyes's own failure at "male

continence" with a woman he presumably loved is described by Ernest R. Sandeen, "John Humphrey Noyes as the New Adam," *Church History* 40 (1971), pp. 85–90.

7. Muncy, *Sex and Marriage*, pp. 176–177.

8. Children were raised communally in an effort to rule out the notion of the parents' "ownership" of their offspring. See Robertson, *Oneida Community*, pp. 311–334. Noyes believed that in traditional marriage, the wife and children were "owned" by the male head of the household; exalting "family spirit" merely made selfishness (insofar as owning personal property led to selfishness) appear to be a virtue. See Pierrepont B. Noyes, *A Goodly Heritage* (New York: Rinehart & Company, Inc., 1958), p. 4. Noyes's socialist views exerted a strong influence on his notions of marriage and the family.

9. Robertson, *Oneida Community*, chap. 10.

10. John Humphrey Noyes, *History of American Socialisms* (Philadelphia: J. P. Lippincott & Co., 1870), p. 636.

11. Robertson, *Oneida Community*, p. 294.

12. *Circular*, March 18, 1872, in Robertson, *Oneida Community*, p. 284.

13. *Circular*, January 23, 1858, in Roberston, *Oneida Community*, p. 300.

16. Sarah Grimké: From Abolition to Suffrage

1. Gerda Lerner, *The Grimké Sisters from South Carolina: Pioneers for Woman's Rights and Abolition* (New York: Schocken Books, 1971), pp. 187–188.

2. See Eleanor Flexner, *Century of Struggle: The Woman's Rights Movement in the United States* (New York: Atheneum Press, 1973), pp. 45–49, for a discussion of this episode.

3. *Letters of Theodore Dwight Weld, Angelina Grimké Weld and Sarah Grimké, 1822–1844*, vol. 1, ed. G. H. Barnes and D. L. Drummond (New York: Appleton–Century Co., 1934), p. 424.

4. Ibid., p. 427.

5. Lerner, *The Grimké Sisters*, p. 203.

6. Ibid., p. 366.

7. For example, Grimké's calling Genesis 2 a "recapitulation" of chapter 1 shows she was not aware of the scholarly opinion accepted later in the century that these chapters are the products of different authors.

17. Elizabeth Cady Stanton and The Woman's Bible

1. Aileen Kraditor, *The Ideas of the Woman Suffrage Movement, 1890–1920* (Garden City: Doubleday & Co., 1971), pp. 65 and 76, n. 2.

2. Elizabeth Cady Stanton, *Eighty Years and More: Reminiscences 1815–1897* (1898; New York: Schocken Books, 1971), chap. 2.

3. Ibid., p. 80.

4. Ibid., p. 357.

5. Kraditor, *Ideas*, p. 75.

6. William O'Neill, *Everyone Was Brave: The Rise and Fall of Feminism in America* (Chicago: Quadrangle Books, 1969).

7. E. C. Stanton, S. B. Anthony, and M. J. Gage, eds., *The History of Woman Suffrage* (Rochester: Susan B. Anthony, 1881–1922), vol. 1, p. 806.

8. Stanton, *Eighty Years*, pp. 390–393.

9. Ibid., p. 467.

10. For example, see the collection of papers on *The Woman's Bible* in *Women and Religion: 1973 Proceedings*, American Academy of Religion Annual Meeting.

18. Women and Marriage, Vatican Style: The *Casti Connubii*

1. The vulcanization of rubber in the mid-nineteenth century had made the mass availability of condoms a reality; later in the century, the modern diaphragm was developed. See John Noonan, *Contraception: A History of its Treatment by the Catholic Theologians and Canonists* (New York: The New American Library, 1967), p. 469 and p. 485.

2. For papal pronouncements on these and other themes, see William Faherty, S.J., *The Destiny of Modern Woman in the Light of Papal Teaching* (Westminster, Md.: Newman Press, 1950), chap. 2–5.

3. Although a papal encyclical does not possess the same infallible status as does a dogmatic pronouncement, that is, the salvation of the individual does not depend upon adherence to its precepts, the Vatican has always urged that faithful Catholics accept the teachings of the encyclicals as binding upon their lives.

4. Such as "Woman's Duties in Social and Political Life," printed in *Catholic Mind*, December 1945; "Woman's Apostolate," in *Catholic Mind*, November 1949; and "Morality in Marriage," in *Catholic Mind*, May 1952.

5. The text of this famous speech can be found in *Catholic Mind*, January 1952.

6. For the discussion at Vatican II regarding contraception, see "The Church in the Modern World," *The Documents of Vatican II*, ed. Walter M. Abbott, S. J. (New York: Guild Press, 1966), pp. 249–258. Also see Peter Riga, *Sexuality and Marriage in Recent Catholic Thought* (Washington, D.C.: Corpus Books, 1969) for a discussion.

7. The full texts of the Majority and Minority Reports are in Daniel Callahan, ed., *The Catholic Case for Contraception* (New York: The Macmillan Company, 1969).

8. The text of the *Humanae Vitae* is in Daniel Callahan, ed., *The Catholic Case for Contraception*. The document affirms that "grave motives" must be present for a couple to use even the "rhythm" method (p. 229).

9. Articles by Catholic clergy and laypersons critical of the Vatican's position are in Callahan, *The Catholic Case for Contraception*. Especially recommended is Michael Novak's "Frequent, Even Daily, Communion," pp. 92–102.

Most recently (December, 1975), the Vatican has reaffirmed its traditional condemnation of various sexual practices in "Declaration on Certain Questions Concerning Sexual Ethics." Premarital sexual experimentation, homosexuality, and masturbation are singled out for special censure.

19. The Triumph of Patriarchalism in the Theology of Karl Barth

1. Edward Thurneysen, *Zwischen den Zeiten* (1927), pp. 514–515, translated in Wilhelm Pauck, *Karl Barth: Prophet of a New Christianity?* (New York: Harper & Bros., 1931), p. 59.

2. John Godsey, in Karl Barth, *How I Changed My Mind* (Richmond: John Knox Press, 1966), p. 23.

3. Karl Barth, *Die Lehre vom Worte Gottes* (München: Chr. Kaiser Verlag, 1927), cited in *How I Changed My Mind*, p. 25.

4. Karl Barth, *Church Dogmatics*, ed. G. W. Bromiley and T. F. Torrance (Edinburgh: T & T. Clark, 1936), 2. 1, p. 635. Hereafter, references to the *Dogmatics* will be to *CD*, followed by the volume and section numbers.

5. It has frequently been noted that Barth's idea of the Trinity is really one of three "modes" rather than three "persons." It is difficult, then, to understand how the Trinity can really be an archetype for human relationships. See Robert Willis, *The Ethics of Karl Barth* (Leiden: E. J. Brill, 1971), p. 433, and Cyril Richardson, *The Doctrine of the Trinity* (New York: Abingdon Press, 1958), pp. 105–106.

6. Arnold Come, *An Introduction to Barth's "Dogmatics" for Preachers* (Philadelphia: The Westminster Press, 1963), pp. 78–79.

7. Karl Barth, *Christ and Adam: Man and Humanity in Romans 5* (New York: Collier Books, 1962), p. 107.

8. *CD* 3. 2, p. 274.

9. *CD* 3. 2, p. 243.

10. Barth's notion of freedom involved submitting oneself to God's order for the universe as that has been revealed in the Bible. Thus we are truly "free" only when we are living in accordance with God's command. Barth uses this notion of freedom in ways which would provoke the wrath of feminists. For example, when he discusses Paul's injunctions to the Corinthian women (1 Corinthians 11) to veil themselves, he argues that Paul was reminding them of their "peculiar dignity and rights. . . . In resisting the women of Corinth he was contending for their own true cause" (*CD* 3. 4, p. 156). Feminists might remark that being ordered to embrace the conservatism toward women found in that passage is scarcely their idea of freedom.

11. Robert Willis, *The Ethics of Karl Barth*, pp. 98ff. There are a number of puzzles about Barth's ethics. For one thing, although he is often claimed as a contextualist who believes that we should not bring principles or "isms" to our consideration of particular problems, he has plenty of rules at his fingertips when he so desires! He assumes rather easily that the Bible gives us precise commands for our daily lives. For example, his strong condemna-

tion of homosexuality as a "physical, psychological and social sickness, the phenomenon of perversion, decadence and decay" (*CD* 3. 4, pp. 165–166) leaves little room for God to act in loving freedom toward the confirmed homosexual. If the "good news" of the Bible, the content of the gospel, always comes to man in the form of law, as Barth asserts (*CD* 2. 2, p. 511), it is not clear that the individual really does have any "freedom" of interpretation, in the ordinarily recognized meaning of that word.

12. *CD* 3. 2, p. 243.
13. *CD* 3. 2, pp. 250–261.
14. *CD* 3. 2, pp. 261, 269–270.
15. *CD* 3. 2, p. 286; 2. 1, p. 186.
16. *CD* 3. 4, p. 154.
17. *CD* 3. 4, pp. 161–162.
18. *CD* 3. 4, pp. 155, 190; 3. 2, p. 314.
19. *CD* 3. 4, p. 171.
20. *CD* 3. 2, p. 287.
21. *CD* 3. 1, p. 301.
22. *CD* 3. 1, p. 303.
23. *CD* 3. 2, p. 311.
24. *CD* 3. 4, p. 172.
25. *CD* 3. 4, pp. 177–179.
26. *CD* 3. 4, p. 168.
27. See the discussion of Genesis 2 in *CD* 3. 1, pp. 298–303.
28. Joan Arnold Romero discusses this point in "The Protestant Principle: A Woman's-Eye View of Barth and Tillich," *Religion and Sexism: Images of Woman in the Jewish and Christian Traditions*, ed. Rosemary R. Ruether (New York: Simon and Schuster, 1974), pp. 320, 327.
29. Paul K. Jewett, *Man as Male and Female: A Study in Sexual Relationships from a Theological Point of View* (Grand Rapids: William B. Eerdmans Publishing Company, 1975), pp. 71, 84.
30. Clifford Green, "Liberation Theology? Karl Barth on Women and Men," *Union Seminary Quarterly Review* 29, no. 4 (Spring-Summer 1974), p. 230.
31. *CD* 3. 2, p. 311.
32. *CD* 3. 4, p. 172.
33. Karl Barth, *How I Changed My Mind*, p. 58.
34. *Ibid.*, p. 79.

20. Radical Feminism, Radical Religion: Mary Daly

1. See William O'Neill, *Everyone Was Brave: The Rise and Fall of Feminism in America* (Chicago: Quadrangle Books, 1969) for a discussion of this point of view.
2. For information about the role of women in these movements, see

Judith Hole and Ellen Levine, *Rebirth of Feminism* (New York: Quadrangle Books, 1971), pp. 108–135.

3. Betty Friedan, *The Feminine Mystique* (New York: Dell Publishing Co., 1963), chap. 1.

4. The various laws passed to aid women in their quest for equality are summarized in Judith Hole and Ellen Levine, *Rebirth of Feminism*, pp. 17–77.

5. Elizabeth Farians, "Justice: The Hard Line," *Andover Newton Quarterly*, 12, no. 4 (March 1972), p. 199.

6. For the various arguments pro and con which have been given regarding women's ordination, see Emily Hewitt and Suzanne Hiatt, *Women Priests: Yes or No?* (New York: Seabury Press, 1973). For the story of one woman's struggle to become a priest, see Carter Heyward's *A Priest Forever* (New York: Harper & Row, 1976).

7. Mary Daly, *Beyond God the Father: Toward a Philosophy of Women's Liberation* (Boston: Beacon Press, 1973).

8. Ibid., p. 19.

9. Ibid.

10. Ibid., chap. 1.

11. Ibid., pp. 6, 32–33.

12. Ibid., pp. 48, 51–55.

13. Ibid., pp. 67–68.

14. Ibid., p. 72.

15. Ibid., p. 55.

16. Ibid., p. 71.

17. Ibid., p. 50.

18. Ibid., chap. 4.

19. Ibid., pp. 114–122.

20. Ibid., pp. 127–131.

21. Daly notes that there is one statistic on abortion which is absolutely not open to challenge: 100 percent of the Roman Catholic bishops prohibiting abortion are male and 100 percent of the persons seeking abortions are female! Ibid., p. 106.

22. Ibid., p. 140.

23. Ibid., p. 96.

24. Ibid., pp. 169–178.

25. Ibid., p. 190.

26. June O'Connor, "Liberation Theologies and the Women's Movement: Points of Comparison and Contrast," *Horizons* 2 (Spring 1975), p. 108.

27. Robert Kress, *Whither Womankind? The Humanity of Women* (St. Meinrad, Ind.: Abbey Press, 1975), pp. 266–267.

28. Emily E. Culpepper, in *The Women's Movement: An Exodus Community, Religious Education*, 47, (September/October 1972), p. 334.

29. Mary Rodda, in *The Women's Movement*, p. 335.